Longfellow's Tattoos

Longfellow's Tattoos

TOURISM, COLLECTING, AND JAPAN

CHRISTINE M.E. GUTH

UNIVERSITY OF WASHINGTON PRESS

SEATTLE AND LONDON

MM Publication of this book has been aided by a grant from the Millard Meiss
Publication Fund of the College Art Association.

University of Washington Press
P.O. Box 50096, Seattle, WA 98145
www.washington.edu/uwpress

Library of Congress Cataloging-in-Publication Data

Guth, Christine.
  Longfellow's tattoos : tourism, collecting, and Japan /
  Christine M.E. Guth.
      p.   cm.
  Includes bibliographical references and index.
  ISBN 0-295-98401-5 (alk. paper)
  1. Japan—Social life and customs—1868–1912. 2. Longfellow, Charles
Appleton—Travel—Japan.   I. Title.

  DS822.3.G88 2004
  915.204'31'0092—dc22   2003066592

The paper used in this publication meets the minimum requirements
of American National Standard for Information Sciences—Permanence
of Paper for Printed Library Materials, ANSI Z39.48–1984.

Design by Echelon Design

Printed in China

"The same waves wash the moles
of the new-built California towns,
but yesterday planted
by the recentest race of men,
and lave the faded
but still gorgeous skirts
of Asiatic lands, older than Abraham;
while all between float milky-ways
of coral isles, and low-lying,
endless, unknown Archipelagoes,
and impenetrable Japans."

— Herman Melville,
Moby-Dick (1851)

"Is not this the very hour
when the wonderful flowering
of the Japanese mind could best
influence, and for most good,
the Western mind?"

— Thomas Gold Appleton,
"The Flowering of a Nation,"
Atlantic Monthly (1871)

CONTENTS

ACKNOWLEDGMENTS

I had no idea when I first visited Longfellow House in the spring of 1997 that it would lead me to learn as much about nineteenth-century New England as about Japan. I was lucky to have as my guides in this learning process two extraordinarily knowledgeable and enthusiastic individuals: Jim Shea and Anita Israel, the director and the archivist of Longfellow House National Historic Site. Throughout the course of my research, I profited enormously from their intimate knowledge of the Longfellow family, their relatives, and the intricacies of the Cambridge sociocultural environment.

Along the way many other people helped as well. I am grateful to Ellen Conant and Allen Hockley for lively conversations that helped me develop and clarify the ideas that eventually found their way into the chapters of this book. They also read and commented thoughtfully on the manuscript. Luke Gartlan and Sebastian Dobson generously shared their knowledge of Meiji-era photography. Christine Laidlaw patiently answered my Americanist questions. Melinda Takeuchi also provided invaluable help by reading, commenting on, and tightening my prose. I particularly want to acknowledge the generosity of Jay Fliegelman, who took the time to share with me his rich knowledge of nineteenth-century American literature and culture.

This book would never have been written without the assistance and encouragement of more individuals than I can name at museums and libraries throughout the United States. I am especially indebted to Deborah Muller at the Museum of the Rhode Island School of Design; Valrae Reynolds at the Newark Museum; Ruth Simmons, Curator of the William Elliot Griffis Collection at the Rutgers University Libraries; Keiko Thayer at the Peabody Essex Museum; and Emiko Usui at the Museum of Fine Arts, Boston. With their aid I was able to compare the nineteenth-century photographs acquired by Longfellow with those in their collections. They also brought to my attention objects in their institutions brought back from Japan during the 1860s and 1870s. Janet Heywood, Vice President of Interpretive Programs at the Mount Auburn Cemetery in Cambridge, Massachusetts, helped me complete the epilogue by throwing light on the history of cremation in New England, especially as it pertained to the Longfellow family. My research in New England institutions and purchase of some photographs were carried out with the assistance of a short-term travel grant from the Northeast Asia Council of the Association for Asian Studies.

Last but not least, I want to thank my husband, Tom, who read draft after draft of this manuscript, offering valuable suggestions for improvement.

Note to the Reader

The modified Hepburn system of romanization has been used throughout this book for Japanese words (e.g., *shinbun* not *shimbun*). Words in common English usage and the place names Tokyo, Osaka, and Kyoto are written without macrons when they appear in the text. Japanese names are given in Japanese style, with family name followed by given name.

Introduction

On June 1, 1871, Charles Longfellow (1844–93) telegraphed his father, the poet Henry Wadsworth Longfellow, "Have suddenly decided to set sail for Japan today. Good-bye. Send letters to the Oriental Bank Corporation, Yokohama."[1] The younger Longfellow arrived in Yokohama twenty-five days later, part of the wave of American tourists who, by the end of the century, would make Japan an obligatory stop on their round-the-world tours. Nascent American imperialism in the years following the Civil War had led to an unprecedented boom in leisure travel to Japan. In the early 1860s, the country was still too inaccessible and dangerous for all but the most intrepid, but this changed with the inauguration of regular steamship service between San Francisco and Yokohama in 1867 and the completion of the transcontinental railroad and opening of the Suez Canal two years later. By 1872, the ease, speed, and safety of travel to and within Japan even led Thomas Cook to begin group tours to the Far East.

Whether taking a tour with Thomas Cook or making the voyage on their own, most tourists of the late 1860s and 1870s stayed in Japan only a few weeks—long enough to buy curios in Yokohama, to admire the Great Buddha in Kamakura, and to stroll around the ornate shogunal temples at Shiba in Tokyo. Longfellow himself followed this routine; like many of his peers, he also bought photographs and other souvenirs to authenticate his experiences. Such activities characterize the class of visitors many local resident foreigners derisively labeled "globe-trotters."

Although the twenty-seven-year-old Longfellow arrived in Japan intending only a brief stay, he so enjoyed the country that he remained for nearly two years. He even built a house for himself in Tokyo's Tsukiji district, newly opened to foreign residents. At the time, most Euro-Americans lived in the port settlement of Yokohama, where they had a professional agenda—usually teaching, missionary work, trade, or diplomatic service. Longfellow, a young man of ample independent means, did not. The primary impetus for his journey was adventure and escape, not the development of a career. In his eyes, Japan was an uncharted and unexplored land where he could live out his heroic fantasies. It also provided a refuge from the conventional expectations of his own society and a climate more congenial to his ideals of personal and cultural authenticity. The artistic tattoos Longfellow carried home on his person are emblematic of the complex and often conflicting images, associations, and values that Japan assumed in the mind of this and other nineteenth-century American globe-trotters.

This book began in 1997 with my own "discovery" of more than 350 unpublished albumen photographs mounted in four albums, all dating from Longfellow's stay in Japan. I first examined these and other Japanese artifacts at Longfellow House National Historic Site in Cambridge, Massachusetts, in preparation for teaching a seminar on collecting. This little-known local collection of Japanese art, I thought, might make a good student project.

Decades earlier, as a graduate student in Japanese art history, I had often walked past the Longfellow family's historic colonial home on Brattle Street but had never entered it. This shrine to the man once known as "America's favorite poet" brought back memories of sixth-grade recitations of "Under the Spreading Chestnut Tree" and other verses that have since come to seem sentimental. I was unaware that the poet's son had been a pioneer collector of Japanese art. Like other students of Japanese art history at that time, my gaze was fixed on the internationally acclaimed collection of painting and sculpture in the Boston Museum of Fine Arts formed and acquired by Ernest Fenollosa (1853–1908), William Sturgis Bigelow (1850–1926), and Charles Goddard Weld (1857–1911). At the time, "Japanese art" was understood to mean the painting, sculpture, and decorative arts created before the Meiji era (1868–1912). Works of the late nineteenth century, having been compromised by contact with Western art, were "inauthentic," and therefore not deserving of serious study. Had I examined the Longfellow collection then, I would have dismissed it as little more than a cache of Victorian tourist souvenirs. Since that time, visual culture studies have opened up new avenues of investigation, prompting art historians to examine previously ignored materials and to ask questions of them that go beyond traditional connoisseurial concerns.

Longfellow's collection of photographs ranges from commercial views of Japan and its people and rare scenes of Ainu coastal settlements on the northern island of Hokkaidō to portraits of his many Japanese acquaintances and himself. The latter include several startling shots of the New Englander elaborately decorated with Japanese tattoos: a giant carp ascending a waterfall on his back and a Buddhist deity seated in the mouth of a dragon on his chest. Also in Longfellow House are a small number of Japanese screens, scrolls, lacquer furniture, illustrated books, ceramics, and clothing, all that remains of the "half a shipload" of curios Longfellow sent home. Most of his collection was either given to family and friends during his lifetime or dispersed after his death in 1893. Photographs of the home's interior dating from shortly after his return, however, provide evidence of the way he and his family displayed these exotic treasures. These, along with his personal photograph albums, journals, and letters from 1871–73, shed further light on his activities in and views of Japan.

Hand-colored photographic views of Japan, nineteenth-century arts and crafts, full body tattoos, and a "Japan Room," featuring a ceiling decorated with painted fans, comprise a seemingly disparate and, in many ways, challenging corpus for study. Yet their acquisition, preservation, organization, and display during Longfellow's lifetime disclose an underlying logic that offers provocative insights into the formative stages of the modern American conceptualization of Japan. Why such artifacts do not figure in the consecrated artistic hierarchy today raises important historical and interpretive questions that need to be addressed if we are to understand the roots of modern assumptions about Japanese art and culture.

Longfellow's expectations and experiences, while not typical of all American travelers, help to chart the new ways of seeing associated with the growing enthusiasm for world tours. Japanese art and culture were used to further current agendas: what tourists collected was grounded in the concerns, self-understandings, and perceived needs of their time. Many individuals went to Japan with the belief that its culture had qualities lacking in their own. In the American imagination, Japan was peopled with individuals who, regardless of class or education, were innately artistic. Such a vision was particularly attractive in the decades following the Civil War, when Americans had become increasingly attentive to how they might make their own lives more culturally refined.

During the 1860s and 1870s, especially as the nation's centennial approached, American ideas of culture underwent profound changes. These new meanings are revealed in the changing definition of the term *culture* in Webster's dictionary. In the 1841 edition, culture is defined as "an act of tilling; the application of labor to improve good qualities; and any labor or means employed for improvement." In the 1869 edition, the primary meaning is "labor that improves," followed by "the state of being cultivated," or "enlightenment and discipline acquired by mental training."[2] These new attitudes stimulated intense debates about the role, meaning, and forms of art in national life.[3] Europe remained an important touchstone, but the American encounter with Japan also shaped and reflected the contours of this debate. Japan offered a prism through which to see, scale, and reorder American culture and society at a time when growing numbers of immigrants from Catholic Ireland and Italy were forcing Americans to negotiate differences within their own country.

Travel to Japan played a central role in these cultural developments. Though often maligned, globe-trotters helped to mediate America's growing appreciation of Japanese products. Their arrival there also set off a chain reaction that helped to rewrite understandings of Japanese art both domestically and internationally. Collecting was central to the image of a country that was often characterized as a paradise of curios. With the opening of its ports to tourism, Japan, like its goods, became a marketable commodity. Travelers collected visual experiences as well as photographs and souvenirs to authenticate them. The articles they purchased to display upon their return are often characterized today as bric-a-brac, but these contributed mightily to what William Hosley has called "the Japan Idea."[4]

Vision is essential in the apprehension of any exotic country, and this was especially true for the nineteenth-century traveler to Japan, who was unable to read or speak the language. While there was no overarching way of envisioning the country at the time, it is fair to say that the expectations and experiences of most travelers were heavily shaped by pictures. Japan's own visual and material culture—painted fans, folding screens, as well as bronzes and ceramics, already widely available in Europe and America—played a central role in these constructs. Scenic photographic views of the country and people were also important. So too were Western representations of Japanese art. Illustrations in magazines and newspapers based, often only very loosely, on "pictures by native artists" were equally, if not more, potent.[5] The power of such images often remained strong even after the traveler arrived in Japan, since communication with Japanese who might be able to explain or correct preexisting ideas was limited. Even the photographs tourists purchased portraying samurai in formal attire, tattooed grooms, or courtesans gorgeously clad in kimonos, which seemingly presented the objective reality of Japan, helped to create and perpetuate myths. America's Japan was based on images that were frequently distorted, imaginary, and lacking in substance. Tourists and long-term foreign residents of Japan alike often denied to themselves and others what their eyes saw in favor of what their hearts desired.

This mythmaking was not a unidirectional process, of course. When tourists looked at Japanese, they looked back. European and American visitors liked to think that their authority was uncontested, but just as they could impose their fantasies on Japan, so too Japanese could reinforce, manipulate, or subvert them for their own purposes. Japanese were not passive, innocent bystanders, but active participants in their self-presentation to the West, both at home and abroad. Japanese artists and merchants were especially attuned to foreign visitors' expectations and created or adapted the goods they purveyed accordingly.

Most previous studies have directed attention either to the Japanese or to the American contexts without fully examining the nature or consequences of their mutual interaction. Instead of dwelling on one side at the expense of the other, I attempt here to weave together both views. Just as Japanese employed art to help reinvent themselves, so too American travelers bought it for their own self-representation. This cultural encounter was mutually modifying.

The 1860s and 1870s were key years in the crystallization of American perspectives on Japan and Japanese perspectives on America. In the United States, these two decades span the Civil War and the surge of economic growth and industrial progress that followed it. The horrors of the Civil War did much to reconfigure the terms of Americans' encounter with non-European cultures. Shattered illusions about their own world prompted many young men to seek out cultures they believe to be more innocent and uncorrupted by the modern world. During this era also, under the banner of "manifest destiny," the United States set in place a policy of economic imperialism in Asia that was deeply implicated in both American leisure travel to and trade with Japan. New affluence spurred middle-class Americans to surround themselves with exotic *objets d'art* and furnishings from that country. Japan's participation in the 1876 Philadelphia Centennial further encouraged these developments. The hunger for Japan was driven as much by supply as by demand.

In Japan these decades span the periods known as Bakumatsu (1853–68) and Meiji (1868–1912). The former refers to the waning years of the feudal Tokugawa shogunate following the arrival of Commodore Perry, the latter to the reign of Mutsuhito (1852–1912), known posthumously as Emperor Meiji. The Bakumatsu and early Meiji eras saw rapid changes as the country opened its ports to Western commerce, missionaries, diplomats, and tourists. For the first time, numerous Japanese began making journeys abroad for diplomatic and educational purposes. The publicity surrounding the groups that traveled across the United States in 1860 and 1871–73 did much to stimulate popular interest in Japan.

The cultural impact of Japan before the Philadelphia Centennial has been the subject of only limited critical analysis by historians of American art, and virtually none by historians of Japanese art.[6] Longfellow's journals and correspondence are uniquely valuable because the views he expresses are candid and idiosyncratic. Longfellow was not a political creature. He saw Japanese society in a highly subjective way, discussing only what directly touched him. He ignored the larger ideological issues confronting that country and its relationship with Western nations. Yet he was a keen observer of his surroundings and wrote quite eloquently of his experiences. His perspective on Japan is also noteworthy because it is unmistakably American, informed by an education and upbringing in a New England family that was unusually cosmopolitan and, perhaps for that reason, extremely sensitive to America's own cultural heritage. Longfellow's photographs, moreover, document a picaresque life whose existence has been largely excised from American accounts of that period. Although photographs of Japan from the 1860s and 1870s can be found in museums throughout the world, few are as precisely dated, documented, and contextualized through supporting materials as those preserved in the Longfellow family's house.

Longfellow's responses paint a richly textured picture of the ambiguities and contradictions of the ideas associated with Japan. Yet, as important as the facts we learn about him are the way they may be woven into the larger picture of America's understanding of Japan, and Japan's understanding of America. The particularities of the Longfellow collection offer a point of departure for considering how other American travelers of the time negotiated difference by appropriating Japanese products to fashion themselves as individuals and Americans.

The tourists from the United States and Europe who flocked to Japan in the late 1860s and 1870s offer a fresh vantage point from which to examine the emergence of many enduring images of Japan. Most studies of the formative stages of this phenomenon have not distinguished between the views of American Japanophiles who experienced the country firsthand and those who interpreted it through the romanticizing prism of printed books, wood-block prints, and literature. Nor have they taken note of the significant differences between European and American responses to Japan or the fact that not all Japanophiles belonged to the artistic avant-garde. The interpretation of cultural relations between the United States and Japan in the nineteenth century has been further limited by its emphasis on the reception of Japanese prints among modernist artists, writers, and the cultural elite, and on the formation of museum collections. Most of these approaches do not take into account the plethora of sources for American images of Japan. They also fail to acknowledge the profound attitudinal and institutional changes that swept the art worlds in Japan and the United States over the last quarter of the nineteenth century, and their role in reshaping their mutual responses to Japanese art.

Building on the foundation provided by the written and visual materials in the Longfellow archives, and using a variety of methodologies, this study investigates collecting in Japan from four different perspectives. Chapter 1 opens with a discussion of the ideology of tourism and the place of Japan within round-the-world travel. The arrival there of large numbers of globe-trotters of widely different geographic and cultural backgrounds created a new kind of "imagined community" that altered and accelerated the traffic in ideas, styles, and images between Japan and America. Although tourists undeniably helped to shape American perceptions of Japan, their role is generally ignored, because their impressions were often partial and filled with half-truths and misunderstandings. Furthermore, their authority to speak of Japan was frequently challenged by long-term residents who sought to capitalize on their experience and knowledge of the country. Tourists, however, created cultural attitudes that endured long after their lifetimes.

Commercial photographs of Japan and its people, often hand-painted by Japanese artists, were popular souvenirs. The photograph commanded a special kind of visual authority for actual and would-be tourists, and over the last quarter of the nineteenth century, photographic vision became a key referent for Western interpretations of Japan. Easily manipulated, both by their creators and their viewers, photographs helped to give focus to notions about Japanese culture that were rarely consonant with reality, creating and reinforcing some stereotypes, even as they displaced others. The advent of photography seemed to bring with it a new era of truthfulness, but, like any form of visual culture, it was not value-free.

Chapter 2 offers a close reading of the hundreds of photographs preserved in four albums assembled by Charley Longfellow to better understand how this medium contributed to the ways that Americans saw Japan, and Japanese saw themselves. These include scenic views of the country by Felice Beato, the leading commercial photographer in Japan during the 1860s and early 1870s, rare photographs of the Ainu and northern Hokkaidō taken during a British coastal survey of 1871, and two highly personal albums offering a microcosm of Longfellow's activities and friendships in Japan.

What tourists chose to collect involved a complex interplay of personal and culturally ascribed meanings. Longfellow's experiences underscore that there was no preordained standard against which Japanese art, either old or new, was evaluated at the time. One of the greatest difficulties in trying to understand the artistic world of the 1860s and 1870s is the modernist effort to hide the commodity status of all Japanese art by disparagingly classifying the articles appreciated at that time as bric-a-brac, bibelots, knickknacks, tourist art, or curios. Chapter 3 examines what and where globe-trotters collected and the meanings that they attributed to their acquisitions. It focuses particular attention on their ambiguous attitudes toward authenticity and how these have informed modern readings of Japanese art.

Clothing is a system of communication that exposes many ideas about a people, by including questions about race, class, ethnicity, gender, and attitudes toward the body. Nineteenth-century tourists were especially prone to read inner meanings about Japan from the external appearance of its inhabitants. Clothing and full-body tattoos were among the arsenal of picturesque stereotypes used in this discourse. Tattoos provide an especially resonant metaphor for the complex, subtle transformations in attitudes toward Japanese culture brought on with the advent of global tourism. Tourists were fascinated by these exotic manifestations of the "artistic nature" of the Japanese people. Some men even "went native" by having themselves tattooed. In so doing, they celebrated the natural life, freedom from convention, and aestheticization of the male body they had discovered in Japan. The costumes Longfellow had made for himself and tattoos he "collected" on his back and chest dramatically illuminate the process through which Euro-American visitors claimed Japanese heritage to fashion their self-identity.

How Americans absorbed cultural difference, transforming its threat into something comforting and compatible with their own lives, is the subject of the final chapter, "Domesticating Japan." Most interpretations of the nineteenth-century reception of Japanese art in America take the museum as their paradigm, but until the beginning of the twentieth century, the primary settings for the public's encounter with Japanese art were fairs and expositions, bazaars and curio shops, and private residences. The décor of Longfellow House, and especially its "Japan Room," filled with Charley Longfellow's souvenirs, serves as the basis for analyzing some of the ways that aesthetic transactions with Japan influenced the American home. The 1870s saw the publication of many guides to interior décor for middle-class Americans. Such publications, though not explicitly about Japan, were filled with images showing how Japanese screens, paintings, ceramics, bronzes, and other decorative furnishings could be integrated into the American home—just as they were in Longfellow House. How homes were decorated reveals many unspoken, and often gendered, Victorian assumptions about the island nation and how it became associated with sophistication and cosmopolitanism.

Charles Longfellow has been overlooked in accounts of New England exchanges with Japan.[7] This neglect is especially surprising given the abundance of literature on the subject by Japanese and American scholars. Although Longfellow's journals and letters were not published during his lifetime, knowledge of his trip was by no means limited to his immediate family. In the nineteenth century, oral communication was more powerful than today, when it is assumed that to participate in cultural discourse requires that ideas be articulated in writing. To gather in the parlor for public readings of a traveler's letters home was common practice in Victorian America.[8] When Charley's letters arrived, his father and siblings read them aloud, often in the presence of visitors with a special interest in Japan. Longfellow's collection of Japanese artifacts enjoyed an even wider public audience. Visitors who called on the elderly poet and his family were often guided to the second-floor suite of rooms Charley had decorated in Japanese style. The Longfellow family's social importance led a number of these visitors to extol the décor of this historic home as a model for other Americans.

Longfellow's absence from the historical record is even stranger in light of the fact that he was acquainted with many of the men from the Boston area who later traveled to Japan. Charley, as he was known to his friends, saw "a good deal" of Ernest Fenollosa and his wife in Nikkō during his second trip to Japan in 1885.[9] He also knew William Sturgis Bigelow, whose father was the family doctor. During his second visit to Japan, Longfellow was among the guests at a "spree" Bigelow hosted.[10] Longfellow was especially close to Charles Goddard Weld, with whom he shared a passion for sailing and collecting. In 1885, they yachted together in Japan and went to the Yokohama tattoo artist Horichō to have themselves tattooed. It is also likely that he knew Edward Morse (1838–1925), who made his first trip to Japan in 1877, ostensibly in search of brachiopods, and his second in 1878 to teach zoology at newly founded Tokyo University. Morse, like Henry Wadsworth Longfellow, was from Portland, Maine, and had studied at Bowdoin College.

One reason Longfellow does not figure in modern art-historical scholarship is that, unlike Morse and Fenollosa, he did not participate professionally in the great cultural exchanges of the last quarter of the century. Nor did he, like so many globe-trotters of his generation, publish an account of his travels. A further contributing factor may be that he was something of an eccentric in a sociocultural community that held its members to high philanthropic standards. Unlike Bigelow and Weld, Longfellow donated no Japanese art to the Boston Museum of Fine Arts or the Peabody Academy of Science (now the Peabody-Essex Museum) in nearby Salem.

Perhaps most important, Longfellow first went to Japan at a time when definitions of Japanese art were in flux. These definitions underwent profound change during the two decades between his first and last trip to the island nation; with the advent of modernism, evaluations of Japanese art saw still further reinterpretation; and, of course, they continue to evolve. As a result, many collections formed in the early years of the Meiji era became objects of derision. The eclectic Victorian domestic taste in Japanese art was regarded as "lowbrow," and Japanese art enshrined in public museums "highbrow." This transformation was part of a broader American phenomenon embracing theater, music, and literature characterized by Lawrence Levine as the "sacralization of art and culture." Sacralized art, he observes, is "an art that makes no compromise with the 'temporal' world; an art that remains spiritually pure and never becomes secondary to the performer or to the audience; an art that is uncompromising in its devotion to cultural perfection."[11] Late-nineteenth-century Bostonians' romanticized view of Japan and its culture lent itself particularly well to such sacralization. The development of Japanese art history, led by aesthetic professionals dedicated to the celebration of art and artists outside the market economy, further clinched this process.

Modern interpretations of Edward Morse and his collection are in many ways emblematic of this shift. In 1893, the Museum of Fine Arts purchased at considerable cost his encyclopedic collection of ceramics. A zoologist, not a professional art historian, Morse did not share the near religious cult of ideal beauty that developed among many Japanophiles of the 1880s and 1890s. After the turn of the century the artistic quality of his collection was widely deprecated. His biographer, Dorothy Wayman, writing in 1942, asserted that "Edward Morse was endowed with an observant eye, an amazingly retentive memory for form and fact, and an analytical mind. He had, however, no aesthetic feeling."[12] Henri Cernuschi (1821–96), a French globe-trotter in Japan at the same time as Longfellow, met a similar fate. Historians of Japanese art until quite recently ignored his collection, which consists predominantly of bronzes, ceramics, and other decorative arts fashionable in 1871. This assessment began to change only in 1998, with the publication of scholarly catalogs and symposia papers occasioned by the centennial of the museum he founded.[13]

Collecting Japanese art in America in the 1860s and 1870s was still primarily a private passion; public museums, which were only then being formed, were not yet recognized as "temples of authenticity." Most American globe-trotters acquired exotic goods, both old and new, in response to personal needs that were met by their display in the family home. The hierarchy of artistic values of the American middle and upper classes developed in the domestic context, a bulwark against the threats of the outside world and a privileged site of culture.

The idea of authenticity is a powerful undercurrent that runs through these changing attitudes. As the anthropologist Richard Handler has written, authenticity is a cultural concept central to the emergence of the ideology of individualism in the modern Western world. It is also closely allied to the emergence of the notion of the nation-state. "The existence of a national collectivity," he writes, "depends on the 'possession' of an authentic culture." Today, the museum is "the temple of authenticity" that sanctifies a nation or a culture. Visiting a museum enables people feeling a sense of anxiety about their own existence to appropriate something of that authenticity as part of their own personal experience.[14]

The nineteenth-century Euro-American idealization of non-Western societies as somehow more authentic than their own led Japan and its products to become highly desirable commodities. Tourists went to the island nation with the expectation that they would come into contact with a culture having qualities either lacking or rapidly vanishing in their own. Acquiring photographs that documented the "traditional" sights, people, and customs of Japan assuaged these modern anxieties. "Going native," by adopting Japanese kimonos or tattoos, was a way of becoming part of this culture while at the same time constructing an individual identity in opposition to one's own. Carrying home souvenirs enabled tourists to authenticate their own experiences, while collecting "antiquities" fulfilled a larger function of preserving what was culturally distinctive about Japan. Yet if what is authentic is first recognized by its function within a given sociocultural context, paradoxically, its "authenticity" is confirmed only by the fact of its removal. Herein lies the dilemma of tourism and collecting.

Longfellow's Tattoos

CHAPTER 1

Globe-Trotting in Japan

The American is a migratory animal. He walks the streets
of London, Paris, St. Petersburg, Berlin, Vienna, Naples, Rome,
Constantinople, Canton, and even the causeways of Japan, with
as confident a step as he treads the pavements of Broadway

—Robert Tomes,
Harper's New Monthly Magazine, 1865

When Phileas Fogg and his companion Passepartout set out on their fictional
eighty-day journey around the world, globe-trotting was the rage among
wealthy Europeans and Americans wanting to visit sights more exotic than
those of Europe and the Middle East. Jules Verne capitalized on this phenomenon in his 1873 novel by combining fantastic adventures with accurate information about people and places that new or improved transportation and
communication were bringing ever closer to his readers. Most of the places where
Verne's two heroes set foot—Suez, Bombay, Calcutta, Singapore, Yokohama,
Hong Kong, Shanghai, San Francisco, and New York—were routine stops on
the itinerary of world travelers. Verne himself hadn't been to any of these cities
but was able to describe them and their strange inhabitants by drawing on the
burgeoning literature of travel.

Like many of his own readers, Verne was a fan of *Le Tour du Monde,* a bian-
nual publication featuring true accounts of hair-raising shipwrecks in the South
Seas, daring Arctic expeditions, treks across India, and adventures in the American Far West.[1] His description of the amazing feats of the Japanese acrobats,
whose troupe Passepartout briefly joins in Yokohama, was in all likelihood
inspired by the richly illustrated articles written by Aimé Humbert, the Swiss
minister to Japan between 1863 and 1864, that were serialized in this periodi-

cal before being published in a book titled *Le Japon illustré*.[2] Verne also had available travelogues written by French-speaking globe-trotters such as Ludovic de Beauvoir, a twenty-one-year-old French count who had visited Japan as part of a tour that included Australia, Java, Siam, Canton, Peking, Yeddo (Edo), and San Francisco.[3] Jacques Siegfried, another Frenchman, chronicled a similar journey in his *Seize mois autour du monde, 1867–1869, et particulièrement aux Indes, en Chine et au Japon*.[4] Verne may not have had an opportunity to read it before the completion of his own book, but Baron von Hubner's *Promenade autour du Monde*, one of the most informative publications of its genre, also appeared in 1873.[5] Written in French by a noted Austrian diplomat who had been ambassador to Paris and the Vatican, this round-the-world account became so popular that within four years of its initial publication it went into a sixth edition. Like Aimé Humbert's book, it was translated into English, enjoying wide readership both in Britain and the United States.[6]

Even as Verne was helping European and American armchair travelers imagine the sights they might encounter in Japan, Japanese were themselves writing accounts of journeys, both real and imaginary. Among the first of these was the best-seller *Conditions of the West (Seiyō jijō)*, which appeared in 1866, just a year before the end of the Tokugawa feudal regime. Its young author, Fukuzawa Yūkichi (1835–1901), had been a member of the first diplomatic mission to the United States. The fictional *Shanks' Mare to the Western Seas (Seiyōdōchū hizakurige)*, an adaptation of a popular story about two bumbling Laurel and Hardy-like travelers, appeared a few years later.[7] Its author Kanagaki Robun (1829–94), like Jules Verne, had never left Japanese shores. By 1878, readers could read about themselves in a Japanese translation of *Around the World in Eighty Days*.[8]

These publications coincided with the growth of Japanese travel overseas. Diplomatic envoys were dispatched to the United States in 1860 and to European capitals in 1862, 1864, and 1867 (fig. 1.1). During the final decade of its rule, the Tokugawa shogunate sent about 150 students abroad, leading Laurence Oliphant to declare, "There is scarcely a capital in Europe now which has not been visited by young Japanese students making the 'Grand Tour.'"[9] Unlike their Euro-American counterparts, however, their objective was not recreation, but the study of Western technologies and institutions. The new Meiji oligarchy, which succeeded the shogunate, was even more eager to send students and diplomats abroad as part of its campaign to develop "civilization and enlightenment" *(bunmei kaika)*.[10] Between 1871 and 1873, hundreds of Japanese toured Europe and the United States to inspect and compare their respective military, educational, legal, and cultural institutions.

Verne's fictionalized account shaped and reflected the dramatic changes in world travel during the early 1870s. With the inauguration of regular crossings between San Francisco and Yokohama in 1867, the opening of the Suez Canal and completion of America's transcontinental railway two years later, and the

1.1 "Reception of the Japanese Ambassadors by the President at the White House, May 17, 1860," from *Harper's Weekly*, May 26, 1860.

improvements in rail and steamship service in Asia, theoretically it *was* possible to circle the globe in eighty days.[11] Most travelers, however, allowed themselves more time. As one returnee warned: "To be benefited by travel, time must be taken for study and reflection. No man can eat all the time; if he attempts it, digestion ceases. A person had better remain at home than go round the world in ninety days."[12] Even Thomas Cook, who introduced a personally conducted world tour in 1872, allowed for 222 days, of which only one was spent in Shanghai, two in Singapore, and three in Ceylon.[13] A year or more was the norm for solo travelers, but even at this more leisurely pace, they rarely stayed in one place for long. Their journey was, to borrow the title of one young American's account, but "dottings round the circle."[14]

While world travelers were proud of the wealth and leisure time that enabled them to undertake such journeys, the European and American residents of the port settlements where they congregated were not pleased by their arrival. William Elliot Griffis (1843–1928), an American teacher in Japan between 1870 and 1874, complained, "Already the circummundane tourists have become so frequent and temporarily numerous in Yokohama as to be recognized as a distinct class. In the easy language of the port, they are called 'globe-trotters.'"[15]

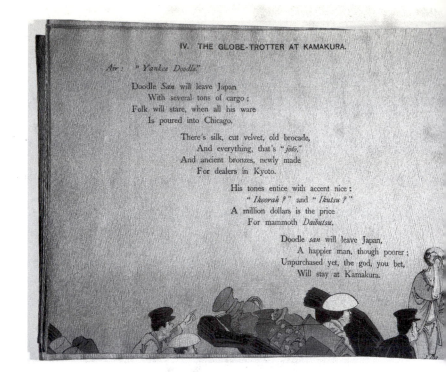

IV. THE GLOBE-TROTTER AT KAMAKURA.

Air: "*Yankee Doodle.*"

Doodle *San* will leave Japan
    With several tons of cargo;
Folk will stare, when all his ware
    Is poured into Chicago.

There's silk, cut velvet, old brocade,
    And everything, that's "*joto*,"
And ancient bronzes, newly made
    For dealers in Kyoto.

His tones entice with accent nice:
    "*Ikoorah ?*" and "*Ikutsu ?*"
A million dollars is the price
    For mammoth *Daibutsu*.

Doodle *san* will leave Japan,
    A happier man, though poorer;
Unpurchased yet, the god, you bet,
    Will stay at Kamakura.

Criticism of globe-trotters in fact became a common refrain in the writings of many Europeans and Americans living and working in Japan. In his *Things Japanese* (1890), the British scholar Basil Hall Chamberlain identified numerous species within the "*genus globe-trotter.*" Among them may be included "*globe-trotter communis,*" whose "object is a maximum of travelling combined with a minimum of expense; *globe-trotter scientificus,* who travels with "spectacles, microscope, a few dozen note-books, alcohol, arsenical acid, seines, butterfly-nets, other nets"; *globe-trotter elegans,* "provided with good introductions from his government, generally stops at a legation, is interested in shooting, and allows the various charms of the country to induce him to prolong his stay"; *globe-trotter independens,* "who travels in a stream-yacht, generally accompanied by his family. Chief goal of his journey, an audience with the Mikado"; *globe-trotter princeps,* "princes or other dignitaries recognizable by their numerous suite, and who undertake the round journey . . . either for political reasons or for purposes of self-instruction; and *globe-trotter desperatus,* who expends his uttermost farthing on a ticket to Japan with the hope of making a fortune there, but who, finding no situation, has at last to be carted home by some cheap opportunity at the expense of his fellow-countrymen."[16]

Men and women working in Japan as diplomats, missionaries, traders, or teachers resented the carefree big-spenders who arrived in Yokohama, enjoyed a few days in Tokyo, visited Kobe and Osaka, and after boating through the scenic Inland Sea, concluded their stay with a bit of sightseeing in Nagasaki. Griffis and Chamberlain saw themselves as privileged insiders engaged with Japanese

1.2 *The Globe-trotter at Kamakura*, from Osman Edwards, *Residential Rhymes* (Tokyo, 1899) Photograph by Mark Sexton; courtesy Peabody-Essex Museum.

society on a professional level and were threatened by the invasion of these newer arrivals, who, by their sheer numbers, were transforming life in Japan. Deep-pocketed globe-trotters accelerated the development of a tourist industry that endangered the "authentic" Japan as they knew it. Furthermore, the narratives many published upon returning home enjoyed wide readership, and by confirming the clichéd expectations of armchair travelers, challenged the knowledge and cultural authority of those who aspired to make their living writing about the "real" Japan.[17]

These unflattering references to globe-trotters lend themselves to interpretation in the context of the distinction between "traveler" and "tourist." Although these two terms had been synonymous in the late eighteenth century, by the middle of the nineteenth, the latter was widely understood to have negative connotations. While the notion of travel was linked to work (Fr. *travail*), tourism implied little more than aimless movement.[18] Tourists (always someone else) were denounced for their preoccupation with conspicuous consumption, their lack of aesthetic sensitivity, and above all, their failure to recognize what was culturally authentic and what was not. This stereotype reflected the ambivalent response to the democratization of travel among members of industrialized societies. At its core was a modern preoccupation with distinguishing between "genuine" travel and its commodified manifestations. The rhetoric of tourism was thus deeply implicated in the West's confrontation with and escape from modernity and in the invention of the dichotomy between the traveler and the tourist or globe-trotter (fig. 1.2).[19]

This prejudice has led many modern scholars to dismiss tourist narratives as fragmentary and flawed representations of the culture they describe. Billie Melman, the author of a study of women travelers to the Middle East, has observed that regardless of background, the "overall approach to cross-cultural representation is often synecdochical. The participant-observer cannot reconstruct a culture in its totality. He or she cannot record all that was seen on the spot. Instead they select a detail, a custom, an institution, a ritual, a group of people. The detail is then used to evoke the cultural whole."[20] Travelogues are further criticized because they often fall into the category of what the cultural anthropologist James Clifford has called "salvage ethnography," nostalgia-filled attempts to save the vanishing primitive by means of textual representation.[21]

Such views have also led historians to discount the importance of early tourists in constructing images of Japanese culture. To overlook these individuals, however, is to ignore their transformative role and interpretive power in Japan as well as in their homelands. Their influence led many Japanese social and cultural institutions to assume new forms and meanings. Tourists were often part of the very changes they deplored. By their extensive written and pictorial legacy, they did not simply leave records of themselves but also created a vast repository of information about Japan for others.

Travelogues were compendia of information about places visited that also conveyed attitudes and expectations for both those at home and future visitors. The European and American public had a voracious appetite for travel, both real and imaginary, and magazines and newspapers routinely published their dispatches from abroad. Publishers issued many books by world travelers, some of which were widely read at the time but are now forgotten. Even those who did not leave a public record of their experiences had an impact on family, friends, and acquaintances through their journals and letters. Since returnees often gave lectures at churches and clubs, oral transmission was also important in disseminating nineteenth-century globe-trotters' views.

Equally influential in representing Japan for their fellow Americans were the photographs and souvenirs that most globe-trotters carried home for display in their parlors. Commercial photographs of Japan from the 1860s and 1870s, often mounted in albums entitled "Views and Costumes," combined education and entertainment in discrete units that armchair travelers could readily take in. Even as they helped to transport the sights of "real" Japan home to America, these representations also helped to insure that Japan remained safely in the realm of myth. The romantic sensibility was too intricately interwoven into the American vision of Japan to be disengaged by photographs. The curios deployed throughout the American domestic interior further reinforced imaginary visual projections of "artistic" Japan, often revealing as much about the aspirations of those who had acquired them as about the culture in which they had originated.

In this chapter I look at the changing nature of the world traveler's motivations, expectations, and experiences in Japan during the 1860s and 1870s. Here, and throughout the book, the terms *tourist, globe-trotter,* and *traveler* are used synonymously to designate persons who traveled primarily for leisure. (It is not always possible, however, to draw a clear line between recreational travel and journeys undertaken with a professional agenda.) While all adhered to certain protocols, there was no "typical" globe-trotter. Attitudes toward Japan and its culture varied widely depending on nationality, social background, age, and gender, often combining attraction and revulsion in equal measures. Americans' views differed significantly from those of their British and continental counterparts, but there was considerable heterogeneity even among those of the same nationality. Charley Longfellow's responses to Japan bear the stamp of a distinctly American worldview, but as someone who could be fairly characterized as a member of the New England aristocracy, he had money, connections, and culture, which gave him enormous advantages over most of his peers. His experiences and impressions of Japan, therefore, are not necessarily representative of other American tourists.

American Travel to Japan

Affluent Americans traveled abroad in considerable numbers throughout the nineteenth century.[22] Travel was a ritual long sanctioned and encouraged by American society for self-improvement and education. Indeed, for those who could afford it, it was an acceptable surrogate for formal education and professional occupation. Seeing the world, it was held, helped to develop both the mind and the eye. A young man who left home ignorant of the world returned better informed, maturer, and better prepared to deal with the future. His worldly education often included sexual experiences not so easily gained at home. Travel not only served to open up or develop new professional opportunities; it could also be a way of turning over a new leaf following failure. Most important, encounters with other cultures were understood to play an important role in producing enhanced understanding and appreciation of what it meant to be an American. As Emerson declared in 1847, "We go to Europe to be Americanized, to import what we can."[23]

Individual motives for travel were varied and complex, with the professed reasons often disguising hidden ones. Travel could help an individual to recover from physical or mental illness and provide a temporary refuge from other personal or professional problems. It could satisfy the desire for adventure and escape from routine. Although no American admitted to traveling for the sheer fun of it, this was often a primary goal. William Perry Fogg, a successful businessman from Cleveland, Ohio, was careful to note in the prologue to his *Round the World Letters from Japan, China, India, and Egypt* (1872) that his "motive was not merely the pursuit of pleasure, but the desire to gratify a long cherished passion to see strange and curious nations of the Orient."[24] His claim also served to mask the fact that the leisure to spend a year or more circumnavigating the globe was a way of broadcasting one's worldly success. Undertaking such a journey required, according to an estimate of 1869, a minimum of $3,500 to $3,800 to cover the cost of steamship and train fares, hotel accommodations, and other living expenses.[25] At a time when personal ostentation was not condoned in many American cultural circles, travel was a socially sanctioned form of conspicuous consumption. Writing about it, moreover, was an important way of assuaging one's guilt and justifying the life of leisure. Some travelers, in fact, helped to defray their expenses and give the appearance of time well spent by writing newspaper reports on their travels.

By freeing an individual from the institutional restraints of work and home, the experience of travel also fostered reflection that could lead to new self-knowledge. The constantly changing surroundings predisposed travelers to reconsider their lives, assumptions, and goals. These conditions also provided a stage for demonstrating independence and acting out new identities that sometimes had a questionable relationship to the real world. Since tourists lived a life of casual acquaintances and chance encounters, there were rarely any long-term consequences from such activities. Casting themselves in a wide range of roles and identities within the culture of the countries visited was often an important part of this quest for self-identity. This was possible in Europe, where many Americans had mastered the local language, but was more difficult in the Middle East or Japan, where foreign visitors were insulated from the local culture both linguistically and ethnically.

Before 1850, when already thousands of Americans were crossing the Atlantic annually, "going abroad" meant going to Europe.[26] These numbers increased dramatically following the Civil War, owing to increasing prosperity and improvements in transportation that lowered the cost and time required for continental travel. By making it possible for men, women, and even entire families to see Europe safely, conveniently, and economically, these developments also lessened the cachet associated with the time-honored European "Grand Tour." Consequently, in the postbellum era, Americans with the means and leisure to do so began to turn their attention to more distant and less well-trodden places where they could still discover strange new sights, feel the satisfaction of physical exertion, and even experience the frisson of danger that had all but disappeared with the advent of mass tourism in Europe. As Charley Longfellow's friend Allen Macrough wrote in a letter of introduction before Longfellow set off for India, the first leg of his round-the-world journey, "Longfellow intends visiting the three Presidencies, getting what shooting he can and then going on to China! This is what you may call a tour with a vengeance, and one which would I think astonish Mr. Cooks [sic], who yearly leads herds of English to Switzerland and Rome."[27]

Although Japan was only one of many stops on the route of the round-the-world traveler, it held special allure for Americans because of Matthew Perry's role in "opening" the country. As the only non-European nation to resist formal colonization and to embrace modern technology and institutions, it also enjoyed considerable prestige vis-à-vis the rest of Asia. The contrasts between China and Japan in globe-trotters' accounts are particularly striking: "Passing from China to Japan is like a change between two worlds," wrote one. "China is stationary, fixed and immovable; Japan, on the contrary, is turning a somersault, and transmutation is visible in everything."[28] Visitors found Japan more scenic, comfortable, and clean than China, although the Japanese habit of mixed bathing was a frequent subject of criticism on the part of prudish Americans. They also deemed Japanese men and women more courteous and attractive. The Japanese, said one observer, were the "Frenchmen of Asia."[29] The tourist's appreciation of the modern creature comforts available to them, however, were generally tempered by dismay that such innovations were contributing to the loss of the very qualities that had drawn them to Japan in the first place.

American travelers' curiosity about and expectations of Japan were largely dependent on presentations by others who were often little more knowledgeable than themselves. Misinformation continued to be purveyed in the popular press long after more accurate data were available: fanciful accounts that confirmed the image of Japan as strange and mysterious tended to be more appealing to the public. Some of this misinformation was a legacy of the large body of writings cutting across many aspects of Japanese culture published by the Dutch more than a century earlier, when they were the only Westerners officially allowed in Japan. Even those who wrote in the 1860s and 1870s based on personal observations did not necessarily try to disprove myths about the island nation. This problem was not unique to American authors, but also prevailed in Britain, prompting Sir Rutherford Alcock (1809–97), the first British Minister to Japan, to declare in 1861 that more photographs were necessary to provide authentic information on Japan.[30]

Alcock's belief that the photographer would be an objective witness to and recorder of the people and events in Japan proved to be misplaced. In fact, photographs fostered a new kind of pictorial romance with the country that often began even before the tourist set off on his journey. During the 1860s and 1870s, photographs as well as lithographs, engravings, and woodcuts based on them, sometimes only loosely, appeared with growing frequency in European and American books and newspapers. Lithographs copied from daguerreotypes taken in 1854 by Eliphalet Brown, who had accompanied Perry, figured in the official record of the first American mission to Japan.[31] *The London Illustrated News* featured engravings based on photographs of Japan taken by

1.3 Mrs. de Long and five young Japanese women, c. 1872. Carte de visite. Photographer unknown. LNHS.

Felice Beato, and, although less frequently, American periodicals did as well.[32]

Although some globe-trotters read publications such as *Across America and Asia* (1870), the geologist Raphael Pumpelly's narrative of his work and travels in Japan, or *The Mikado's Empire* (1876), William Elliot Griffis's wide-ranging introduction to Meiji-era Japan, most Americans' perceptions were based primarily on accounts in the popular press.[33] The steady stream of illustrated articles that appeared in *Harper's Weekly, Frank Leslie's Illustrated Newspaper, The Nation,* and other periodicals following Perry's expedition gave birth to a vast and enduring repertory of images of the island country. American coverage was most intense in the years during the visit of the first Japanese embassy in 1860, the tour of the Iwakura Mission in 1871–73, and the Philadelphia Centennial Exposition of 1876, events that brought Japanese men, as well as a few young female students, to American soil (fig. 1.3).

The 1860 embassy's cross-country journey and visits to Washington, Baltimore, Philadelphia, and New York aroused enormous enthusiasm and pride, since the United States was the first country visited by such a mission. Walt Whitman celebrated the procession of envoys down the streets of Manhattan in a poem published in *The New York Times.*[34] Stereoscopic photographs of the envoys were made available to the public (fig. 1.4). Photographs and autographs of the Japanese ambassadors, as well as Japanese swords, sandals, smoking

1.4　Japanese Embassy to the United States, 1860. Albumen print mounted on stereocard. Photographer unknown. Courtesy Peabody Museum, Harvard University (photo H 15343).

pipes, razors, tobacco pouch, and coins, were added to the displays at P. T. Barnum's New York Museum. The museum even featured a wax figure of the charismatic young member of the 1860 embassy the American press had nicknamed Tommy.[35]

These developments attest that in the eyes of the public, the political implications of this and the subsequent Iwakura mission were overshadowed by fascination with the Japanese visitors' exotic appearance and customs. For most Americans, the diplomats and students who toured the United States, like the indigo-jacketed carpenters who erected the Japanese buildings for the 1876 Centennial Exposition, were little more than a form of public theater staged for their enjoyment (fig. 1.5).

Western powers had signed treaties with the Tokugawa shogunate opening the ports of Nagasaki, Hakodate, and Shimoda to Western residents and trade six years after Commodore Perry's arrival at Uraga in 1853. These were soon followed by Kanagawa (Yokohama), Niigata, and Hyogo (Kobe). As part of these accords, diplomatic missions were also permitted in Edo, later Tokyo, although the city was not opened to international trade until 1869. Kyoto was accessible to tourism only briefly in 1872 on the occasion of a special exhibition, and until 1874 foreigners were allowed free movement only within a twenty-five-

1 Japanese workmen preparing their meals.   2. The chief workman and his assistant consulting their books and charts.   3. Bringing joists and timber from Machinery Hall.   4. Erecting the Japanese dwelling house.   5. Mortising
6. Sawing.   7. Using the adz.   8. Around the fire.

ERECTION OF THE JAPANESE BUILDINGS ON THE CENTENNIAL GROUNDS, IN FAIRMOUNT PARK.

1.5   Japanese carpenters preparing for the 1876 centennial, from *Frank Leslies' Illustrated Historic Register of the Centennial Exposition* (New York, 1876). Photo courtesy Felice Fisher.

mile radius of these cities unless given special travel passes by the government. Despite these limitations, young American men seeking adventure, fame, and fortune flocked to the port settlements of Nagasaki, Yokohama, and Hakodate, much as they had to frontier towns in the American Far West during the Gold Rush. Yokohama, where a large expatriate mercantile community had developed by the mid-1860s, epitomized the world of those who went to Japan "without much capital to make a livelihood, or, if possible, something more, and hastened to the attainment of their object without being troubled with much scruple."[36]

Although there were hotels and other services catering to foreigners in Yokohama and Tokyo, political instability made Japan a dangerous tourist destination during the 1860s and even the early 1870s. The opening of the ports to Western trade, and especially the extraterritorial rights that were integral components of these treaties, were made under duress, when shogunal authority was waning. The treaty ports were sovereign territories where foreigners had the right to be tried under the judicial authority of their own country. Japanese did not enjoy similar rights abroad. Extraterritoriality was abolished only in 1899, after bitter and prolonged Japanese diplomatic efforts.

Some of the shogun's feudal retainers also opposed the growing foreign presence, fearing that it jeopardized their sinecure. Foreign diplomats and merchants were frequent targets of attack: in January 1861 Henry Heusken, the Dutch interpreter and secretary to Townsend Harris, the American minister in Japan, was killed by a band of assassins, and in September of the following year, Charles Richardson, a British merchant from Shanghai, was murdered. The German tourist Margaretha Weppner had a close brush with death in Tokyo in 1869, when the Europeans in the hotel where she was staying were attacked.[37] Travel beyond the foreign settlements remained so dangerous that the Meiji government often appointed soldiers to accompany diplomats and tourists. When Charley Longfellow and his companions toured the foothills of Mount Fuji in 1871, they carried revolvers in their belts for added protection.

As many scholars have noted, travel was a highly gendered experience in the nineteenth century, and the Europe of the Grand Tour, with its emphasis on the pursuit of high culture and art, was coded as feminine.[38] For Americans of the 1860s and early 1870s, Japan, by contrast, was decidedly masculine terrain. Travel there not only satisfied the urge for personal independence, but offered the potential for heroic adventure and exploration of the unknown. A climb to the summit of snowcapped Mount Fuji or an expedition across the remote northern island of Hokkaidō, both outside the officially permitted travel zones, were among the exploits that lent themselves to such interpretation, although a few women did make such treks. The masculinity of the experience of Japan was reinforced by the fact that the port settlement was a homosocial environment. With the exception of missionaries, there were few Euro-American women, and these were generally regarded with disdain by their less religious male compatriots. For a young unmarried woman, travel to Japan was to flirt with danger, as Margaretha Weppner (d. 19?) discovered upon her arrival in Yokohama. Assumed to be a libertine, she was particularly outraged by the less than courteous treatment she received at the hands of her fellow Germans. Her dismay at the depravity of life in Yokohama colored her disapproving assessment of nearly everything she saw and experienced in Japan.[39]

Warning "parents against sending their sons to the wild immoral settlements of Asia," Weppner declared:

> There is a vast difference between life in such places and life in Europe or America. . . . The foreigner in Japan leads an expensive, luxurious life, and I have often noticed the consequences with unfeigned disgust. These consequences are, it is said, attributable to the climate, which requires that liquors should be taken before breakfast, wine, beer, and champagne at breakfast, and again liquors after breakfast; the same routine before, at, and after dinner, and brandy and soda all day long. Short hours of business are a necessity, wild exercise on horseback, much pleasure, and long sleep are the concomitants. The moral consequences of this life, among a people like the Japanese, I have already sufficiently dwelt upon. . . . Another cause of the ruin of young foreigners in Japan is the high salaries usually paid to unmarried men. It places every pleasure within their reach, and leaves them prey to their passions. . . . I heard in Boston of a merchant who sent his son to Japan, simply because he was dissolute, and Japan could neither harm nor cure him! Fatal folly![40]

As Weppner and others observed, most foreign residents who could afford to do so took a Japanese mistress—and sometimes several. "One American in Tokio" claimed Griffis, "enjoyed a harem of ten native beauties."[41] In the 1860s, those who didn't have mistresses frequented the Gankirō, an establishment in Yokohama's Miyozaki brothel district, which the Japanese authorities had opened to cater specifically to this Euro-American bachelor society. Later, many patronized prostitutes in the Shinbashi district of Tokyo, which was closer to Yokohama than the older and more celebrated Yoshiwara brothel district.

Descriptions of the brothels in Yokohama, Tokyo, and other cities, usually couched in disapproving terms, figure more often in the travelogues of European than of American men.[42] Despite the moralistic rhetoric, the promise of sexual adventure was an important component of Japan's allure as a tourist destination for men of all nationalities. Perceptions of Japanese women had much in common with and drew on a stock of Orientalist stereotypes deeply implicated in the colonialist discourse on the Middle East. A few teachers and diplomats in Japan tried to present a more balanced picture, but informed and informative discussions, such as appeared in William Griffis's *The Mikado's*

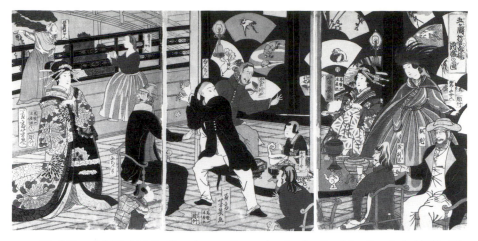

1.6   Yoshiiku (1833–1904), *Foreigners Carousing in the Gankirō Brothel*, 1860–62. Wood block print, ōban triptych. 37.8 x 75.3 cm. (14 7/8 x 29 11/16 in.). Arthur M. Sackler Gallery, Smithsonian Institution; gift of Ambassador and Mrs. William Leonhart (S1998.66).

Empire, carried less weight than globe-trotters' titillating accounts.[43]

Far from home, beyond the oversight of family and friends, men could sow their wild oats with few personal consequences—except perhaps the risk of venereal disease. Japanese, like all "Oriental" women, were understood to be not only promiscuous, but also racial and cultural inferiors who didn't need to be treated with the same respect accorded women of one's own background. Brief liaisons followed by unacknowledged and abandoned children were common. In this sense, travel to Japan was a kind of ritual in which Euro-American travelers could use their political and economic power symbolically to reconcile their sense of themselves as men.

American travelogues never explicitly refer to the sexual activity in which their authors engaged. Many, however, acknowledged being impressed by the décor of the Gankirō, the brothel built in Yokohama expressly to cater to foreign visitors (fig. 1.6). In the journal of his 1860 world tour, Richard Henry Dana Jr., the author of *Two Years Before the Mast* (1840), recounts going with a companion to "inspect" the Gankirō, which, he wrote, "looked like a temple, it is so large and handsome. Within are parlors, reception rooms, dining rooms, a dancing hall, a theatre etc. etc. The chief rooms were beautifully carved and elaborately painted. The chief artists of Yeddo contributed each a panel, for the walls and ceiling. Lacquered furniture and screens abound, and great neatness everywhere."[44] This detailed description should be read in the context of Dana's sexual double life. According to his biographer, after his marriage, "Whenever he got the chance, usually while away from Boston on his frequent trips, Dana would slip into a sailor's disguise—varnished cap, loose trousers, and a peacoat—and 'cruise,' as he put it, the brothels, and dives of the town."[45]

Suggestive pornographic photographs and references to sex also can be discovered in other private papers. The Japanese vocabulary list, including "iro-onna, mistress; iro-otoko, lover; and iro-shitai, let us consummate," in Charley Longfellow's pocket diary leaves no doubt that he took advantage of the easy access to prostitutes in Japan.[46] A souvenir photograph in one of Longfellow's albums showing two Euro-American men with Japanese women offers further confirmation of this aspect of life in Japan (fig. 1.7). The two blond men, bearing some resemblance to Charley himself, casually dressed in white cotton kimonos *(yukata)*, are stretched out on a futon gazing intently at two fully dressed prostitutes kneeling in front of them. Charley has suggestively labeled the picture "Teachers in Toke," presumably a reference to Tokyo, which was sometimes referred to at the time as Tokei. Pornographic photographs by both Japanese and European photographers were widely available in Japan in the 1870s and figure in many collections, such as that formed by William Bigelow, now in the Peabody Museum of Harvard University (fig. 1.8).[47] Charley himself also acquired a selection, which he did not mount in his album but kept separately in a box of miscellaneous cartes de visite.

1.7 *Teachers in "Toke,"* c. 1871. Carte de visite. Photographer unknown. LNHS.

The attractions of Japanese women had much to do with American discourses on gender that called into question the way men saw themselves. In contrast to America, where women were demanding a more prominent public role in society, in Japan women's lives were still largely confined to the domestic sphere, where they remained deferential and subservient to the wishes of men. Although the debate about women's rights to freedom and equality became

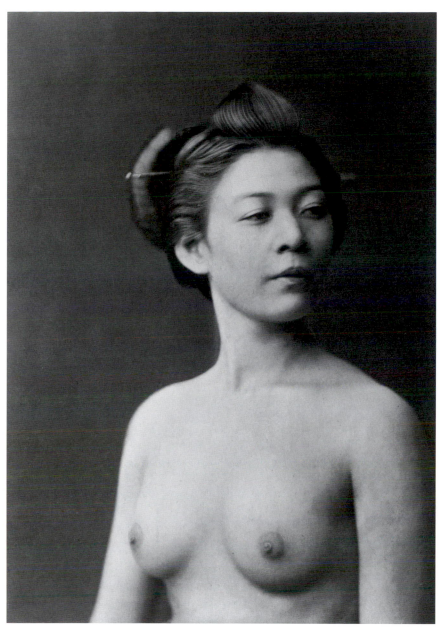

1.8 Prostitute, 1870s. Hand-colored albumen print. Stillfried and Anderson Company. Courtesy Peabody Museum, Harvard University.

particularly intense in the last quarter of the century, a cartoon in *Harper's Weekly* reveals that the Victorian ideal of the woman as homemaker was displaced to Japan as early as 1858 (fig. 1.9). The picture features six attractive young women tending to a tired dandy's needs—removing his shoes, washing his hands, fanning him, brushing his hair, supplying his pipe, and bringing drinks.

1.9 "Japanese Manners," from *Harper's Weekly,* December 18, 1858.

The caption, quoting "From a Letter from Japan" states: "The traveler, wearied with the noonday heat, need never be at a loss to find rest and refreshment; stretched upon the softest and cleanest of matting, imbibing the most delicately-flavored tea, inhaling through a short pipe the fragrant tobacco of Japan, he resigns himself to the ministrations of a bevy of fair damsels, who glide rapidly and noiselessly about, the most zealous and skilful of attendants. – AND BY ALL MEANS LET US HAVE JAPANESE MANNERS AND CUSTOMS HERE"[48] This visual projection also underscores the image of Japan as a refuge from work and retreat from modernity.

Japan's popularity as a tourist destination grew steadily over the course of the 1870s, as travel beyond the treaty ports became safer, restrictions on travel eased, and transportation, accommodations, and food improved. The new accessibility of the former imperial capital of Kyoto and the shogunal tombs at Nikkō, some ninety miles north of Tokyo, provided visitors with a greater range of picturesque sight-seeing possibilities. The grand opening of Japan's first railway between Yokohama and Shinbashi (Tokyo) in 1872, followed a few years later by the Kobe-Osaka-Kyoto line, made it possible to visit more sights during a limited stay. Before the advent of the train, at least three hours were required to cover the approximately eighteen miles between Yokohama and Tokyo. By 1875, passengers disembarking in Yokohama could choose among the Grand, International, and Hotel du Louvre, and a few years later, one globe-trotter reported that he dined in a Tokyo hotel on food prepared by a French chef, "specially imported."[49]

The publication of reliable guidebooks, establishing what the author of *Going Abroad*, William Stowe, has called "the liturgy of travel," was emblematic of the institutionalization of tourism in Japan.[50] Two early examples, *The Tokio Guide* and *The Yokohama Guide* (1873), were both written, ironically, by William Elliot Griffis—whose dismay at the ubiquity of globe-trotters was cited above. The author begins the former with instructions on what to read: "The tourist will do well to read Mr. Mitford's *Tales of Old Japan* (2 vols.), or at least the notes preceding or subjoined to each story. It is well to have it in hand to read at the places to which it refers, or even to peruse it after a visit to Tokio."[51] Next he gives clear instructions on railway travel between Yokohama and Tokyo, and what to look at along the way: "On the [Kawasaki] river flats will be noticed pear-orchards . . . to the right of the road, before crossing the bridge, may be seen a small but famous shrine gaily decorated, and approached by a numerous series of sacred red portals."[52] This is followed by a vocabulary list; a general description of Tokyo; detailed descriptions of places of special interest; suggested one-, two-, three-, and four-day trips; shopping places; a chronology; and fees. Many American globe-trotters followed Griffis's guide, and in their travelogues, some quoted—with and without credit—passages describing the sights he had certified.[53]

Photographers, committed to producing what visitors would purchase, reinforced the itinerary of recognized tourist sights. Among the places Griffis singled out as being of special interest in Tokyo were the great Buddhist mortuary temples constructed by successive shoguns at Shiba and at Ueno and the "charming rural retreat" of Oji. Views of the shogunal tombs, among the most elaborately lacquered and painted monuments accessible to early tourists, figured especially prominently in commercial photographs. Carefully framed shots of a quaintly picturesque canal flanked by small residences and teahouses at Oji were also tourist favorites (fig. 1.10).

1.10   Felice Beato, teahouse at Oji, c. 1870. Albumen print. LNHS.

1.11 Felice Beato, view of Shiba temples, c. 1870. Albumen print. LNHS.

If travel to Japan in the 1860s and 1870s provided Americans with a cultural education, it did so in ways quite different from travel to Europe. No Americans visited the great cities of Europe with their ancient monuments, palaces, and museums without becoming keenly sensitive to their own nation's lack of such traditions. Sightseeing in Japan, by contrast, was profoundly empowering. The manifestations of Japanese culture, relatively modest in scale by European standards, strengthened feelings of racial superiority. Since Japan had no permanent museum until 1882, the visitor's appreciation of Japanese art was limited to what might be seen in industrial exhibitions or was available in curio shops. With the exception of the walled and moated Imperial Palace in Tokyo, and the shogunal mausoleums and temples of Shiba and Ueno, visitors were on the whole little impressed by Japanese architecture (fig. 1.11). Olive Seward, who visited Japan in 1870, declared the architecture of Japanese towns and villages to be "monotonous."[54] Furthermore, to many Americans, the scale, refinement, and decorative qualities of Japanese art, architecture, and gardens suggested a warmth and homey intimacy associated with the private rather than the public realm. This domestic "femininity" was encoded in one traveler's view that Japanese art "has been content to remain solely decorative," and had yet to reach "creative and imaginative power."[55] This tendency intensified as a result of the glowing press coverage of the Japanese displays of porcelains, silks, lacquers, and bronzes at the 1876 Philadelphia Exposition. "They are the sweetest-voiced, gentlest-manner folk," said one report on the fair, "and it is impossible to look from their small forms to their exquisite productions without an uncomfortable misgiving that they may feel like so many Gullivers in Brobdingnag."[56] For many Americans, the idealized image of the Japanese people became inseparable from the delicate, finely crafted domestic goods produced there, a perception that was often tinged with a sense of imperialist superiority.

Globe-Trotters of the 1860s and 1870s

Only a handful of the many globe-trotters who visited Japan in the 1860s and 1870s for a few weeks or months can be identified today because they left journals, correspondence, sketches, or photographs; published travelogues; or others took note of their activities. We may imagine their considerable numbers from a remark by Benjamin Robbins Curtis (1855–91), a globe-trotter who sailed from San Francisco to Yokohama aboard the *Great Republic* in 1875. In addition to himself and his companion, he noted in his book, there were among the 150 cabin passengers, "five gentlemen making a tour of the world."[57] Of these, he was the only one to publish a travelogue. Similarly, the minister Edward D. G. Prime was the sole author among a group in 1869 that included his wife, B. B. Atterbury Esq. and his wife and son, Miss Mary Parsons, and Mr. Kilian Van Rensselaer, all of New York.[58]

Despite the paucity of written records, it is also clear that American men and women of surprisingly diverse regional backgrounds, professions, and ages visited Japan on their world travels. Their expectations and experiences were by no means homologous. They had minds and voices of their own, and were often sharp, critical observers and interpreters of what they saw. A few were even prepared to revise the biases they had when they left home. As Prime declared: "We entertain altogether too high an opinion of our modern perfection in art as compared with some people whom we have been wont to place on the borders of barbarism."[59]

A significant number of these globe-trotters were from the affluent cities of Philadelphia, Boston, and New York, which had a long tradition of trade with the Far East. Richard Henry Dana Jr. visited Japan in 1860 to recover from a nervous breakdown, leaving at home a wife and infant.[60] The journals recounting his experiences were not made public during his lifetime, but he gave a lecture at the Saturday Club in Boston, which Henry Wadsworth Longfellow, Oliver Wendell Holmes, Charles Eliot Norton, and other prominent cultural figures attended.[61] Alfred Dupont Jessup (d. 1881), who visited Japan in 1872, joining Charley Longfellow on an ascent of Mount Fuji, was a cosmopolitan Philadelphia businessman (fig. 1.12). Before visiting Japan, he summered in England, where he leased a country mansion. Later, he purchased a villa in Rome.[62] Edward Prime, a frequent contributor to the *New York Observer,* was equally well traveled, having served in 1854–55 as chaplain to the American diplomatic mission in Rome. Benjamin Curtis, whose *Dottings round the Circle* was cited above, was a Bostonian who circumnavigated the globe with his classmate Andrew Fiske after graduating from Harvard. The written record of the Boston painter Winckworth Allan Gay (1821–1910), who traveled to Japan in 1877, is limited to a few letters, but he left numerous paintings. Whether or not he went to Japan with the intention of living there is not clear, but the fact that his brother was an employee of Walsh, Hall and Son, the largest American trading concern in China and Japan, may have played a role in his decision to remain there for four years.[63]

Midwesterners were also represented. William Perry Fogg, a wealthy merchant from Cleveland, toured the world in 1870, later publishing the letters he had written during his journey.[64] William H. Metcalf (d.1892), a successful shoe manufacturer from Milwaukee and amateur photographer who crossed the Pacific in 1877 with Edward Morse, left no written record, but some of his stereographic photographs are still extant.[65] Enoch Mather Marvin (1823–77), a Methodist bishop who traveled round the world with his wife and son in 1876, was from St. Louis. In his introduction to the posthumously published narrative of Marvin's journey, Reverend Summers explains that "This is not a trip for pleasure, merely, with him, nor one of curiosity; but prompted mainly by a desire to see the battle as it rages along the front lines of the army of invasion and occupation, by which the Son of God is going forward to the conquest of the world."[66] While few wrote with such verbal intemperance, many of those who went to Japan for rest or recreation also went with a religious mission that deeply inflected their responses to the country.

The line between recreational and professional considerations was in fact often blurred. Although the catalyst for his 1874 round-the-world tour was a desire to visit his daughter in Australia, David Dudley Field Jr. (1805–94), a noted New York jurist and legal reformer, attended conferences in Europe en route. He was accompanied by his eleven-year-old grandson, Addis Emmet Carr, who became the youngest globe-trotter to publish his impressions of Japan. His *All the way Round: or What a boy saw and heard on his way round the world, a book for young people and older ones with young hearts* (1876) was the first of many books touching on Japan that aimed to inform young readers of the world beyond American shores. His youthful views on subjects ranging from ruins to collecting curios are often refreshingly unguarded by comparison with those of his elders.[67] Andrew Carnegie (1835–1919) ostensibly had no business in Japan, but his professional background predisposed him to take special note of Japanese trade, industry, and currency problems.[68] Although undertaken as a private citizen, the world travels of William Seward (1801–72), secretary of state under Lincoln, also had economic and diplomatic overtones. When the Japanese minister of foreign affairs asked Seward to intervene in Japan's border dispute with Russia over the Sakhalin islands, the American replied that the United States had resolved a similar dispute by purchasing all Russian possessions on the American continent. "What would you think," he added playfully, "of a suggestion that Japan shall, in the same way, purchase Saghhalien?"[69]

No American globe-trotter caused a greater sensation than Ulysses Grant (1822–85), who headed east in 1877, spending two and a half years circumnavigating the globe in the company of his wife, younger son, and an entourage that

1.12   Raimund von Stillfried, "The Fusiyama Pilgrims," 1872. Carte de visite. LNHS.

included John Russell Young, a reporter for the *New York Herald*. Its publisher, James Gordon Bennett Jr., had achieved a coup in 1871 when Henry Stanley, whom he had sent to Africa, discovered Dr. David Livingston on the shores of Lake Tanganyika. By sending Young to cover Grant's travels, he hoped to achieve a similar boost to the newspaper's circulation.[70] Young's *Around the World with General Grant,* based on the almost daily reports he sent to New York, and written in the lively prose for which he was renowned, offers an unparalleled record of the extraordinary efforts Japanese authorities made to welcome the former president.[71] One reason Grant was so warmly welcomed was his outspoken support of Japan's urgent desire to revise the treaties granting Western powers extraterritorial rights and economic advantages in trade. His role in helping to mediate a dispute between Japan and China over control of the Ryūkyū Islands further contributed to his popularity.[72] Although Grant went to Japan for pleasure, because of his status as a war hero and former president, he received porcelains, cloisonné, and other artistic gifts, which he later put on display in the parlor of his New York residence (fig. 1.13).

Grant's visit also engendered a Japanese biography and souvenirs aimed at the domestic market. Edward Morse, who was teaching in Tokyo at the time, commented on the degree to which Grant had captured the popular imagination: "You find rude engravings of the General in the shop-windows. Sometimes these pictures are in a heroic stage of color. . . . Most of these engravings depict the General as a military athlete doing marvelous things with his sword. This, however, is how history becomes mythology."[73] This romanticized image of Grant was further promoted by a three-volume illustrated "biography" that began appearing in serial form during his stay in Japan. Written by Kanagaki Robun, who had earlier written a comic narrative of two Japanese travelers abroad, it tailored Grant's life and accomplishments to the theatrical expectations of the Japanese public. Illustrations of dancers, clad in kimonos fashioned from fabric patterned with the American flag, who had purportedly performed for the distinguished visitor, enhanced this exotic drama (fig. 1.14).

While a few European women of this era, most notably Margaretha Weppner and the intrepid Isabella Bird (1813–1919), fulfilled their desire for personal freedom through solo travel to and within Japan, most American women globetrotters accepted their socially sanctioned roles as good wives and mothers or companions to elderly relatives.[74] Many, however, expressed themselves by writing of their experiences, often with considerable verve and interpretive insight. Olive Risley Seward accompanied her adoptive father, and upon their

1.13   General Grant's parlor, from *Artistic Houses* (New York, 1883).

1.14   Utagawa Kunisada II, illustration from Kanagaki Robun's biography of Mr. Grant, 1879; property of Mary Griggs Burke.

return, edited the narrative of their world travels. Fifteen-year-old Ellen Hardin Walworth (1858–1932), took a year off from the Sacred Heart Convent School she attended to travel around the world with her uncle, a Catholic priest. Her chatty letters home were published in an Albany newspaper before being issued in book form.[75] In 1879, Lucy Bainbridge (1858–1932) accompanied her husband, who had just completed a decade of service as a minister in Providence, Rhode Island. At the request of the editor of the *Providence Daily Journal,* she too wrote a series of letters during her two years' journey chronicling her *"personal* sight-seeing and experiences."[76] In her *Round the World Letters*, she found it necessary to justify her leisure voyage to those of her readers who believed: "A woman's business is to stay to home and look after things and save."[77] In response to these imaginary readers, she argued that travel makes a man *and* a woman wiser.

Aspiring professional travel writers also made round-the-world journeys, later publishing their experiences and advice in the form of travelogues. Prospective globe-trotters may have prepared for their journeys and formed opinions about Japan on the basis of Charles Carleton Coffin's *Our New Way Round the World* (1869). A famous Civil War correspondent known for his uncompromising eye-witness accounts of the brutal battles of the Civil War, Coffin (1823–98) went to Japan in 1866–67. In his book he described his journey in considerable detail, often drawing analogies designed to help his readers appreciate each country and culture in terms of their own. He likened the beauty of Japan's Inland Sea to Arcadia and its temples and their many deities to those of ancient Greece. In discussing the introduction of Christianity, he noted that Jesuit missionaries were driven from the Japanese islands "in 1620, when the Mayflower was making her lonely journey across the Atlantic."[78] Coffin provided an appendix supplying globe-trotters with practical advice on recommended readings, the time required for each leg of the journey, costs, best routes, and even the most comfortable clothing. He also cautioned them to allow enough time—at least a year—for the trip, or else "the brain, instead of retaining distinct pictures, will be in the condition of a sportsman whose horse turns a somersault in a steeplechase, and the unfortunate rider beholds a whirling landscape of fields, trees, hounds, hedges, and blinding stars!"[79]

Although the publication of a travelogue by someone as young as Carr was exceptional, such writings were an extension of the journals, letters, and sketches that were integral to the experience of most nineteenth-century travelers. As Ellen Walworth declared, "These long letters, written at odd times and in old places, had become to me a part of the pleasure of the journey."[80] On the surface, they present a certain sameness, since they do not vary greatly in form or content. Japan did not deliver a cultural experience like that of Europe, but the rhetoric of travel throughout the world demanded similar narrative strategies and structural devices. Travelogues lack a conceptual framework, following instead a temporal and spatial program that takes the reader from day to day and one place to the next. They share the same relatively limited range of source materials, since even the best informed globe-trotter had access to very little information about Japanese history, literature, and art, and what was available was often dated and not necessarily accurate. Most writers incorporated some historical background but felt safer keeping to an ocular account. The two to four weeks they spent in Japan did not give them the time, knowledge, or inclination to move beyond the surface. Ellen Walworth's uncle, however, was rare in admitting that "in a stay of twelve days in a strange country, one does not become very learned, although one sees a great deal that is novel and interesting."[81]

The tendency of nineteenth-century globe-trotters to present their impressions of Japan within clichéd frames of reference may be attributed in part to the fact that tourism is grounded in an ideology of distinction wherein social cultural capital is accrued through the citation of place names that others recognize. Retracing the route of earlier travelers made it one's own. The search for novelty within Japan was not yet the dominant concern it would become later in the century. It was as important to visit and thereby personally authenticate known places as to seek out new ones.

Attitudes toward Japan and Its Culture

American travelogues disclose a wide range of attitudes, but to a one they reveal a strong sense of pride and even proprietorship over Japan's relationship with the West, owing to Perry's role in its "opening." Just as the West's mapping of Japan was not neutral, so too travel was never far from the politics of power. By traveling there Americans were symbolically laying claim to and consolidating this authority. Bayard Taylor (1825–78), the most popular and enterprising travel writer of his day, gave clear expression of this imperialistic worldview in his *A Visit to India, China, and Japan in the Year 1853* (1855). To travel to Japan, Bayard had managed to get permission to join Perry's squadron, despite the latter's notorious unwillingness to have on board anyone who was not in the navy. Taylor's chief concern was how Americans should manage their efforts to gain a foothold in the Pacific. The opinions about Japan that he voiced reveal that he also brought with him many racial prejudices that would be common among later globe-trotters as well.[82] Although Taylor never returned to Japan, he continued to capitalize on his early visit in various publications, including *Japan in Our Day* (1872).

We may read similar political and economic overtones in the 1860 journey of Richard Henry Dana Jr., who perhaps qualifies as the first American tourist in Japan. His youthful experiences aboard a ship that plied the California coast collecting hides and tallow for use in manufacturing shoes, harnesses, soap, and candles in New England (the inspiration for *Two Years before the Mast*) had made Dana a lifelong advocate of American hegemony in the Pacific. This imperialistic self-interest was also a leitmotif in William Seward's 1870 visit. As secretary of state, Seward had advocated the purchase of Alaska in the belief that territorial and maritime expansion was not merely in the national interest but was America's "Manifest Destiny."[83]

In the 1860s and 1870s, when Americans aspired to overtake the British as the leading traders in Japan, their sense that they had a special relationship with the island empire fueled considerable rivalry, which often extended to representatives of other European nations involved in commerce with Japan. An offhand remark by the British globe-trotter William Simpson suggests that long before the advent of McDonald's, the United States was exporting its culinary tastes.

> That which struck me first was the number of what I may call "American Institutions" in China and Japan. American steamers are doing the local traffic on the rivers and at all the treaty ports. At hotels, clubs, and all such places, American bars, with drinks of wondrous names, may be found. I had never tasted a "cock-tail" till I reached Hong Kong, but afterwards I found that there is not a house in China or Japan where the switch for frothing it up is not to be seen.[84]

A second leitmotif that cuts across globe-trotters' accounts closely related to Euro-American imperialism is the sense that going to Japan was an excursion into history that made the past tangible in a way books could not. For some Americans, the historical progress they observed in Japan revealed divine will; for others it revealed the evolution of the species, a much-debated topic in the wake of the publication of Darwin's theories. "A new horizon opened up to me on this voyage," Carnegie wrote of his 1878 journey. "It quite changed my intellectual outlook. Spencer and Darwin were then high in the zenith, and I had become deeply interested in their work. I began to view the various phases of human life from the standpoint of the evolutionist."[85] Americans, as representatives of a powerful and wealthy nation, saw Japan as a young nation much like their own—a land of opportunity for its inhabitants as well as themselves. They assumed that it would follow the same pattern of development as their own country and eventually "catch up."

It was in this developmental context that globe-trotters often likened Japanese institutions, customs, and arts to those of ancient Greece, Rome, or medieval Europe. Encoding Japan within such Eurocentric frameworks was, as many modern scholars have underscored, a form of Orientalism, but it was also a natural way of using familiar paradigms to interpret a still unfamiliar culture. It was a double-edged sword that, by opening up a way of examining other civi-

1.15 Felice Beato, *View of the Great Buddha of Kamakura*, c. 1870. Albumen print. Miriam and Ira D. Wallach Division of Art, Prints and Photographs, New York Public Library. Astor, Lenox, and Tilden Foundations.

lizations, could also call into question their own. The analogy to Greece simultaneously implied backwardness and promise, since Greek culture was the point of departure for and measure of Western civilization. The dichotomous responses to the Great Buddha of Kamakura suggest that those visitors who looked for historical parallels with the West were sometimes more open to Japanese culture than those who didn't. Disgust at the sight of the Buddha statue because it was a heathen icon or admiration because it possessed the serene presence of a Greek statue suggests that comparisons were sometimes the first step in the reordering of American thinking and taste (fig. 1.15).[86]

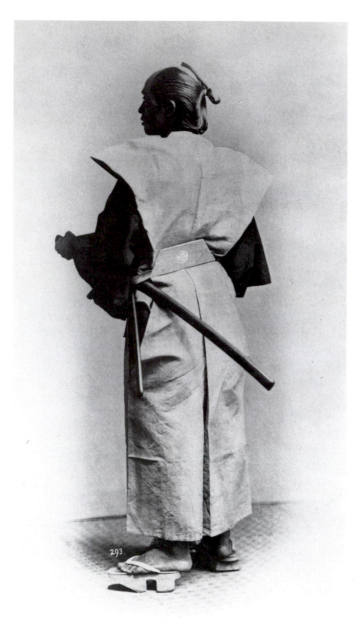

1.16 Samurai, 1870s. Albumen print. Stillfried and Anderson Company. Peabody Museum, Harvard University.

Mitford's *Tales of Old Japan* (1871), a collection of stories of feudal passion and politics that, as noted above, Griffis recommended to globe-trotters, fueled popular mythology of Japan as a chivalrous society populated by brave knights comparable to those of medieval Europe.[87] The samurai heroes of Mitford's tales stirred the imagination and admiration of readers because they possessed the virtues of honor, loyalty, and daring believed to be increasingly rare in the Western world. Their exploits also confirmed and celebrated the romance and adventure that awaited the visitor to Japan. Few travelers acknowledged that such literary images presented a skewed picture of the realities of the country in the 1860s and 1870s. Photographers catered to their desire to authenticate "old Japan" by producing portraits of "samurai" attired in dramatic, starched *kamishimo* and *hakama* (fig. 1.16).

Even as Japan was associated with and admired for having the nascent institutions of modern society, the development of such institutions was deplored by those seeking to discover in Japan ways of life absent in their own society. Many shared the strong sense of urgency about seeing the country before it was too late that informed a letter Richard Henry Dana wrote his son before the latter's departure for the East in 1860: "When Captain Johnson was here, he said he had [heard] you [were] going to Japan. I hope you have been able to look in upon that peculiar people. Now is the time; for soon they will be as uninteresting as the rest of the world."[88] This ambiguity is a recurrent theme in globe-trotters' narratives. After visiting Japan in 1869, Edward Prime lamented, "Foreign commerce and foreign intercourse have not been a blessing thus far to the Japanese. Foreign communications and trade have broken in upon the quiet habits of a people that were living in almost Arcadian simplicity."[89] Not all "authentic" features of Japanese culture merited preservation, however. This inconsistency is revealed in attitudes toward nudity and mixed bathing, which all globe-trotters deplored. Public nudity inspired fascination and fear because it transgressed the boundaries of Western normative behavior and exposed the observer to sexual temptation. Responses to the Japanese tattoo underscore this tension: positive evaluations of the practice tended to focus on the tattoo's decorative qualities rather than on the body it served simultaneously to conceal and reveal.

No tourist experience was more emblematic of the desire to turn back the clock, to return to a less mechanized pace of life than the jinrikisha, a kind of lacquered, hooded pram mounted on two wheels with a pair of shafts connected by a bar at the front end that could be pulled by one or two men (fig. 1.17). The origins of this "man power vehicle" are uncertain, but soon after its appearance between 1867 and 1870, it became a favorite mode of transportation among both locals and tourists. "The gin-rik-shar holds one man, but it is *the* thing in Japan—everybody uses it, natives and foreigner," declared Ellen Walworth.[90] Bishop Marvin was a lonely voice of moral indignation over this mode of travel: "Imagine my feelings, to be drawn by a man in shafts, as if he were a horse! I was literally ashamed of myself. Talk about Southern slavery! The average negro in the south was a lord, compared to the coolie of the East."[91] While it was possible to travel considerable distances at a fairly fast pace, this vehicle retained the rhythms of time and space lost by modern travel. Because of its appeal among tourists, the jinrikisha remained popular long after trams, trains, and other more convenient modes of travel had been developed. The jinrikisha, bound up in the search for authenticity yet itself a "tradition" perpetuated for the globe-trotter, vividly underscores the irony of tourism.

Although it is often assumed that all Americans shared the Emersonian idea that God was revealed through nature—a view that led to a consecration to the American landscape—there is little evidence that this idealization informed globe-trotters' apprehension of Japan. The fin de siècle nostalgia that would lead American visitors of the 1880s, such as William Bigelow, Henry Adams (1838–1918), John La Farge, and Percival Lowell (1855–1916), to visualize the country in highly aesthetic and spiritual terms was not yet pervasive. Americans of the 1860s and 1870s saw Japan, its people, and its culture through the prism of romanticism, an important catalyst for the nineteenth-century interest in the Orient. Most, however, still had too much faith in their own religion—not to mention the religion of progress—to seek transcendent meaning in their experience of the physical environment of Japan. British travelers of the 1870s were more apt to see Japan in a spiritual and aesthetic light since they were more conscious of the downside of progress, the smoke and other pollutants from coal mining and ironworks having spurred intellectuals such as John Ruskin to decry industrialization. On the whole, Americans tended to write more effusively about the skill and care with which Japanese farmers tended their fields than about the spiritual qualities of the landscape. "Culture" was still understood primarily to refer to tilling rather than personal cultivation.

Only the "peerless" beauty of the 12,385-foot, snowcapped peak of Mount Fuji seems to have evoked the qualities of the sublime—a nineteenth-century aesthetic ideal applied to phenomena so awe inspiring that they partook of the divine. (There were a few dissenters: Bishop Marvin remarked, chauvinistically, "My recent familiarity with Mount Hood, in Oregon, had in some degree disqualified me for the enthusiasm expected of every one on his first view of this peerless monarch of the great Nippon range."[92]) But it is important to take into account the fact that globe-trotters visited only limited coastal regions—short stretches of the Tōkaidō Road, the foothills of Mount Fuji, and the Inland Sea—that were among the most intensely cultivated and heavily populated in Japan.

Winckworth Allan Gay's visions of Mount Fuji are revealing in this respect. This painter, who had achieved modest success as a landscapist in Boston before traveling to Japan in 1877, imbued his views of the still-active volcano with an atmosphere of pastoral calm and order reminiscent of a New England landscape (fig. 1.18). None of the mountain's dangerous associations is apparent; the tone is one of perfect tranquility, with the distant snow-covered peak a foil for the fishermen's activities in the foreground—man and nature in perfect harmony.

The ban on foreign travel by Japanese in effect during much of the Edo period had stimulated the growth of domestic tourism among people of all walks of life.

1.17 Raimund von Stillfried, Charles Longfellow in jinrik-isha, 1871–73. Carte de visite. LNHS.

1.18 Winckworth Allan Gay, Mount Fuji, c. 1877. Oil on canvas. LNHS.

This long tradition of sightseeing and pilgrimage had endowed natural sites throughout Japan with special literary, religious, and historical meanings. Mount Fuji, as well as scenic sights on or near the Tōkaidō Road, temples and shrines in Tokyo and Kyoto, and the hot springs of Miyanoshita were all famous places, *meisho,* well before the arrival of Euro-American tourists. Their particular attractions had been packaged for the domestic market through guidebooks, and wood-block prints that celebrated their religious powers and scenic beauties, often with glosses about their historical or literary importance. Many Japanese pilgrims to Mount Fuji, for instance, would have been familiar with a poem about it in the tenth-century *Tales of Ise,* the source of inspiration for countless paintings.

Americans, though for the most part unaware of the *meisho* tradition, experienced its significance through its impact on designs in lacquer, ceramics, and textiles, as well as paintings and prints. They in turn often overlaid these scenic Japanese places with names and meanings of their own. The *New York Herald* reporter John Young, for instance, asserted lexical sovereignty over Mount Fuji by visualizing it through the eyes and words of Henry Wadsworth Longfellow, America's favorite poet. Longfellow's own visual projection of Mount Fuji in turn was based on a motif on a porcelain jar, possibly one carried back from Japan by his son:

> All the bright flowers that fill the land,
> Ripples of waves on rock or sand,
> The snow on Fusiyama's cone,
> The midnight heaven so thickly sown
> With constellations of bright stars,
> The leaves that rustle, the reeds that make
> A whisper by each stream or lake,
> The saffron dawn, the sunset red,
> Are painted on these lovely jars.[93]

If the Japanese landscape did not reveal the qualities of the sublime, the country and its inhabitants more than fulfilled the American tourist's pursuit of the picturesque, another central trope in travel writings of the period. *Picturesque* is a term that implies a way of seeing the world through pictorial compositions.[94] Deeply ingrained in nineteenth-century tourism, it presumed that what was seen became meaningful primarily in terms of viewers' experiences rather than what presented itself before their eyes. The habits of seeing a scene from a particular point of view or time of day or framed in a certain way were all symptomatic of this picturesque response.

Lucy Bainbridge's evocation of the scenery on the way from Yokohama to the Great Buddha of Kamakura is typical of this sensibility:

Like a panorama of strange and beautiful pictures, the landscape opened up before us. The grand old trees, always green; the feathery bamboo and brilliant japonica blossoms; the fields of rape and of barley; the patches of wet ground, where the rice-stalks a foot high are left to rot until the time of seed-sowing; the farm-houses with thickly thatched sloping roofs, so like the color of the hillside near by that it was sometimes difficult to tell where the roof left off and the hill began; the hedges of green; the quaint costumes of a new people, made up a picture of Japan—a thing of beauty, a joy forever.[95]

The tourist's cult of spectatorship also focused on the exotic novelty of the human environment. As Prime declared, Japan is a "living and moving museum."[96] Euro-Americans concerned themselves with how Japanese ate, drank, smoked, worked, played, and slept, glamorizing and sentimentalizing the facts of everyday life (fig. 1.19). They made endless observations on the details of Japanese clothing—or the lack thereof. They were delighted, if overwhelmed, by the chaotic spectacle of street life, with its basket sellers, itinerant priests, soothsayers, barbers, candy sellers, blind musicians, and child acrobats. To make order out of this visual hodgepodge, they often classified activities as "things they [the Japanese] do the wrong way." Enoch Marvin declared, "Both in sawing and planing, they draw the tool toward them instead of pushing it . . . the tailor holds his needle stationary in his left hand, and wriggles his seam upon the point of it, working his cloth with his right hand. They also mount their horses from the right instead of the left side."[97] Readers of Aimé Humbert's *Le Japon illustré* (or its English edition, *Japan and the Japanese Illustrated*) would have learned that Japanese topsy-turvydom extended to artists, who painted horses upside down (fig. 1.20).

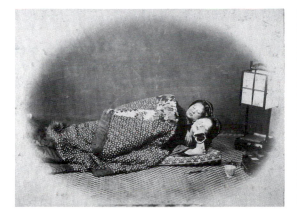

1.19   Felice Beato, *Sleeping Beauties*, c. 1870. Hand-colored albumen print. LNHS.

1.20   *Japanese Artist Painting a Yema*, from Humbert, *Japan and the Japanese Illustrated* (New York, 1874).

The perception of Japan as a consumer paradise, formed on the basis of the Japanese goods that had been flowing into ports on the west and east coasts since the 1850s and crystallized by the 1876 Philadelphia Exposition, was another recurring motif in many travelogues. Although Americans believed that it was the fate and duty of America to lead the world in all things economic, spiritual, and political, they nonetheless felt a sense of inferiority toward European art and culture. This anxiety contributed to the enormous enthusiasm that they evinced for Japanese arts and crafts. Although few globe-trotters knew much about Japanese art, many already owned examples of the kinds of goods that were commonly exported at the time. For the most part, these were articles of personal and domestic use—furnishings and clothing accessories imported from Japan having become stylish accoutrements of daily life in both Europe and the United States. Lacquers, bronzes, and porcelains topped the list of artistic and decorative goods for home use and display recognized and appreciated as being distinctively Japanese. Lengths of silk, "dressing gowns," buttons, and fans were also desirable among fashionable ladies. The images of Japan travelers carried with them were often based on such goods. "I had not a very grand idea of Japanese art, judging from the specimens I had seen in America on paper fans," wrote young Ellen Walworth. "Now I can fully appreciate their genius and correctness of drawing from nature—those fans give you a better idea of the natives of Japan than the most learned descriptions possibly could. The dress, the attitudes, the expressions are perfect."[98]

The Western public's growing appreciation of Japanese artifacts was embedded in new relativistic schemes of social and technological progress. While Western culture was still held to represent the pinnacle of achievement, in the late nineteenth century, cultural differences were beginning to be explained in a conceptual framework where "primitive" and "civilized" were not fixed categories, but evolutionary stages. In stressing the potential for development, these new paradigms contributed to a perceptual shift in which primitive cultures were identified temporally as being less advanced and thus belonging to the past vis-à-vis the modern West. As Richard Henry Dana Jr. declared of a set of paintings of birds, reptiles, insects, and flowers of Japan that a fellow traveler had acquired, "They are as good as Audubon. The attitudes of the birds are full of spirit, and every *hair* is painted. The silver hues are so well given that they seem to quiver in the air. The insects are done with exquisite taste and finish. The pencil is as fine as the cobweb. They interested and pleased me more than anything of the kind I ever saw before. These people are not to be treated as uncivilized, when, unknown to the world, unaided, uninfluenced fr. abroad, they produce such works."[99]

As this passage suggests, the forms and styles visitors championed tended to refer back to European and American culture. This process of valorization often involved drawing analogies with Greek and medieval art. The Great Buddha of Kamakura expressed a certain "classical" simplicity. The absence of illusionism in Japanese pictorial arts suggested comparison with those of ancient Greece. The grotesque imagery and complex ornamentation of Japanese crafts showed an affinity to those of Medieval Europe. Like the artists of the medieval world also, those in Japan were said to approach art intuitively, with the result that their creations were infused with spirituality and authenticity lacking in the products of the industrial world. This kind of cultural sensitivity, in which Japan is simultaneously celebrated for its strangeness and its familiarity, underscores the interpretive ambiguities of the era.

The American globe-trotters who were the backbone of Japan's nascent tourist industry were men and women of means and leisure, whose expectations and responses to Japanese culture were determined by the often very different milieux in which they lived. They did not necessarily have similar judgment in matters of art. Most Americans of the 1860s and 1870s who purchased souvenirs of their journey viewed these as curios, not as high arts comparable to European painting and sculpture. Despite the growing interconnectedness among artists, art, and taste in the United States and Europe, we must be cautious about assuming that American globe-trotters who went to Japan all held the same highly developed artistic enthusiasms and sensibilities. Even those who were well educated and cosmopolitan by the standards of the day were not necessarily aware of or even interested in the kinds of artistic issues addressed by British intellectuals such as John Ruskin and later disseminated in the United States by the painters James MacNeil Whistler (1834–1903) and John La Farge and the collector and critic James Jackson Jarves (1818–88)—none of whom had yet visited Japan.[100]

The awakening of interest in Japanese arts and crafts of all kinds was closely tied to the growth of commodity culture in the United States. Despite efforts to escape the modern world, and clichéd criticism of growing materialism at home, no tourist could or even wanted to escape the dictates of the marketplace. Travel in fact often whetted acquisitiveness. When an admiral showed Addis Carr his collection of Chinese and Japanese curiosities, the eleven-year-old wrote, it "made me feel quite miserable for a time, I wanted one so much. But of course it takes years and years and a great deal of money to get such a collection, and may be I shall have one just as fine some of the coming days. I have come to wish for a good many things since I have been abroad, that I have never thought about before, and I expect to have some of them if I live."[101] The satirical poem "The Globe-trotter at Kamakura," in Osman Edwards's *Residential Rhymes* (1899), illustrated in figure 1.2, underscores both the importance that Americans attributed to the acquisition of curios and the snobbish sense of its British author that they often had more money than taste.

Charles Longfellow: American Globe-Trotter

Charles Longfellow seems to fit Chamberlain's stereotype of the *globe-trotter elegans,* who is "provided with good introductions from his government, generally stops at a legation, is interested in shooting, and allows the various charms of the country to induce him to prolong his stay."[102] With his striking good looks and aristocratic bearing—part the self-assurance of class and perhaps part bravado—he cut a dashing figure wherever he went. He also had the ease of entry into any society that comes from having a famous name, a substantial income, and a willingness to spend it liberally. It was no doubt these assets that led Minister Charles de Long (1831–76), the ranking American diplomat in Japan, to extend a welcome to young Longfellow that included an honorary appointment that enabled him to live and travel with the American legation. Captivated by the manifold pleasures of Tokyo, and with no job or family responsibilities to return home to, young Longfellow lingered in Japan for nearly two years.

The extensive written and visual record he left, none of which was published during his lifetime, reveals that Longfellow's experiences of and attitudes toward Japan and its culture, while comparable to those of his peers in some respects, were strikingly different in others. He was more cosmopolitan and cultivated than most Americans who ventured to Japan in the 1860s and 1870s. He was also unusually tolerant of religious and cultural differences, perhaps owing to his family's outlook on these matters. The Longfellows were Unitarians, whose adherents held that all people are innately good. Charley's openness to Japanese culture—in all its manifestations, but most notably tattoos—however, was a decidedly personal trait.

Charley Longfellow was already a well-seasoned traveler in 1868 when he first formed the idea of traveling around the world. In June 1866, he had crossed the Atlantic on the *Alice,* his uncle Tom Appleton's fifty-six-foot sloop, and later the same year he participated with his friend, the publisher and sailing enthusiast James Gordon Bennett Jr. (1841–1918), in a daring midwinter trans-Atlantic race from Sandy Hook, New York, to Cowes, England.[103] The next year he accompanied his step-uncle Nathan Appleton Jr. (1843–1906) on an extended tour of Russia followed by a sojourn in Paris during the International Exposition.[104] The following summer found him once again in Europe, this time with his father, siblings, uncle, and other relatives. While his younger sisters made their first grand tour of Europe's capitals and scenic spots, he went off on a yachting trip along the French coast.

When Charley left Paris for India via Marseilles and Alexandria, the intended first leg of his journey to China and Japan, he was as well equipped with hunting gear as with letters of introduction. Among these was one from the novelist Charles Dickens to his son Frank, a Bengal Police Officer, requesting him to do everything in his power "to remind this gentleman of my great affection for his father."[105] In India Charley visited the temples and other sights as well as devoting time to big-game hunting. He also made a strenuous trek high into the Himalayas, as far as Ladakh, where he stayed for several days, visiting Lamaist monasteries. Longfellow's famous name gave him entrée to British colonial as well as Indian high society. In Benares, he and Comte Alexis de Gabriac, a fellow globe-trotter, visited a Nepalese prince, a local raja named "Naring-Sing," and the Maharaja of Benares. In his *Course humoristique autour du monde: Indes, Chine, Japon* (1872), de Gabriac describes the travel companions' misguided efforts to return this hospitality by inviting Sir Naring-Sing and the Maharaja to their lodgings, unaware that the two men are mortal enemies.[106] Charley and the Maharaja's shared interest in hunting helps to overcome some of the awkwardness, and the latter is delighted by the American's arsenal of guns, until he discovers to his horror that the Spencer rifle that he has been handling has just been oiled. His hosts assure him that the sticky substance is mutton fat, not beef or pork fat, but the damage is done, and the occasion ruined.

In India, as he would later in Japan, Charley chronicled his activities in journals, letters to his family, sketchbooks, and photographs. His writings permit us to imagine his journey by train, elephant, horse, camel, and foot as well as his arduous ascent of the Himalayas.[107] Longfellow had studied drawing and painting since childhood, and under the guidance of the New England landscapist John Kensett (1816–72), had even done some *plein air* sketching in Newport.[108] Although Longfellow was not talented, long habit led him to make a number of drawings during his Indian journey, among them some showing the tent in which he camped, the game he bagged, and the bloated stomachs of some of the malnourished children he encountered. He further documented his trip through the purchase of hundreds of photographs, filling three large albums with views of Hindu, Islamic, and British monuments in Delhi, Lucknow, Kanpur, and Agra sold by the firm Bourne and Shepherd. He acquired a generous selection of their spectacular shots of the high reaches of the Himalayan ranges (fig. 1.21). Longfellow, who in a sense fashioned his life as a perpetual performance, also had professional photographers take souvenir portraits of him in appropriate costumes and poses wherever he went (fig. 1.22).

Most globe-trotters purchased photographs as travel souvenirs, but Charley amassed exceptionally large numbers of them. His enthusiasm may reflect his family's special interest in the medium. His uncle Samuel Longfellow (1819–92) was an early photography enthusiast who, together with his classmate Edward Hale, experimented with the Talbotype process while a student at Harvard. The poet himself also collected photographs to serve as visual inspiration for his poems.[109] As a literary figure whose photographic portrait was taken often and widely disseminated, Henry Wadsworth Longfellow was also keenly aware of the relationship between photography and international celebrity.

Charley's ambition to circle the globe was cut short at the end of 1869, when

1.21 Spiti Pass, c. 1866. Albumen print. Shepard and Bourne. LNHS.

he was confined in Delhi with a sprained leg and advised by a doctor to return to Europe to recuperate. On January 25, 1870, he sailed from Calcutta to Marseilles through the newly opened Suez Canal, and thence to Paris. By April, he was sufficiently recovered to participate in the Grand Atlantic Race on the *Dauntless*, a schooner belonging to Gordon Bennett Jr.

A little more than a year elapsed before he resumed his world travels, this time westward to Japan across the United States and Pacific by transcontinental railway and steamship.[110] En route he stopped to sightsee, hunt, and buy curios. In Omaha he discovered a shop filled with tomahawks, bows, arrows, moccasins, and even scalps and other Indian trophies from which he made a selection to send home to Cambridge. He paused in Salt Lake City, whose Mormon inhabitants were exotic even to American globe-trotters because of the controversy surrounding their practice of polygamy. In California he rode

1.22   Charles Longfellow in India, 1869. Albumen print. Photographer unknown. LNHS.

out to see the giant sequoias, whose astonishing dimensions he recorded in his journal. On May 31, he purchased for $260 a ticket to travel from San Francisco to Yokohama, and the following day, having telegraphed his father of his plans, he left on board the *Idaho.*

Although Longfellow had an appetite for world travel that remained unabated throughout his life, Japan seems to have occupied a special place in his imagination since childhood: a sketchbook kept by his family dating from 1855 to 1860 includes Charley's tracing of the cartoon "Japanese Manners" that had appeared in the December 18, 1858, issue of *Harper's Weekly* (see figure 1.9).[111] Perhaps his youthful fascination with Japan was also piqued by the Chinese and Japanese lacquer, porcelain, ceramics, bronzes, and other curios commonly displayed in fashionable homes, including his own. Many families involved in the China and India trade lived in Boston, and especially in Newport and Nahant, where the Longfellows summered. His enthusiasm for Japan also may have been whetted by the tales of the many family and friends who had traveled there. Lieutenant George Henry Preble, who had accompanied Perry's expedition to Japan, was a relative by marriage.[112] Bayard Taylor corresponded with Henry Wadsworth Longfellow and visited him on occasion.[113] Richard Henry Dana Jr. was a neighbor, and his children close friends. The Longfellows were also acquainted with Raphael Pumpelly, whose travelogue Charley's sisters read while he was in Japan. In addition, several of Charley's Cambridge and Boston contemporaries were involved in trade with Japan. His friend Kirk Lothrop, a partner in Walsh Hall and Co., with whom he shared an enthusiasm for sailing, would be the first person to greet Charley when he disembarked in Yokohama on June 23, 1871.

Henry Wadsworth Longfellow (1807–82) came from a family of relatively modest means from Portland, Maine, but his wife Frances (1817–61) was the daughter of Nathan Appleton (1779–1861), a Bostonian who had made his fortune in the textile industry. Henry had met and fallen in love with Frances in Salzburg in 1836, but the two did not marry until 1843. Then a professor of modern languages at Harvard College, Henry was in Europe to improve his German. He had published (anonymously) his first book, *Outre mer: A pilgrimage beyond the sea* (1835), a collection of European travel sketches, but was not yet the celebrity he would become following the appearance of *Hyperion, A Romance* (1838), *Evangeline: A Tale of Acadie* (1847), *The Song of Hiawatha* (1855), and other epic poems. As a wedding present, Nathan Appleton purchased for the newlyweds a colonial house in Cambridge, Massachusetts, where George Washington had stayed for nine months in 1775. When Nathan died in 1861, each of his children from two marriages inherited $100,000.[114]

Frances and her brother Thomas Gold Appleton (1812–84) shared a deep interest in the arts and, having traveled widely in Europe, had very cosmopolitan tastes. "Uncle Tom" was an avid collector of European art, and a patron of

American painters, including John Kensett and Winckworth Allan Gay. A founding member and benefactor of the Museum of Fine Arts, Tom Appleton gave much of his collection of European paintings, Cypriot ceramics, as well as Japanese lacquers, bronzes, and tortoise-shell boxes to the museum.[115] In later life, Appleton became a noted Boston *bon vivant* and wit. In *Windfalls*, a collection of essays, he spoke out against hard work and the belief that pleasure is sinful: "Here, we only retire from business when the strength to continue it retires from us; business is our life, and, in the rush, we stumble over our grave before we have time to pull up. . . . Nature invites us to a table magnificently spread, if the proper artist were there to intelligently profit by its bounty. Heaven has sent us its food, and the Puritan has sent us his cook. . . . All over New England, the doctrine taught by the Puritans is fading away; but, alas! their kitchen remains."[116] Charley was close to his uncle and emulated him in many respects, including his bachelorhood.

Charley's first days in Japan were filled with sightseeing in and around Yokohama. This was followed by a trip to Miyanoshita, a hot-spring resort in the foothills of Mount Fuji. In the large and well-appointed Naraya, an inn popular among both Japanese and foreign visitors, Charley met Yamanouchi Yōdō (d. 1872), a former daimyo, and Iwasaki Yatarō (1835–85), a businessman. Influential figures in the new Meiji government who shared Charley's enjoyment of parties and theater, they later introduced him to their favorite Tokyo teahouses. Charley also went pleasure boating on the Sumida River and to the Kabuki theater with them.

A letter Charley wrote his sister Alice recounting the first evening on a pleasure boat in Iwasaki's company, conveys both his infectious enthusiasm and his descriptive powers:

> At every turn, we would meet other parties like ourselves bound for the more open water of the river. . . . It is about a quarter of a mile broad, and as we glided along among the other boats in the bright moon light, with the cool evening breeze refreshing us, the shores lit up from the rows of lanterns hung out from the teahouses, the sound of many "samisens," and snatches of song and laughter that came floating over the water from the hundreds of boats gliding about looking like fire flies with their paper lanterns . . . was charming—and I thought of the remarks of my acquaintances in Yokohama, that Yedo didn't amount to much. I don't know what *they* want but I know such evenings are only too short for me.[117]

It was evenings spent in this way that led him to conclude that the Japanese "really know how to enjoy themselves quite rationally" and that he would like to stay in Japan longer.[118]

Charley led a life of cultivated leisure in Japan. The words *ukiyo,* floating world, and *ukiyo-e,* pictures of the floating world, were not part of his vocabulary—or indeed of most Japanophiles of the time—but the life he led in Japan between 1871 and 1873 might well have led Japanese to characterize him as a "man of the floating world" *(ukiyo otoko)*. He certainly had all the qualities of the Japanese bon vivant. Stylish, witty, and urbane, he moved smoothly in many circles. He took an interest in the arts and had ample funds to form a personal collection. He enjoyed all manner of food and drink. He delighted in Kabuki theater. He was a big spender. He was also a connoisseur of women.

Charley's ample means and family name also gave him many opportunities not available to most globe-trotters. Since Minister de Long appointed him Acting Secretary of the Hawaiian mission, on August 14, 1871, he was able to attend a diplomatic audience where he caught a glimpse of the young Emperor Mutsuhito in his last appearance in official court garb. In reporting this event, the *New York Times* mentioned the presence of "a son of HENRY W. LONGFELLOW, who is en route around the world."[119] The following month, he accompanied de Long and other members of the American mission on a journey to Hokkaidō that included a tour of the island's small coastal Ainu settlements. Twenty days later they returned to Hakodate, crossed the Tsugaru Straight back to the main island of Honshū, and began the long overland journey back to Tokyo along the old Oshūkaidō Road. Charley's vivid narrative of his travels in northern Japan conveys the sense of exhilaration he experienced in exploring this region off the beaten track. He may have hoped to publish it, but these plans were never realized.

Charley's chronicle of his travels in northern Japan suggests that he shared the exploratory fever common among many young men of his generation, and perhaps even aspired through such endeavors to achieve fame and glory. Seafaring and ships, which his father and other literary figures had helped to make an important part of New England mythology, were central to Charley's heroic ideal. Already in 1866, Charley had adopted personal stationery decorated with a view of Sir John Franklin (1786–1847), the arctic explorer who died while searching for the Northwest Passage.[120] His accounts of his trek into the Himalayas and his expedition in northern Japan are informed by pride that he was participating in the exploration of little-known regions. In 1878 he considered, but owing to family pressure decided against, joining the expedition to the Arctic of the ill-fated *Jeannette,* sponsored by James Gordon Bennett Jr., to increase his newspaper's circulation.[121] It is perhaps more than a coincidence that Charley was staying with Bennett in New York in 1871 just before he set off across the country for Japan.[122]

Longfellow's decision to have himself extensively tattooed while in Japan was one expression of his identification with the heroic ideal of the seafaring explorer. He did not mention his tattoos in his letters or journals, but commemorated this unusual form of self-transformation photographically. Although he projected a confident image in his writings, the photographic portraits he had taken while in Japan reveal a more fragile, uncertain individual who craved attention and approval. Wherever he went, he lived theatrically, happiest when he was on display.

Not long after his return from Hokkaidō, Longfellow began looking for a Japanese house in Tokyo, with the thought of remaining in Japan for a further five months. The Japanese government had first permitted the sale of land in the foreign concession of Tsukiji in 1870, but Westerners began moving there only after a terrible fire in 1872 made possible the construction of new buildings suited to their needs. While Charley's house was being built, he lodged at the American mission in Tokyo and made excursions to Osaka, Kobe, and Kyoto, newly opened to foreign visitors for the duration of a special exhibition. During these journeys he purchased many articles with which to furnish his house. He also traveled through the scenic Inland Sea and climbed Mount Fuji with Alfred Dupont Jessup, a Philadelphia acquaintance of his father's who was touring Japan.

Although Charley was twenty-seven, he had never had a house of his own. His obvious pride in his Tokyo residence is evident in the series of photographic views he sent home to his family, along with detailed descriptions of each room. The women who appear in several of these include his mistresses. It is more than likely that young Longfellow was the nameless individual whom the prudish Griffis had in mind when he declared, with some exaggeration, that an American living in Tokyo "enjoyed a harem of ten native beauties."[123]

A little more than a year after settling into his new house, Charley suddenly decided to leave Japan. The reasons are not altogether clear, but his precarious finances were in all likelihood a contributing factor. Charley's income of approximately $6,500 a year was a considerable sum that should have enabled him to live in comfort almost anywhere in the world, but in Japan, as elsewhere, he had incurred large debts, which his indulgent father invariably paid off after a flurry of admonitory letters. When he left Japan he owed more than $18,000.[124]

On March 13, 1873, he left Nagasaki by Pacific mail steamer for Shanghai. Despite his financial predicament, Longfellow did not return home immediately but spent four months in China, traveling up the Yangtze River, visiting the Great Wall, and sightseeing at the Summer Palace in Beijing. After a brief stop in Hong Kong, he sailed for the Philippines, where he injured his leg during a hunting trip. Having returned to Hong Kong to recover, in February 1874, he finally headed home via Saigon, Bangkok, and Singapore. He arrived in Cambridge in mid-June of 1874, remaining only briefly before leaving for a summer of yachting on the New England coast.

This was not the end of his globe-trotting, however. In March 1875, he traveled to Cuba and Mexico in the company of the painter William Morris Hunt (1824–79) and Greeley Stevenson Curtis (1830–97), a relative by marriage.[125]

He also returned to Japan twice, first in May 1885, for about seven months, part of it spent sailing from Yokohama to Nagasaki on a yacht chartered by Charles Weld, a fellow Bostonian and boating enthusiast. Charley made a third trip to Japan via Australia and New Zealand in January 1891.[126]

Since Charley had no bent for introspection, his letters and journals offer few clues to the reasons for this wanderlust. Even as a child, however, he seems to have been propelled by a sense of rebelliousness and love of risk that later manifested itself in a yearning to engage in activities that might enable him to evade comparison with his father. Both his parents were pacifists, yet at age twelve, despite maternal opposition, he received as a birthday present a rifle with which he soon accidentally blew off his finger. Despite this accident, he developed a lifelong love affair with guns. Longfellow arrived in Japan equipped with a large number of American hunting rifles—so many that he had to pay an extra fee for them on the transcontinental railroad.[127]

In his journal, Charley's father described the fourteen-year-old boy as "active, impetuous, skillful in all out-of-door sports, not a lover of school-books, and with a strong will of his own."[128] The escapades that earned him the nickname "Enfant terrible" continued in later life: in 1863, he was arrested for bathing in the nude at the Nahant shore. Just after his return from India, his younger sister noted in a letter: "Charlie is at home now and beginning to settle down into his new room. He is more wild, extravagant and childish than ever and we can hardly keep him within the bounds of propriety."[129] Even more embarrassing to his family, in 1877 his name was linked to a scandal, widely reported in the New York and Boston press, involving his fun-loving friend, the publisher Bennett.[130] Although accounts of the affair vary, it appears that Bennett became inebriated at a New Year's Eve party hosted by his fiancée, and urinated into the fireplace, causing many young ladies at the gathering to faint. The hostess' brother responded to this affront to his family by assaulting Bennett. Bennett then challenged him to a duel, sending Charley to announce the challenge.

It is possible that Charley's malaise was related not only to his failure to live up to his family's expectations, but also to his mother's tragic death in 1861 and his Civil War experiences two years later. Her death, when her dress caught fire as she was melting sealing wax to apply to a letter, left Charley and his four younger siblings, Ernest (1845–1921), Alice (1850–1928), Edith (1853–1915), and Anne (1855–1934), in the care of their devoted but busy father. Two years later, while still too young to enlist, Charley ran away to join the Union Army. After gaining his father's permission, he became a private in the Massachusetts Artillery, and later, thanks in all likelihood to family intervention, he was promoted to second lieutenant of the First Massachusetts Cavalry. Despite his superior officers' efforts to keep the son of America's favorite poet away from the most dangerous battlefields, on November 27, 1863, Charley suffered a gunshot wound just under the shoulder, which disqualified him from further military service.[131] Letters he wrote home during the war reveal little of the horror he saw—indeed, if anything, life on the battlefront seems to have satisfied his need for excitement and action. Nonetheless, his injury was later used as a euphemistic family explanation for his inability to settle down, marry, and find a suitable profession.[132]

Despite these personal tragedies, young Longfellow does not seem to have been caught up in the mood of uncertainty that informed the worldview of many fin de siècle Bostonians.[133] He did not belong to that self-conscious and anxious group of Japanophiles that included William Sturgis Bigelow and the historian Henry Adams, who later turned to Japan for solace because science, industry, and immigration were encroaching on their world. Japan did offer him a refuge, but it was primarily because it allowed him to lead an autonomous life devoid of adult professional or family responsibilities.

By devoting himself to a sybaritic life of travel, sports, and parties, Charley was not only evading adult responsibilities, but also evading his family. Even his sister Edith, who was nine years younger than he, regarded him with patronizing affection. Like other family members, she referred to him throughout his life by the diminutive Charley. Her correspondence with her cousin suggests that his sense of inadequacy made it uncomfortable for him to remain for long under the paternal roof. "Charley came home after a 'splendid time in New York,'" she wrote. "It delights me to have him so gay but he never can be so for more than a few hours when he gets home, for he has to face the stern realities and things throw him all down. His only way at present is to keep dashing away and forgetting them in some new pleasures. Dreadful isn't it?"[134] Her letters also reveal the depressions he fell into at home, in one instance, due to his inability to form a lasting relationship with a female friend.[135]

Some of Charley's problems may reflect a struggle with unresolved contradictory sexual impulses. Yet we must be cautious about an anachronistic homosexual reading of his lifelong bachelorhood. Many men of this generation valued the camaraderie of men above the society of women, as evidenced in the enormous success of *Reveries of a Bachelor* (1850, 1863, 1888), a panegyric to the unmarried state by the essayist Donald Mitchell (a.k.a. Ik Marvel). In decrying the institution of marriage, Mitchell posed a question one can well imagine Charley asking himself: "Shall a man who has been free to chase his fancies over the wide-world, without lett or hindrance, shut himself up to marriage-ship, within four walls called Home, that are to claim him, his time, his trouble, and his tear, thenceforward forever more, without doubts thick, and thick-coming as Smoke?"[136]

Charley's flight from domesticity and desire for an exclusively male sphere was also socially sanctioned through his membership in elite social and sports clubs. He belonged to Boston's Somerset Club and took up residence there after his return from Japan. Sports such as swimming, hunting, and yachting also offered opportunities for socially and physically validating all-male activities. Treaty port Japan during the 1860s and 1870s was an analogous environment, where men could enjoy the companionship of other men while engaging in heterosexual pursuits without committing themselves to marriage.

It is assumed that Americans who went to Japan wrote and commented on their visit from the relative security of their status as members of an advanced imperialist society, yet this was not necessarily the case. Travel was an acknowledged therapy for personal problems of all kinds, and many who went to Japan were social misfits. Japan attracted many who wanted to escape a problematic past, hoping to create for themselves a new persona. Charley clearly shared this dream of self-reinvention, and it is likely that the Longfellow family accepted Charley's escape to Japan in this context. His appetite for travel was never sated, however, and he raced around the world, in constant pursuit of a change of scene.

In Japan, Charley did not try to thrust himself into the intellectual limelight or to promote himself as a critical voice on Japanese culture. He never became a professional pundit, nor is there any direct evidence that his opinion was sought by other globe-trotters. As far as we know he was essentially a fun-loving adventurer, not unlike the heroes of Jules Verne's novels. In the Unitarian mode, he was not one to make moral judgments about "heathen" Japan. This globe-trotting son of Henry Wadsworth Longfellow nonetheless may tell us much about the formation and reception of Japanese art and culture in America during the last quarter of the nineteenth century.

CHAPTER 2

Picturing Japan

Some such impressions of photographic accuracy are
becoming more than ever needful in the plethora of new
compilations, and the dearth of new authentic matter to
fill them with.

—Rutherford Alcock, 1861

Widely disseminated in the form of albumen prints and recycled as illustrations in books and newspapers, photographic images were part of the wave of visual information—true, false, and absurd—that began flowing from Japan to the West in the 1860s. Pictures captured the imagination in a way that the written word alone could not, contributing to stereotypes that endure to this day. Views of Japan and its people made for foreign consumption were premised on articulating an image of the island country as different in both time and space. As John Urry has observed, the "tourist gaze" by definition focuses on the extraordinary, on that which contrasts with what we encounter in our daily lives.[1] Yet like the new modes of transportation and communication that made the Far East more accessible, photographs were emblematic of the very modernity that tourists sought to escape.

Until the advent in 1888 of the Kodak handheld camera, there were few amateur photographers among globe-trotters. Most pictures they carried home were taken by commercial photographers. These professionals, through their choice and treatment of subjects, played a major role in shaping the visitor's expectations, experiences, and memories of Japan. Unlike picture postcards, which would become widely available only in the last decade of the nineteenth century, tourist photographs were luxury souvenirs. Those available in Japan were generally albumen prints ranging in size from 2 $\frac{1}{2}$-by-4-inch cartes de visite to 10-by-13-inch full plates. They were produced initially by the wet-plate collodion process: for each image a glass plate had to be coated with collodion emulsion, sensitized with silver nitrate before being exposed, and developed immediately afterward. Sometime after 1873, this cumbersome technique was superceded by the dry-plate process, in which gelatin was used as emulsion, and prepared plates could be purchased and stored. Many prints were hand-colored by "native artists," a practice that rendered them more authentic even as it transformed each one into a unique work of art. A price list from 1864–65 indicates that views and costumed figures of Japan cost $2.00 each; a 7-by-9 portrait, $15; and a 13-by-10-inch photograph $25.[2] Prices may have gone down by the 1870s, but a pair of screens with gold background that Charley Longfellow purchased for $35 in Osaka in 1872 is likely to have cost considerably less than an album of fifty photographs.[3]

Photographers of many nationalities—British, Russian, American, Italian, Austrian, Chinese, as well as Japanese—were active in Japan during the 1860s and 1870s.[4] Some, like their clients, were roving adventurers who went from one country to another in pursuit of new experiences and professional opportunities. Felice Beato (1825/1834–1904/1907) was a Venetian with British citizenship. He had launched his career in 1855 photographing the Crimean war, later working in Jerusalem, India, China, Japan, Korea, and Burma.[5] He arrived in Japan in 1861. Baron Raimund von Stillfried-Ratenicz (1839–1911), an Austrian nobleman, also made a career as an itinerant photographer.[6] Active in Yokohama from 1871, he gained an international reputation when his picturesque views of the country and aestheticizing portraits of its people were displayed at the 1873 Vienna and 1876 Philadelphia Expositions.[7]

Beato was among the first in Japan to capitalize on the mass market potential for photographs. He had an innate feel for the sensibilities of the foreign market and created a complex, multilayered visual narrative of the country and its people. As a result, in the 1860s, he commanded extraordinary authority in framing Japan for the West. The fact that he had made a name for himself with photographs of the gruesome realities of the wars in Crimea, India, and China no doubt enhanced the documentary weight of those he took in Japan.[8] His quasi-encyclopedic, pictorial record of places, manners, and customs, perhaps more than any other photographs of the era, gave Japan an identity and presence abroad. By creating a commodity that engaged the interests and fantasies of an emerging tourist audience, Beato made his viewers want to experience Japan for themselves. Once tourists were in Japan, Beato's photographs drew attention to places they might otherwise miss, as well as provided them reference points against which to measure their own experiences. Beato's pictures were also in a sense self-perpetuating, since tourists invariably wanted to go to the same places others had already been and needed visual proof of their visits.

Because he developed an infinitely recyclable vocabulary of images that could be emulated by other photographers, his impact endured well into the twentieth century.

Many photographs produced in Beato's studio were accompanied by informative printed captions written by his business partner, Charles Wirgman (1832?-91), a correspondent and illustrator for the *London Illustrated News*.[9] These entrepreneurs recognized and sought to capitalize on their role as guides to and interpreters of Japan's sight-seeing attractions. Like the guidebooks indispensable to the European Grand Tour, Wirgman's texts "provide[d] an order of worship at the shrines of the beautiful, the historic, and the foreign, telling the potential tourist what kind of behavior is appropriate to each site and indicating what kind of fulfillment to expect from it."[10]

The long captions accompanying Beato's views were both factual and opinionated. The descriptive text about the Great Buddha of Kamakura, for instance, underscored the statue's monumentality, antiquity, and picturesqueness, all values of importance in its aesthetic appreciation. A photograph of a pair of deeply bent women was characterized as *The Original "Grecian Bend"* (fig. 2.1). This allusion to the posture affected by fashionable Victorian women reveals how a union of text and image could make Japan appear simultaneously exotic and familiar. One globe-trotter's comment about kimono-clad women walking in the "Grecian bend," testifies to Beato and Wirgman's role in mediating tourists' interpretations of Japan.[11]

2.1   Felice Beato, *The Grecian Bend*, c. 1870. Albumen print. Miriam and Ira D. Wallach Division of Art, Prints and Photographs, New York Public Library. Astor, Lenox, and Tilden Foundations.

Although Beato, von Stillfried, and other European photographers did not have an explicitly political program, as did their counterparts in colonial India, a Eurocentric agenda was encoded in their photographs. As commercial photographers whose success depended on shaping their ideas and attitudes to the demands of the foreign market, they selected subjects their Western clientele wanted to see. Yet even during their lifetimes, their pictures invited multiple readings: while each was witness to Japan at a particular historic moment, many were reproduced decades after they were taken, investing the sights they recorded with an aura of timelessness.

When William Simpson, a British globe-trotter, visited Japan in 1872, he was astonished to see in Nagasaki a shop selling a camera, complete with tripod and all the requisite photographic materials. "As Europeans get such things direct from England," he concluded, "this establishment was principally for supplying the Japanese, and while it indicates the extent to which the art is practiced by them, it becomes in itself one of the many evidences of the rapid changes now going on."[12] When he wrote this, Japanese photography, which had first developed in the 1840s under the patronage of feudal lords interested in Western science, already had been practiced in Japan for nearly a quarter of a century.[13]

Growing domestic demand in the 1860s led enterprising Japanese photographers to open studios in cities and towns throughout the country. Ueno Hikoma (1838–1904) and Shimooka Renjō (1823–1914) opened theirs in Nagasaki and Yokohama in 1862. Kizu Kokichi (1830–95) launched operations in Hakodate (Hokkaidō) in 1864, Uchida Kyūichi (1846–74/75) in Osaka in 1866, and Hori Masumi (Yohei: 1826–80) in Kyoto in 1866. These represented only a tiny fraction of the numerous Japanese who were operating in the vicinity of temples and shrines or were traveling around the country with their cameras, waiting for prospective customers along busy thoroughfares, such as the Tōkaidō Road linking Tokyo and Kyoto. These and other Japanese professionals both contributed to and competed with their European counterparts in the aestheticization of the Japanese countryside, its inhabitants, and the photographic medium itself.

In Europe and the United States at the time, photography generally was not held to be a fine art but a mechanical process that offered great promise as a means of recording external reality accurately and objectively, like "a mirror with a memory."[14] When the poet Charles Baudelaire reviewed the debut photographic exhibition at the 1859 Paris Salon, for instance, he dismissed photographs as tools for lazy artists and *aides mémoire* for travelers. "Let photography quickly enrich the traveller's album, and restore to his eyes the precision his memory may lack; . . . Let it save crumbling ruins from oblivion. . . . But, if once it be allowed to impinge on the sphere of the intangible and the imaginary, on anything that has value solely because man adds something to it from his soul, then woe betide us."[15]

Alexander von Hubner, despite his keen interest in the medium, shared Baudelaire's conviction that the camera was a soulless tool, whose products were chiefly of documentary and archival value. Upon visiting the Asakusa temple in Tokyo he noted: "In front of the portal is a temple dedicated to the goddess Kwannon (Kannon). Mr. Beato, of Yokohama, has photographed it, and heaps of travellers have published descriptions of it; but neither photographs nor descriptions give the faintest idea of the mystical charm of the place."[16] Yet in Kyoto, von Hubner met an elderly Japanese photographer whom, he declared, "had never seen a European before, and had learnt his art from a native. From a technical point of view his photographs perhaps might have been improved but he possessed another talent, which is heaven-born; and that is, the art of seizing objects by their prettiest and most picturesque side."[17] This comment suggests that he attributed to this photographer the artistic qualities widely believed to be innate to the Japanese people. Other globe-trotters who patronized Japanese photographers also professed admiration for their aesthetic talents. The Civil War reporter Charles Coffin found in Yokohama "very good photographs taken by a native artist," and illustrated his travelogue with an engraving based on this "artist's" photograph of his wife.[18]

The extraordinary skill with which Japanese painted photographs may have contributed to the tourist's aesthetic receptivity to this medium. Few "painted pictures" produced in Europe and the United States during the 1860s and 1870s can match the delicacy and tonal sensitivity of their Japanese counterparts.[19] No globe-trotter of that time seems to have commented specifically on the subject, but accounts from the early 1880s concerning "their skill at the art of coloring" suggest that this was one of the special attractions of Japanese photographs.[20] The portrait of "My Artist" (fig. 2.2) figuring in Beato's repertory, moreover, testifies to the professional respect these individuals enjoyed among both photographers and their clients. No names are recorded on painted photographs, but a number of pioneers in oil painting in Japan are known to have made a living in this manner.[21] For the most part, these artists sought to learn photographic techniques in order to develop more empirical styles of painting. The nineteenth-century usage of the term *shashin,* literally "true facsimile," to denote a wide range of naturalistic paintings and prints as well as photographs is indicative of this close relationship.

Globe-trotters patronized Japanese photographers, but in the 1860s and early 1870s, carte de visite portraits for the domestic market were the mainstays of their studios. Because of their relatively modest cost, cartes de visite, the rage in Europe and England in the 1850s and 1860s, became equally popular in Japan during the late 1860s and 1870s. (They were inexpensive, because eight small identical prints measuring approximately $2\frac{1}{2}$ by 4 inches could be produced from a single negative plate by fitting a camera with four identical lenses and a repeating back mechanism.) Japanese government officials used them as

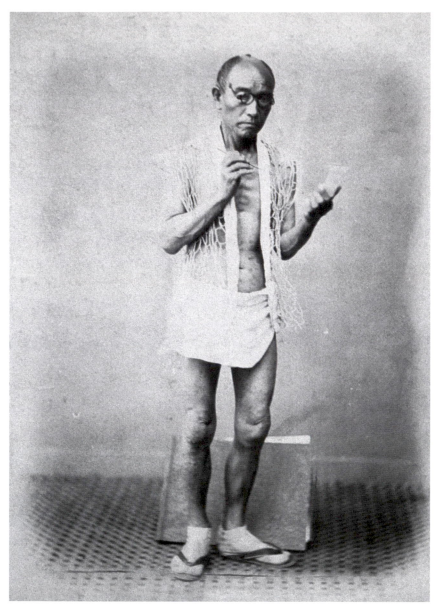

2.2   Felice Beato, *My Artist*, c. 1870. Hand-colored albumen print. LNHS.

visiting cards to present to their foreign counterparts and other visiting dignitaries. Actors and geisha gave them to fans as fashionable alternatives for traditional wood-block printed publicity (see figures 2.3 and 4.6). As noted, above, the young Harvard graduate Benjamin Curtis discovered a pretty teahouse waitress who was willing to give him one of her photographic cartes de visite.[22]

Japanese photographers also carried out various kinds of photographic projects for the Meiji government. In 1872, two years after the emperor had first

2.3 *Hannaogi*, c. 1871–73. Carte de visite. Photographer unknown. LNHS.

appeared in person before the public, Uchida Kyūichi photographed him in monarchical style to comply with European diplomatic practices.[23] That same year, photographers accompanied officials on the first national survey of old temples and shrines.[24] The Hokkaidō Colonization Board began compiling an ethnographic record of the Ainu, much as earlier British colonial authorities had gathered photographic data on local tribes in India.[25] The Bureau of Commerce also ordered photographic albums of goods destined for display and sale at domestic and international expositions.[26] Since glass negatives could be used over a long period of time to produce prints for different purposes, these genres of photographs sometimes found their way into the collections of foreign visitors.

Photographs, which seemed to confirm the reality of the globe-trotter's experiences in Japan, had an ambiguous and invariably essentializing relationship to the world they were intended to document. Although they often served as personal mementos, they did not necessarily represent what those who acquired them had actually seen. Nor were they intended for the educational or scientific purposes to which their Euro-American collectors sometimes put them. Behind many photographs, in fact, there often lay an ideological agenda quite different from that of the person who acquired them. This agenda could be reinforced by the accompanying explanatory text. Tourists wanted "authentic" experiences recorded by the camera, but many of the photographs they bought were representations of representations: because of the long exposure times and other technical limitations of the medium, they were staged in a studio using painted backdrops and other three-dimensional props. Hand-painting, though intended to create a more naturalistic image, could further alter what was recorded by the camera. When the demand for photographs of tattooed men outstripped the availability of photographic subjects, for instance, artists simply painted tattoolike motifs over the black-and-white print.[27]

While most globe-trotters' travelogues contain references to photographs, few albums survive intact from the 1860s and 1870s, and fewer still are as well documented as those preserved in Longfellow House National Historic Site. This chapter uses Charley Longfellow's collection of more than four hundred prints mounted in four albums to explore some of the ways photography mediated his experience of and relationship to Japan and its culture. His photographs raise questions about the ideology of tourism in the nineteenth century and about the role of photography in the mutually constitutive relationship between the imagined and lived reality of Japan. They provide not simply a recital of Longfellow's activities there, but also a dramatization of his image of himself. While helping to map the role Japan played in the life and imagination of one man, they also throw light on the attitudes and assumptions of other Americans of his class and period.

An Album of Tourist Attractions

Given the Longfellow family's long-standing interest in photography, it is not surprising that photographs were among Charley's first acquisitions upon arriving in Japan. Writing from Yokohama on July 20, 1871, he announced to his sister Alice that he was sending her "views of the [sic] Korea taken while the fighting was going on or just over."[28] These were photographs Felice Beato had taken during the military encounter between the United States and Korea two months earlier. In thanking Charley, his sister Annie noted that their receipt "set us girls to reading up in the papers all about the expedition which we knew nothing about before."[29]

Her response is a reminder of the incredible power of photography to incite curiosity and educate viewers about the larger world. In 1871, such photographic prints were still too costly to be widely available, and each was precious and carefully studied in a way that is no longer true today. Reading aloud excerpts from his journals and letters and viewing the photographs that Charley sent home were semipublic rituals that fueled a growing interest in Japan and its culture among the Longfellows and their New England friends.

During his twenty-month stay in Japan, young Longfellow purchased many more photographs from Beato's stock. Among them are fifty-six genre and forty scenic views of Japan, many of them hand-colored, which he had mounted in an album. Both in subject and organization, Longfellow's album roughly follows a model Beato had established in 1868 with the publication of his successful *Photographic Views of Japan with Historical and Descriptive Notes, compiled from Authentic Sources and Personal Observations During a Residence of Several Years.*[30] This mammoth photographic project comprised nearly two hundred albumen prints mounted in two leather-bound volumes divided by subject, the first treating landscapes, cities, and villages, and the second "native types." Charles Wirgman provided long and informative texts for each picture in this compendium, but Longfellow's individually selected photographs lack these printed texts. Instead, he identified each with his own short handwritten caption. He further personalized his collection by having them mounted in a Japanese-style accordion *(orihon)* album, with a brocade cover inscribed with his name in Japanese phonetic syllabary *(hiragana)*.

The pictures Charley selected from Beato's stock were all recognized tourist sights that could be acquired by other globe-trotters. Consequently this album created only an oblique record of his personal experiences in Japan. Although he does not figure in any of them, he no doubt chose those views he believed best evoked his life and travels. One scene, unusual in its domestic intimacy, shows the veranda of a house with a sleeping dog and a garden beyond (fig. 2.4). This house has been identified as belonging to Abel Gower, the British consul in Kobe, and an acquaintance of Charley's, but it was commonly included

2.4   Felice Beato, Gower's house and garden, c. 1870. Hand-colored albumen print. LNHS.

2.5   Raimund von Stillfried, attr., Longfellow's Tsukiji house and garden, 1871–73. Hand-colored albumen print. LNHS.

among commercial tourist views of "typical" Japanese residences. Gower's house, which serves as the opening scene in this album, closely resembles the one Charley later built for himself in Tokyo (fig. 2.5).

Charley's album begins with sights in Tokyo, the city he considered his home in Japan, rather than views of Yokohama, which commonly figure in other photographic collections of the era. There are numerous pictures of Edo Castle and the shogunal tombs at Shiba, architectural monuments in which he in fact had little personal interest. By including them, however, he acknowledged their importance in representing Japan to family and friends. One particularly striking photograph, which he incorrectly identified as "the prince of Satsuma's Palace," features the exterior of a daimyo residence (fig. 2.6). (Whether this was Longfellow's error or he was misinformed is not clear.) Felice Beato took a similar photograph in 1863 or 1864 at the request of the Swiss minister Aimé Humbert, who used it as the basis for an etching in his *Japon illustré*, but this view in fact shows the residence of Arima, another feudal lord (fig. 2.7).[31]

For the most part, the places Longfellow chose to commemorate were those he had personally visited: the scenic Tōkaidō Road, Kamakura, the foothills of Mount Fuji, Kyoto, Lake Biwa, and Nagasaki, a city to which he took a particular liking. Due to the difficulty of travel beyond the treaty ports in effect until 1874, however, the selection of landmarks available to the photographer and the tourist alike was still quite limited. Of Kyoto, for instance, Charley has photographs of only Kinkakuji ("Golden Pavilion") and Chion'in temples, which he visited in 1872, when Kyoto was first opened to Western tourists on the occasion of an exposition (fig. 2.8). Charley's excitement about traveling there is palpable in his letter home: "Every one in Japan who can get away takes a run up

60

2.6 Felice Beato, *Arima yashiki*, c. 1870. Albumen print. LNHS.

2.7 *The Palace of Prince Satsouma at Yeddo*, from Humbert, *Japan and the Japanese Illustrated* (New York, 1874)

2.8 Felice Beato, Kinkakuji, Kyoto, c. 1870. Albumen print. LNHS.

to this most sacred of Japanese cities, and this child was not going to lose the chance."[32] For the occasion, "the government have set apart the extensive grounds belonging to [Chion-in] Temple," and scattered guests "among the houses used by priests and by embassies from different princes in the olden days."[33] This temple apparently was memorable to him not because of its religious history, but rather because it served as a hotel for foreigners. Of the Golden Pavilion, today one of Kyoto's most celebrated sights, he says nothing.

Figural subjects outnumber scenic views, suggesting that Charley was more drawn to Japan's human than to its architectural or scenic beauties. This is not to say that he was oblivious to the charms of the countryside or the grandeur of Japan's mountains. His aestheticizing descriptions of his travels in Hokkaidō and ascent of Mount Fuji testify to a keen appreciation of the natural world. However, the physical rigors of such a trek were too difficult for a photographer laden with equipment, so views of remote locales or mountaintops were still rare. (The photographer Samuel Bourne (1834–1912) was able to take Himalayan photographs like the one reproduced in figure 1.20 because he had an army of porters to carry his cameras and other apparatus.) Longfellow's selection from Beato's photographic repertory is dominated by human subjects whose exotic

2.9 Felice Beato, Yokohama firefighting brigade, c. 1870. Albumen print. LNHS.

professions would contribute to what Dean MacCannell, in his pioneering study on tourism, has called the "mythology of work."[34] Street urchins, men pushing giant carts, peddlers, itinerant barbers, shampooers, masseurs, and other examples of the bustling and colorful street life to be encountered in Japan are especially numerous. Also represented are firemen, who were noted for their bravery and acrobatic skill (fig. 2.9). Such photographs far outnumber those of the elite, because their subjects were more willing to be photographed anonymously. As a result, they better served to create the kinds of personal identities and narratives tourists wanted. The aestheticization of work through spectatorship was one of the privileges of the leisure class.

For the most part, even Beato's seemingly impromptu glimpses of people at work, rest, and play do not record direct experiences, but are carefully choreographed. Beato rarely let his subjects be themselves, and never recorded their personal names. A laborer, his face evocatively hidden by a scarf, is posed before a slatted wooden window that provides a visual foil for the long pole in his left hand (fig. 2.10). A pretty teahouse server holding a cup of tea on a tray for three government officials is photographed in a similar setting, with raking rays of sunlight cutting sharp angles across the vertical bars of the wooden grill (pl. II). Such contrasts of light and shadow were in keeping with the pictorial idioms of

2.10 Felice Beato, laborer, c. 1870. Hand-colored albumen print. LNHS.

European romanticism. As MacCannell has also pointed out, "staged authenticity" is an inevitable by-product of the tourist experience.[35] Yet Beato's photographic vision was also conditioned by the technical requirements and limitations of his medium. Exposure times were long, forcing his subjects to remain immobile for many seconds. These practical considerations explain why so many photographs were shot in the controlled setting of the studio. This setting also had the advantage of allowing the photographer to make his authorial presence felt more strongly by employing devices that dramatized his subjects in various ways. He frequently placed his photographic subjects in shallow, stagelike spaces using emblematic props such as folding screens or painted backdrops as framing devices. For tourist photographers and their viewers alike, the resulting pictures did not represent individuals but "Japanese types," like the human curiosities gathered in Barnum's museum. While such artificiality was not uncommon in the pre-snapshot era, the staginess of Beato's settings and the figures who inhabit them underscore the image of Japan as belonging to an imaginary world. By helping to codify and transmit images that did not accurately reflect Japan's sociocultural spectrum, Beato endorsed and sustained the kind of mystique his European and American clientele wanted.

Even as globe-trotters valued photography as a means of authenticating their travels, photographers themselves sought to exploit its potential as a creative and expressive medium. Beato, like many of his European peers, sought to elevate and legitimate his work through cameo framing, dramatic lighting, and the adoption of European pictorial conventions. His subjects and compositions do not reveal any influence from Japanese wood-block prints as would be the case among later photographers. His selection and interpretation of the celebrated Tōkaidō Road and vistas of Japanese countryside were informed by the ideals of the picturesque that guided European landscape painting at the time (fig. 2.11). In the view with framing trees and receding central vista illustrated here, Beato follows a compositional formula established by the seventeenth-century French

2.11 Felice Beato, *The Tōkaidō Road*, c. 1870. Albumen print. LNHS.

painter Claude Lorrain that was later adopted by many artists. Hand-coloring was motivated by similar aspirations. The detailed coloring of the pictorial tattoos on the back of a groom or the brocade pattern added to a geisha's kimono made the resulting photograph more authentic while investing it with the individuality and aesthetic qualities of the painterly hand (see pls. I and III).

Individually and collectively, Beato's photographs are powerful and resonant records of the unequal relationship between the globe-trotter and Japan. His photographic gaze, in which a foreign presence is never recorded, underscores the separateness of the two worlds. It is a world of privilege, where normal social interaction is suspended. Globe-trotters, like their cousins, *flâneurs*, may roam the city observing and being observed without actually interacting with those they encounter.[36] Beato's selective vision of Japanese life thus matched Charley's own fragmented experiences and understanding of the country, where he lived largely as a spectator, on the margins of both his own and local society. In his wanderings through Tokyo, his gaze was likewise drawn to picturesque types and professions either unknown or in some way distinct from those at home. Charley's apparently random arrangement of Beato's picturesque vignettes reinforces this reading. A Western mental yardstick was the standard of measure for what caught his attention and what he wished to remember of Japan.

Nogootchi's Yesso Album

Of the four albums Charley brought back from Japan, the one containing twenty-one photographs of Hokkaidō, while most valuable from a historical perspective, is perhaps the least informative of Charley's own experiences. Charley went to Hakodate in September 1871 as temporary secretary to the American minister Charles de Long, but his duties were light, and he and fellow members of the delegation spent most of their nearly month-long stay in Hokkaidō exploring the southwestern part of the island. They traveled from Hakodate along the east coast as far as Yubutsu, then crossed the island to Ishikari, continuing west to Otaru and Yoichi before heading south back to Hakodate. Their route took them through the future capital city of Sapporō, which was still in the early stages of planning and construction. The photographs in the album, however, are predominantly of coastal settlements in northern parts of Hokkaidō, which were still exceedingly difficult to reach overland. These include, on the east coast, Akkeshi and Nemuro; on the west coast, Otaru; and at the far northern tip of Hokkaidō, Shibutsu, and Kunashiri Island. Taken during a coastal survey carried out under British auspices by Captain St. John in May 1871, they are part of the vast corpus of visual documentation that was gathered by expeditionary teams of various nationalities during the 1870s, when Hokkaidō was viewed as an uncharted wilderness to be explored, conquered, and exploited.[37]

Charley probably purchased the cloth-covered album readymade, directly from its owner, a certain Nogootchi, since a label on the cover identifies it as "G Nogootchi's Yesso Album." The Chinese characters that identify its contents as "Yesso pictures," *Yessoga,* testify to the still limited use of the modern word *shashin* for photographs. British Admiralty Records reveal that Gen'nosuke Nogootchi was an interpreter from Yokohama who served on board the British surveying ship when the photographs were taken.[38] Whether Mr. Nogootchi also took the pictures is unclear, but his desire to assert his authority over the album's contents is clear from the descriptive and explanatory captions, handwritten in English, that accompany each picture.

Although his identity has not yet been determined, the photographer may have been a locally trained one, hired on in Hakodate. Introduced by Russian visitors in the 1850s, photography had rapidly gained a foothold in Hokkaidō, and by the 1870s there were numerous Japanese photographers active in and around this port city.[39] Many were engaged in projects of political, commercial, and ethnographic importance to Japan and to the Western powers who claimed Hakodate as a treaty port. The Hokkaidō Colonization Board inaugurated a photographic project in 1871, sending the Russian-trained Tamoto Kenzō from Hakodate up the Ishikari River to Sapporo and back. Because of the harsh climate, difficult conditions of overland travel, and cumbersome equipment, Tamoto traveled by boat. He returned with 158 photographs. The following year, von Stillfried was hired by the Japanese government to take still more pictures. He spent two months in Hokkaidō, and with the aid of several Japanese assistants, produced more than one hundred photographs.[40]

The photographer may have been Japanese, but European photographic practices and attitudes conditioned the approach adopted in both the pictures and their arrangement. Like the contents of Longfellow's album of Beato photographs, these are organized by subject matter into two groups, one devoted to views of coastal Hokkaidō settlements and the other to portraits of the Ainu. Unlike Beato's *Views and Customs of Japan,* however, the album was not conceived as a comprehensive photographic project profiling Hokkaidō and its people. Few of the pictures are consciously artistic; whereas Beato's were shot from varied vantage points and carefully composed to create interesting compositional effects, the views of Ainu villages are uniformly presented from eye level with little effort to achieve aesthetic effects.

The camera was among the arsenal of symbolic weapons deployed in the colonization of Hokkaidō. It was used both by Japanese authorities and Western scientific expeditions primarily for constructing an archive of representational types and customs to be viewed against Japanese and Western geographic, social, and cultural norms. The Ainu occupied a peculiar place in both the Japanese and the American imaginations. In the West, during the mid-1800s, when American, Russian, and European ships began refueling in Hakodate, the Ainu were seen as a missing link between Europe and Asia. Captain Henry Holmes, a British merchant navy captain who arrived there in 1859, commented that he "took them to be Jews by their physiognomy and aquiline nose. Maybe they are part of the lost tribe."[41] A few years later, under the guise of scientific study, three British visitors caused a scandal by robbing Ainu graves and sending the bones home to England.[42] In his account of his expedition, Captain St. John, a keen naturalist, also admitted to collecting "two skulls which proved, upon examination, to be very interesting."[43]

Nogootchi's album records a distinctive culture that was rapidly being undermined by the Japanese government in the name of "protection" *(hogo)*.[44] A central goal of its colonization campaign was to integrate Ainu into Japanese society and the Japanese nation-state. To this end, they were encouraged to forgo traditional livelihoods based on hunting and fishing in favor of agriculture. "Uncivilized" practices, including female tattooing, male wearing of earrings, and the use of poisoned arrows, were banned. To further encourage assimilation, whole communities were relocated from the Kurile islands to Hokkaidō, and thirty-five Ainu men and women were sent to a special school in Tokyo, where many fell ill and died. As a result of these and other state policies, the number of Ainu rapidly declined over the course of the nineteenth century.

Ranging from the generic to the highly specific, the photos cover subjects as exotic to Japanese as they were to Europeans and Americans. The photographic gaze here is primarily ethnographic, with little of the romanticizing overtones commercial photographers so consciously invested in their views of Japan and the Japanese. Curiously, despite the uncharted vastness of the island, the photographer seems to have focused almost exclusively on views wherein a human presence is palpable, if not actually visible. Since the camera could not capture motion, and possibly also because of the unwillingness of the Ainu to be photographed, most of the scenes of village life seem strangely devoid of activity.

If the camera helped to record and bring order to the profusion of sights St. John and his team encountered on their journey, the resulting pictures exist in a symbiotic relationship with Nogootchi's words. Each view is framed separately and personalized by a handwritten caption identifying the location and subject. From the very moment one opens the album, both the sequencing and the descriptive text make the viewer aware of Nogootchi's desire to exert control over the response to the images it contained. The images assume representational authority through these captions, even as they confer authority on their author. The first, a bleak scene showing a sloop at anchor in a calm sea made treacherous by the floating icebergs nearby (fig. 2.12), sets the stage for those that follow. Nogootchi's caption reads: "This photography represents A.M.S.S. *Sylvia,* among the icebergs, on the 22nd of May 1871 at the Kunasiri island, on the one end of Yezo." Without this information, there would be no way of identifying this locale or the boat on which St. John's expedition circumnavigated the island.

2.12   Ship *Sylvia* among icebergs, 1871. Albumen print. Photographer unknown. LNHS.

Kunashiri, the southernmost of the Kurile islands, was visited by St. John at midpoint during his coastal survey. The scene that closes the album, also of Kunashiri, is the only other one in the album that approximates a picturesque landscape. With its cameo framing, the spare stillness of the perspective of low-lying land spits jutting out into the sea is as evocative as a Japanese ink painting.

Subsequent photographs are similarly invested with particularistic meanings by captions that often reveal as much about Nogootchi's self-image vis-à-vis the aboriginal inhabitants of Hokkaidō as about the subjects depicted. A bucolic scene of a small meandering river, in which a single canoe with a cluster of dwellings nearby can be made out, is captioned, "This photograph represents a small canoe in the stream, in the Ainos village at Atkish, the Ainos never live together with the Japanese but work together." From the lengthy, detailed comments he appended to a view of the process of extracting fish oil, the chief industry in the region, we may also infer that Nogootchi saw the region in economic terms. Ethnographic considerations are evident in his remarks regarding a view of a cluster of thatched roof buildings: "The picture represents the Ainos bear cage and jos thing on top, the Ainos catch a young bear, in a valley and nourish it by the woman, four or five month, and then put it in a cage made for purpose at Silbeth" (fig. 2.13). The belief that Ainu women raised bear cubs, even nursing them along side their own children, was a ubiquitous theme in travelers' accounts, including St. John's and Longfellow's.[45]

2.13 View of Ainu settlement, 1871. Albumen print. Photographer unknown. LNHS.

The second part of the album is devoted to smaller portrait studies of Ainu men and women the survey team encountered at various settlements. These sharply focused close-ups have a visual intensity lacking in the larger views. Yet, like the rush houses, storehouses, and canoes appearing elsewhere in the album, the portraits accentuate the Ainu's alterity vis-à-vis Japan and the West. Ainu men are distinguished by their short, leg-baring garments and long beards, features that confirmed the Japanese and Western image of them as hairy, half-civilized curiosities (fig. 2.14). Women are dressed in traditional garments made of fabric, bark, and fishskin decorated along the hems, cuffs, and lapels with distinctive geometric patterns. Several also display tattoos on their arms and faces (fig. 2.15).

While technical considerations must be taken into account, it is significant that we are never taken into the homes of these people. All views are outdoors, most showing individuals or small groups before their rush houses, a setting against which we can imagine but don't really see Ainu life. This is a reminder of the photographer's as well as the viewer's status as outsiders permitted to see only the externals of Ainu life. A portrait of a fisherwoman in Etomo staring at the camera uncomprehendingly, or defiantly, but definitely ill at ease, further underscores the fault line between photographer and photographed. A photograph of articles essential to Ainu daily life—bows, poisonous arrows, "jos thing" (made of?) scraped wood, arrow case, sake cup, weaving implements, fish

2.14 Ainu men, 1871. Albumen print. Photographer unknown. LNHS.

2.15 Tattooed Ainu woman, 1871. Albumen print. Photographer unknown. LNHS.

skin boots, and snow shoes—arranged like a display of museum specimens is an even more telling sign that what we are seeing are only photographs, representations of a representation.

While it is hard to separate these photographs from the colonial and ethnographic contexts, they are a far cry from the demeaning anthropological studies commissioned by Henry Wadsworth Longfellow's close friend Louis Agassiz only a few years earlier in Brazil, where subjects are presented in full frontal and profile views, stripped of their clothing and their dignity.[46] They are also qualitatively different from the studio shots later taken under the auspices of the Hokkaidō Colonization Board, where Ainu men and women pose awkwardly next to columns and other props customary in European portraiture. Not only are all the subjects shown in their familiar environment and in their customary dress, but through Nogootchi's inscriptions they retain their status as individuals. By referring by name to "The Aino lady called Kan Kanbi at Silbeth,"

Nogootchi underscores that this album should be viewed within the framework of a personal journey (fig. 2.15).

The contrast between Nogootchi's album and Charley's travel journal is revealing. Charley was a keen observer of his surroundings, but his writing lacks the tone of scientific detachment and high seriousness that characterizes Nogootchi's album. If Nogootchi focuses primarily on subjects that had implications for the development of the island, Charley often took note of the scenic beauty of the region. As his ship approached Hakodate, a little before sunset, he noted that "the effect was very pretty, these dozens on dozens of lights flickering over the water and the dark mountains as a background dimly seen against the clear star-lit night."[47] The pages of his journal are also filled with amusing anecdotes and evidence that, as a tourist rather than a professional observer of Hokkaidō, he sought fun whenever and wherever possible, attending a sumo bout and temple festival in Hakodate and riding, hunting, and fishing outside the city.

Further differences between the album and the journal also may be noted. The photographs and Nogootchi's commentary celebrate the particularity of Hokkaidō vis-à-vis Japan, while Charley's impressions take the United States as their point of reference. Although he does not specifically liken Hokkaidō to the vast wilderness of the American West, it is likely that this was the framework within which he saw Japan's northernmost islands and its aboriginal inhabitants. His view of the Ainu no doubt was also inflected by the romanticized image of the noble savage that his father had helped to popularize in America through his celebrated poem *Hiawatha*. Like all visitors to Hokkaidō, Charley took special note of the Ainu custom of tattooing young women on the hands and just above the lips. This practice was of special interest to him since he had been tattooed already in the United States. His personal engagement is evident from his unusually detailed observations of the distinctive nature of the practice. The climate and vegetation of Hokkaidō, moreover, were similar enough to those of New England that Charley seems to have felt quite at home. In its rich woods, he readily identified familiar maples, oaks, and chestnuts. Much to the amazement of the locals, he even swam in its frigid waters. "The climate here," he noted in his journal, "is charming—fine bracing air and cool one-blanket evenings—also the swimming, and I have had one or two good swims each day."[48]

Nogootchi's album lends itself to multiple readings. Its pictures show the sensibility and interests of a particular photographer, and both the subjects and the inscriptions that accompany them tell us as much about the observer as the observed. Just as the photographs, though intended to serve documentary purposes, became, through their captioning, valuable evidence of Nogootchi's privileged knowledge of Hokkaidō, so too they took on still other subjective meanings for Charley. Despite the fact that they did not specifically depict the places he had visited, he treasured them as souvenirs of his stay in Japan.

"Family" Albums

The two most autobiographical of Charley's four albums are in accordion format and have identical brocade covers inscribed with his name in *hiragana* phonetic syllabary. The photographs, by various photographers, are interleaved between paintings and matching poems on silk celebrating the "Eight Views of Ōmi," scenic spots *(meisho)* in the vicinity of Lake Biwa, just north of Kyoto (figs. 2.16 and 2.17). The "Eight Views of Ōmi" were part of a long Sino-Japanese poetic and pictorial tradition that gained new currency with the growth of domestic tourism in the early nineteenth century. Hiroshige's evocative views of these landmarks, all within easy reach of the Tōkaidō Road, had helped to make them "must-sees" for Japanese tourists.[49] Although Charley visited the area himself, he was probably unaware of the many layers of meaning embedded in the tiny paintings, delicately rendered in pale tones of ink and wash, or the accompanying verses inscribed in cursive script on decorated paper. The two albums were intended as elegant souvenirs of Ōmi, not as photograph albums. Yet by mounting his personal mementos between evocative landscapes and poems, he created a framework that simultaneously confirmed their cultural authenticity and the aesthetic image of Japan.

2.16 One of *Eight Views of Ōmi*, c. 1872. Artist unknown. Ink and colors on silk. LNHS.

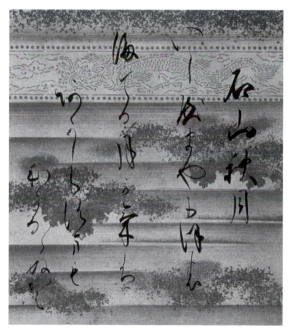

2.17 Poem celebrating one of *Eight Views of Ōmi*, c. 1872. Ink on silk. Calligrapher unknown. LNHS.

One album contains nineteen 8-by-10-inch photographs, most of them hand-colored. Some may be attributed to von Stillfried, whom Charley also commissioned to take photographs commemorating his ascent of Mount Fuji.[50] Others are the work of Uchida Kyūichi. Although each scene is mediated by a professional photographer's eye, by its arrangement, its owner has made himself both the director and star of the album's visual narrative. From the opening view of Charley himself, book in hand, sprawled beneath the bushes in his Tokyo garden, it is clear that its trajectory will exclude anything not directly related to his personal experience of and perspective on Japan (see fig. 2.5).

Individually and collectively, the photographs play to the exotic imaginings of the armchair traveler, while at the same time revealing Charley's need to present himself in a manner that was socially sanctioned by friends and family in Cambridge. By the 1870s, photography had become a ritual that symbolically confirmed normative family life in the United States. This institutionalization of the photograph album to represent personal and family experience went hand-in-hand with the growing division between public and private life in late-nineteenth-century New England. A microcosm of the Victorian cult of domesticity, the family album conferred an aura of sanctity on the home environment. Commercial photographers capitalized on these religious overtones by designing albums bound in leather embossed with gold lettering, like family Bibles. In many households photo albums in fact came to function in much the same way—as sacred records of births, marriages, deaths, and other significant *rites de passage*.[51] This attitude may help to explain why the Longfellow family kept all Charley's albums, but disposed of many of his other souvenirs.

Travel, even as it allowed freedom from familial structures, often reproduced them in subtle ways. Charley needed to see himself and be admired through other eyes, and in the pictorial world of his album, he constructed a self-image he could not achieve at home. Although its setting is Japan, its visual message is bound up with American conceptions of manhood as defined by property ownership, male friendships, and relationships to women. Its predominant theme, Charley as householder, runs counter to his identity as tourist, and in so doing hints at his own conflicting attitudes and insecurities vis-à-vis his family's expectations.

In the culturally conservative New England society where Charley had come of age, a house was a crucial foundation of adult male life. It implied order, stability, and family—the very qualities lacking in Charley's life at the age of twenty-seven. In creating an album that focused on *his* house, he was choosing a subject his family could readily identify with, since their own colonial home loomed large in their collective identity and had been the subject of many private and public photographs. By linking himself with such a potent symbol, Charley seems to have been trying to legitimate a life that was, in fact, devoted chiefly to play.

Six of the photographs in this album focus on Charley's various residences.

He first lived in the foreign settlement in Yokohama, where he rented a house on the fashionable Bluff overlooking the harbor (fig. 2.18). Since it was made of wood in a neo-Gothic style reminiscent of New England, from the outside at least, his family would have found this peak-roofed bungalow with decorative bargeboards in the gables comfortably familiar. Inside the house was a different matter, however. As he wrote his sister Annie, "We live in Japanese fashion, that is, on the floor. And this letter is written lying flat on my belly in front of a charcoal fire and looking out over green fields and Yedo Bay in the distance."[52]

2.18   Cottage on the bluff, Yokohama, 1871–73. Albumen print. Photographer unknown. LNHS.

Another photograph in the album showing twelve Japanese men and women seated on a hill with an aviary behind them and three women standing in the foreground is identified by a small handwritten caption as "my servants." This image is as striking for its subject matter as for its human scope: in the early 1870s, with the exception of commemorative school pictures, photographers in Japan rarely portrayed such large groups. And photographs of servants, seemingly relaxing on grassy hill, are unknown. What prompted this photograph, and whether or not Charley actually had a staff of twelve at his disposal, we cannot know. Nor can we know whether this image, no doubt intended as visual proof of his material well-being, was received by his family in this light or rather as evidence of his profligacy. As noted above, debts of more than $18,000 may have been a factor in Charley's decision to leave Japan in March 1873.

Unlike most of his peers, from the outset, Charley found Tokyo far more attractive than Yokohama. "I have had a splendid and most interesting time here and don't know when I shall leave," he wrote his sister two months after arriving, but it was not until some time the following year that he built a house for

2.19 Raimund von Stillfried, attr., entrance to Charles Longfellow's Tsukiji House, 1872–73. Albumen print. LNHS.

himself there.[53] He used photographs as well as detailed descriptions of its appearance to help his family visualize what he characterized as "all together an awfully snug little place for a weary 'batch' to retire and study in."[54] Charley Longfellow's description of his "snug" cottage is reminiscent of the "cozy" New England farmhouse of Donald Mitchell's *Reveries of a Bachelor.*[55]

To those at home, the actual geographic location of the house within the city mattered less than what it looked like, so Charley never bothered to describe its whereabouts. Recent research has revealed that it was located in the foreign concession at Tsukiji, on the site now occupied by Rikkyō University.[56] With the exception of diplomats and Japanese government employees, foreigners were still rare there. The American teacher William Griffis noted that there were no more than three hundred of them in Tokyo at the time.[57] Although foreigners had been permitted to lease and purchase land and houses in the city in 1868, it was deemed too dangerous, and even by 1872, most Americans still preferred to live in Yokohama, where they could more easily enjoy the safety and comforts of home and the company of their compatriots.[58]

The viewer begins the tour of Charley's "Yedo" house by passing through an impressive wooden gateway flanked by two guards. In the Edo period, such a gateway would have indicated that its inhabitant was of lower samurai status (fig. 2.19). Normally, the wooden gates remained closed and visitors entered through a small side door, but here they have been flung open to allow the camera full access to the entrance, with its line of welcoming servants. Walled compounds were typical of Japanese urban architecture, but at a time when foreigners might still be the target of attack, they also provided protection.

Since the interior of the house was too dark to photograph, Charley provided his family with a detailed description of its appearance. Despite its incorporation of Japanese elements such as tatami mats and sliding doors, its eclectic abundance of furnishings is revealing of its owner's Victorian tastes:

> You enter the portico where stand two large paper lanterns on poles with the monogram C.A.L. on them. Straight ahead is a broad entry [central hall] leading straight through the house, into which four small rooms for visitors open [on the left], one of which I use for a store room. On the right of the [hall], are three rooms opening onto the garden, one entirely Japanese—no furniture, only a chimney place in the corner, papered with blue bamboo paper, large windows, and very jolly in summer and winter. Here we have magic lanterns, acting, etc. The next room is my bed room, quite large with blue bed and window curtains covered with white imitation lace. Half the side of the room opens onto the gardens.
>
> The next is the parlor with long transoms in two of the corners, like a yacht, table in center, porcelain vases in corners and a mantlepiece filled with flowers, mirror over the mantelpiece. Furniture, transoms, and curtains

of marron reps [corded fabric], table covered with a glorious confusion of dictionaries, grammars, novels, photo books, newspapers, and, of course, the Japanese pipe and firebox—which is in pretty constant use. Over the centre, hangs suspended from the ceiling a silver stork with outspread wings. In one corner is a Japanese stand with books and "refreshments." The paper of this room as well as that of my bed room is of a light pearl gray color with little specks of gold showered all over it. And the doors, which all slide into the wall, are of single planks—plain with a border of black lacquer around them and birds, plants, and flowers beautifully painted on them by a well-known Yedo artist. Next [to] the parlor is a little dining room, the chow being passed from the kitchen in through a panel. [At the end of the long hall are] the pantry, kitchen, bathroom, and the house is complete. I have no carpets but thick Japanese straw mats.[59]

This description, though written in response to his sister's request, discloses the deep satisfaction Longfellow derived from arranging his house. While pride in home ownership typified patterns of New England male behavior, this preoccupation with the domestic interior seems to challenge the conventional gender roles of the times. As will be discussed more fully in chapter 5, in middle-class New England society of the 1870s, decorating the home was more properly a woman's vocation.

Three views showing the veranda and the garden beyond, include, as Charley told his family, "some officer's daughters who happened to drop in and insisted on being taken too"[60] (pl. V). In fact, they were women employed by a teahouse he patronized (fig. 2.20). Their stiff, formal poses are in stark contrast to that of Charley himself, who has chosen to be immortalized in his garden, book in hand—a studied pose of leisurely self-cultivation (see fig. 2.5). This view, perhaps unconsciously, conjoins American and Japanese conceptions of the garden as a retreat where its proprietor could enjoy the union of urban and pastoral values and a beneficial communion with nature.

Although Charley lived a life in Tsukiji at some remove from the city's working Japanese residents, he eagerly participated in the urban pleasures available to its men of means. A letter to his sister Annie, written when he was still living in Yokohama, suggests that it was the proximity to these attractions that led him to move to Edo. "We have had a good deal of fun in Yedo lately, at parties, the theatres, and sightseeing. I am never tired of going over the ground and now having turned into a sort of cicerone [guide] of Yedo."[61]

Descriptions of teahouses and their beautifully landscaped gardens figure in virtually all travel accounts. The Yūmeirō teahouse, where Metama, Sokuhe, and Matahe, their attendant, probably worked, may have been a focal point of Charley's social life in Tokyo. His album includes a view of the imposing two-storied teahouse with a pleasure boat this establishment kept on the Sumida river for its guests taken by Uchida Kyūichi (fig. 2.20). Located in the Yanagibashi district, a flourishing geisha quarters in Tokyo, the Yūmeirō was not a teahouse that catered specifically to Western visitors. In fact, in Tokyo, unlike Yokohama, many such establishments refused entrée to foreigners. Early in his stay, Charley wrote in his journal, he and de Long "paddled up [the] Sumidagawa to [a] teahouse. De Long wouldn't take his shoes off, so [they] wouldn't let us in."[62] Charley may have been introduced to the Yūmeirō by Yamanouchi Yodō or Iwasaki Yatarō, two of his Japanese acquaintances. The former daimyo of Tosa, Yodō was a notorious connoisseur of the pleasure districts. He had close personal ties to prominent figures in the Meiji government and forged relationships with Western diplomats and merchants who might be beneficial to Japan's commercial and industrial interests. Iwasaki, a founder of the Mitsubishi Company, was a forward-looking businessman with especially close ties to the American trading firm Walsh, Hall, and Co. Charley also met Iwasaki's younger brother, Yanosuke, before he left to study in the United States under the auspices of Francis Hall.[63]

2.20   Uchida Kyūichi, Yūmeirō teahouse, c. 1871–73. Albumen print. LNHS.

A smiling woman identified as Ohannasan appears in two hand-colored portraits, probably taken in von Stillfried's studio (pls. III and IV). In one she stands with a parasol over her shoulder and in the other, she sits strumming a samisen. Charley never refers to her by name in his journal or letters, but Ohannasan may have been a geisha employed at the Yūmeirō or another teahouse. She seems to have occupied a special place in his affections since he later displayed her portrait in his bedroom in Cambridge.[64] He also made a point of seeing her and a young woman named Osarto, who may have been their daughter, when he revisited Japan in 1885 and 1891.[65]

The portraits of Ohannasan combine time-honored visual conventions from the Japanese painting and wood-block print tradition with new ones borrowed from Victorian photography. Both the parasol and the samisen, the musical instrument of the pleasure quarters, were common pictorial conventions in the portrayal of beautiful women.[66] The beauty beneath a parasol seems to have been something of a fetish for Longfellow. In addition to the portrait of Ohanna, he purchased a painting of a Japanese beauty in this guise, and at some point also added a tattoo of this subject to his arm.

Ohannasan's engaging smile, however, is unconventional. Since female portraiture was relatively rare in Japan before the advent of photography, photographers had to teach their subjects how to sit, stand, and look at the camera. This may have included instruction on suitable facial expressions. In most cases, subjects appear solemn and dignified before the camera, contributing to images that often have an impersonal blankness. Ohannasan's smile is arresting precisely because such expressiveness was so novel in the early Meiji pictorial context.

Yet the smile is also rare in European and American photographs of this era. This absence reflects Victorian standards of portraiture, which held that strong facial expression distorted the subject's beauty. Audrey Linkman, a scholar of Victorian photography, has noted that "smiles do feature on the faces of actresses in the commercial card trade, which suggests a connection with those of an equivocal social standing. The respectable would certainly have wished to maintain their distance from such an association."[67] This may help to explain why photographers promoted the smile in their portrayals of Japanese women made for the Euro-American market.

A photograph by Beato with an accompanying caption by Wirgman, entitled "Declining the Honour," offers clues to the ambiguities the smile encodes. It portrays a "moos'mie," the euphemistic term for a young girl *(musume)*, who is captured, recoiling in surprise with her hand raised, palm facing outward, as if refusing the viewer into a room (fig. 2.21). The caption reads:

She is sweet,—she is gentle;—she is inviting;—she is very coy! Her dark eye has not one atom of what Byron describes as "the flash of a dark eye

2.21 Felice Beato, *Declining the Honor,* c. 1870. Albumen print. Miriam and Ira
D. Wallach Division of Art, Prints and Photographs, New York Public Library.
Astor, Lenox, and Tilden Foundations.

in a woman." Do or say what you will—within the bounds of propriety—she enters into your joke; will chatter and laugh with you; sing to you, accompanying herself on the samisen, and take no offence at your non-admiration of her music; listen with patience and respect to your musical efforts, although quite as incomprehensible to her as hers to you; and she will give no signs of ennui, or make and return of the rudeness all too often accorded to her performance. She will show you all her little toy-like treasures, without taking umbrage at the evident pity you bestow on her simplicity; and she will look with an innocent, wondering curiosity on any foreign trifle, trinket or charm you may permit her to examine. She is never angry at the impossibility of satisfying your lofty ideas of things; nor will she hurt your susceptibilities by allowing you to imagine that you will fail in your attempts to give her pleasure. She is a gentlewoman by nature.

A Japanese moos'mie (girl) will give lessons in gentleness of disposition and consideration for the feelings of others, that her Western sister might copy with advantage. But she has her likes and dislikes like any other daughter of Eve. And if advances are offered to her of an unpalatable nature, she has her own, and a no less effective because kind and graceful way of,—"declining the honour."[68]

2.22 *Full of Fun and Saucy: A Geisha Girl, Japan* (H. C. White Company, 1901). Library of Congress.

Beato's smiling girl is an example of one of the visual codes used in photographic portraiture to present Japanese women as Euro-American men wanted to see them: playful and inviting, yet like "other daughters of Eve," prepared to refuse male advances. This doubleness makes the photograph all the more titillating. It is not hard to understand why Ohannasan was also shown with a smile on her face, a convention that leaves the viewer to decide whether or not she is a "gentlewoman."

The historian of photography Ishiguro Keishō has observed that smiles and laughter became quite common in later tourist photographs.[69] As an American stereoscopic view from 1901 confirms, such facial expressions had become clichés in the portrayal of "geisha girls" (fig. 2.22). This commodification of the smile is a dramatic example of one of the intangible by-products of international tourism, where in the absence of a common language, coded gestures and expressions became an important part of the "hospitality" industry. Since such services generally require "emotional work," notes Urry, "the fact that a great deal of it is provided by women is clearly no coincidence."[70]

Charley personally commissioned from von Stillfried most of the photographs in this album, and they exert a special voyeuristic hold on the modern viewer because their subjects can be identified, allowing us to imagine them as records of particular people and places. Several of them, however, entered the commercial market under the imprint of other studios. Stillfried and Anderson Studios purveyed views of the four kimono-clad women at Charley's house as "geisha on the veranda of a teahouse."[71] A Japanese collector purchased a print of the gate and entryway of Charley's house in Paris, and until recently believed it represented a samurai's residence, a mistake that its American owner would have appreciated.[72]

A "Trophy" Album

Charley used various techniques to make his presence felt in all his albums, shaping how they looked and what they meant, but his personal imprint is strongest in one containing ninety-one photographic cartes de visite spread over eight pages. The album features many of the people he encountered in Japan—predominantly teahouse women, geisha, and Kabuki actors—along with selected photographs of himself, his friends, and a few tourist sights. The care with which the photographs are arranged, creating spatial and temporal unity through physical contiguity, suggests that this was the most personal of his four albums, the most revealing of how he saw and wanted to remember Japan. The narrative structure of this album is not obvious, however, since the pictures are arranged in a collage rather than sequentially. Their studied distribution across the pages suggests that they were mounted at one time, perhaps

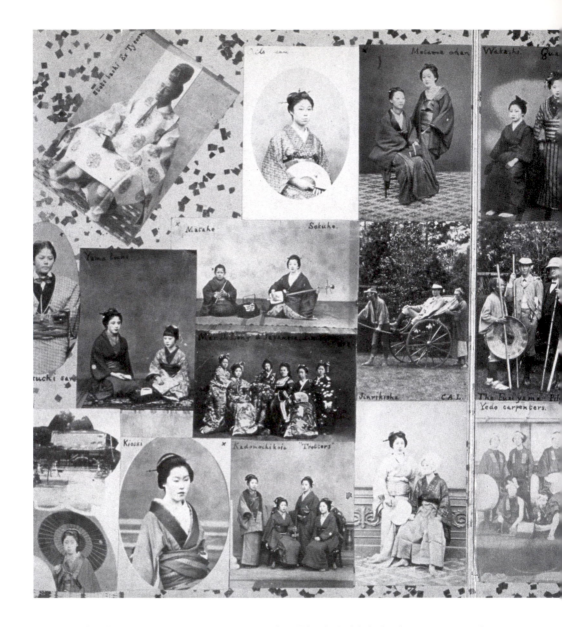

by a professional at a photographic studio. The brief labels, however, are in Longfellow's own hand.

Examination of one double-page spread composed of twenty-four photographs hints at the relationships subtly implied by these juxtapositions (fig. 2.23). The collage is anchored on the upper left and lower right corners by portraits of Prince Hitotsubashi, the last Tokugawa shogun, dressed in full court attire, and of Charley himself, masquerading as a samurai. Their images are both placed at diagonal angles, creating a sense of identification between them while at the same time setting them apart from the other figures. Dominating the center of the collage are two more photographs of Charley; in one he is seated in a jinrikisha with his travel companion Alfred Jessup, and in the other he and Jes-

2.23 Double page from Charles Longfellow's cartes de visite album, 1871–73. LNHS.

sup stand in preparation for climbing Mount Fuji. Both are costumed in pith helmets and hold stout staffs, typical colonial trekking attire. From this vantage point, the two Americans gaze down on the bevy of women—as if from Fuji, their latest conquest. A portrait of Charley's friend Yamanouchi Yodō, labeled "The Old Prince of Tosa, died 1872," is placed in the center on the far right. Its positioning below a view of the Great Buddha of Kamakura may be an allusion to his death.

There is considerable variety among the female portraits, but most appear to be young women of Charley's acquaintance who worked at brothels and teahouses. Their clothing clearly distinguishes them from the ranking geisha, attired in sumptuous brocade kimonos and obis, who appear in other pages in this album (see fig. 2.3). Some women figure individually, others in pairs or small groups. A few photographs seem to portray mothers with their children. Some are shown in three-quarter view with flattering cameo framing, others in a photographer's studio awkwardly standing by or seated on chairs, and still others with more familiar props such as a samisen or hibachi. Since the camera couldn't capture movement, requiring sitters to hold a particular pose for many seconds, many of the photographs look stiff and even uncomfortable to the modern eye.

Most of the women are identified by name. From the viewer's upper left to right, top to bottom, they include Oitsu-san, Metama and Ohanna, Wakashi and Quacho, Omiko and Otayo, Metama, Yamatochi and an unnamed attendant, Matahe and Sokuhe, Mrs. de Long and the Japanese embassy, an unnamed woman in a jinrikisha, teahouse girls from Otsu, Lake Biwa, Kioski, Kadonochikoya Trotters, "Yedo carpenters," and Ogie. Metama, Matahe, and Sokuhe, as noted above, worked at the Yūmeirō and were part of Charley's entourage. Charley's placement of the portrait of Sokuhe, above that of Mrs. de Long and the five young women who traveled with her to the United States in 1872 to study, may suggest a sly wit on his part, since elsewhere he identifies Sokuhe as Charles de Long's mistress (see fig. 1.3).[73] The formal portrait of Mrs. de Long and her companions takes on further sexual innuendoes in light of a passage in a letter Charley wrote to his sister Edith, noting that he had "offered to take charge of two of these princesses and take them to Cambridge, but their guardians didn't seem to see it."[74] The curious photograph of Charley and a young woman dressed in the short cotton jacket of carpenters may have been taken on the occasion of "a festival at the Shiba temples on October 4th in which geisha dressed as artisans in the building trades" (see fig. 4.7).[75] It is likely that Charley had only passing encounters with "the teahouse girls from Otsu, Lake Biwa," and the several other unnamed women whose cartes de visite he saved. He may have received these photos directly from them or even picked them up at a hotel or inn to add to his collection.

Although Charley may have conceived this album as a kind of trophy collection, to be shown off to his male friends at home, many of the photographs it contains were commissioned by their subjects for personal use and not intended primarily to be presented to the male gaze. Japanese women were avid consumers of photographic technology and like their Euro-American counterparts had themselves photographed to commemorate personal milestones, travel, and to give to family and friends. Not surprisingly, women sought to emphasize the glamorous rather than the tawdry aspects of their lives. The studio setting and best attire (perhaps borrowed from the photographer) enabled them simultaneously to conceal their often humble backgrounds and present themselves as fashionably chic. Yet because such portrait photographs were widely disseminated for various purposes, they often helped to create, package, and deliver stereotypes of Japan to the West.

PICTURING JAPAN

2.24　Kumeji, 1871–73. Carte de visite.
Photographer unknown. LNHS.

Paintings and wood-block prints had fostered a culture of feminine celebrity that in the 1860s and 1870s coexisted and competed with photographic portraits.[76] Both exploited the techniques of mass reproduction to express changing feminine cultural ideals, but photographs allowed women a greater role in their self-presentation. In the pictorial realm, male publishers and artists made decisions about who was portrayed and how, but a photographic subject could choose the occasion as well as her dress, props, and pose. One young woman identified as Kumeji stands in a studio next to a pillar draped with a fashionable checkered tablecloth. She holds in her hands an open album of photographic cartes de visite (fig. 2.24) Another asserts her individuality by wearing her kimono in combination with a kind of bow tied around her neck. In her eyes, this was no doubt a fashionable sartorial touch, but for Western viewers who wanted to see Japanese women in authentic attire, her efforts many have appeared incongruous. In this respect the new realism of the camera sometimes served to widen rather than narrow the cultural gap between Japan and the West.

Within the covers of his four photograph albums, Charley has presented a carefully edited, coded, and idealized microcosm of his life in Japan. The albums are deeply autobiographical, revealing conflicting attitudes and impulses not expressed in his letters and journals. His aim is re-collection, both in the sense of memory and in the sense of gathering together. In extracting the particularities of his experiences, both real and imagined, he has subsumed individual lives and relationships and subordinated them to his own. With his personal experiences thus collected, ordered, reduced in scale, and enshrined in an artifact that could be held in the hand, he could recall Japan from the vantage of controlled observation. The miniature, as Susan Stewart has observed, is "the realm not of fact but of reverie."[77]

CHAPTER 3

Paradise of Curios

The places most visited by strangers
in Japan are the curio shops.

—William Perry Fogg, *Round the World
Letters*, 1872

Curios were part of the seductive vision of Japan, inseparable from both the imagining and experiencing of the country. Their pursuit, discovery, and purchase gave focus and personal meaning to travel, while enabling the tourist to maintain a degree of control over and within the unfamiliar environment. Just as the advent of new, faster systems of communication and transportation expanded the tourist's geographic horizons, so too it spurred the demand for exotic products from ever more distant lands. The international trade in curios contributed to new artistic convergences and affinities even as it reinforced old paradigms of difference.

Japan was part of a world of goods whose allure few globe-trotters could resist. As Thorstein Veblen observed, travel is a leisure class ritual in which conspicuous consumption plays a central role as proof of one's own and one's society's economic power.[1] Globe-trotters displayed this power by spending freely to acquire socially desirable goods. By the 1860s, many articles from Japan—furniture, ceramics, lacquer, bronzes, ivories, silks, screens, and fans—were already available in Europe and the United States. When such purchases were made in their country of origin, however, they assumed greater personal value than ordinary commercial exchanges at home, because they authenticated their owners' travels.

Authenticity, in the context of tourism, has very different connotations than it does in modern art history. Both emphasize origins, but what these are and how they are determined are not the same. For art historians, connoisseurship, the careful scrutiny of intrinsic visual evidence, combined with external documentation, guides decisions about what is authentic. The art historian's goal often involves identifying and distinguishing among various artists' personal styles. The tourist's much looser understanding of authenticity is grounded in the idea of "tradition." Generally only those works that are made to serve some function within a particular culture are classified as authentic, while those made expressly for sale to tourists or for export are deemed spurious. Distinguishing between these two classes of artifacts is problematic and often highly arbitrary.

Nineteenth-century globe-trotters recognized that provenance alone did not guarantee the authenticity of their purchases. Many believed that to be "genuine," an article had to be old, the quality of Japanese workmanship having deteriorated since the opening of the country and growth of international trade. Yet this was often a rhetorical stance that had little bearing on reality, since few collectors were able to distinguish between old and new. The perception that goods made in Yokohama were of inferior workmanship and contaminated by Western influence made articles available there especially suspect. Globe-trotters were not aware that Japanese artists had selectively absorbed Western influences long before 1853. Nor were they prepared to acknowledge that many of the artistic changes they decried were a consequence of the very global commerce and tourism of which they were a part.

Travelers of the 1860s and early 1870s acquired a kaleidoscopic range of articles in Japan, many of which were highly regarded at the time but have since fallen out of favor. Within modern art historical discourse, these are often relegated to the realm of "tourist art," "bric-a-brac," "knickknacks," "bibelots," or "curios." Such labels situate them within a culture of feminine domestic consumption that has come to be scorned because it defies the newer conceptualization of both private and public collections according to "universal" principles of art history—nationality, period style, genre, artist, and so on. The advent of modernism, with its prejudice against technical virtuosity, ornament, and realism further sealed the fate of many nineteenth-century Japanese arts and crafts as *objets de mauvais goût,* best relegated to the family attic or museum basement. Such artifacts deserve serious scrutiny, however, because Victorian globe-trotters' tastes played a key role in how Japanese art came to be represented and imagined both within Japan and abroad.

The complexities of production and consumption in the early years of international tourism set the stage for new ways of ordering Japanese material culture. Globe-trotting on the part of both Japanese and Euro-Americans heightened sensitivity to national identity as expressed in art and culture. Growing travel within Japan also contributed to the process by which many distinctive forms of artistic expression first came to be systematically explained in terms of geography, climate, history, and ethnic and/or racial factors.

Mutually modifying exchanges also helped to revise ideas about the relative aesthetic, social, and economic values of individual artists and genres. Since the Renaissance in Europe, the fine arts of painting and sculpture had been regarded as superior to the decorative arts. But the arts and crafts movement that developed in Britain in the 1860s, later spreading to the United States, undermined this hierarchy. Familiarity with Japanese artifacts, many of which were not readily classified as fine or decorative arts, both shaped and reflected these changing attitudes. Conversely in Japan, the terms for art, *bijutsu,* and decorative arts, *kōgei,* were only coined in the Meiji era to accommodate the "universal" classificatory requirements of international expositions. By adopting the categories by which Europeans defined "art," Japanese officials were also assimilating a value system that contributed to the demotion of lacquer and metalwork, "crafts" long held in high esteem among Japanese collectors. These categories also led to new framing and display practices consonant with those employed in European museums and expositions.

In the 1860s and early 1870s, Euro-Americans lacked interpretive paradigms for the wide range of artifacts available in Japan. The same object could be understood differently depending on the individual and the context. The organizers of international expositions generally classified articles within the framework of existing Western categories such as fine and decorative arts, arts and crafts, or industrial arts.[2] Globe-trotters, however, adopted variable, and often highly idiosyncratic terms to refer to their acquisitions. Most were content to let others classify and interpret their exotic souvenirs, often prompting censure by artists and aspiring art critics, especially those who had no personal experience of Japan. This was true of Russell Sturgis (1836–1909), a leading figure in the development of art and architectural criticism in the United States. In an 1868 article titled "The Fine Arts of Japan" in *The Nation,* he observed: "The Europeans and Americans who have visited Japan have done us a good service by bringing away the beautiful things they have brought; but beyond getting together 'curios,' they have done nothing toward the elucidation of the dark questions in Japanese art,—as, indeed, was to have been expected."[3]

Such dismissiveness was not entirely justified. While few American globe-trotters discussed Japanese art at any length, their European counterparts, many of whom were well informed about European art and had some familiarity with Japanese art before their travels, commented with considerable insight on its various manifestations. In his *Ramble Round the World,* the Austrian globe-trotter von Hubner included an extended discussion of Japanese architecture, sculpture, and painting, in which he affirmed, contrary to the then widely held view, "that Japanese painters all know or have understood perspective," but purposefully rejected it.[4] Although their assumptions were not always correct,

Europeans were generally well ahead of their American counterparts in acknowledging and discussing Japanese art on its own terms. They played a key role in guiding American appreciation of Japanese art.

Shorthand for "curiosity," "curio" is a word that came into widespread use in the Victorian era as a result of what modern anthropologists have called the "commoditization of ethnicity."[5] Earlier, curiosity had signified a rare natural or man-made object of wonder or pseudoscientific interest. In the eighteenth century, curiosities had often served as tangible evidence of a male explorer's journey to a distant land. The Japanese wood-block prints that the captain of an American ship acquired in Nagasaki in 1799 were classified as "curiosities," because they provided ethnographic information about a distant and inaccessible land.[6] When donated to the East India Maritime Museum in 1832, each was identified with a number stamped on the front. The prints were then cataloged together with an antelope foot, a compass, a cap worn by an Owhyhee chief, and a Chinese painting (fig. 3.1).

After the opening of Japan, when prints became readily available in Europe and America, they were more commonly referred to as "curios" or "art." "Curiosity" was still used occasionally, however. As the poet Longfellow warned his son: "Don't ruin yourself in buying strange bronzes. You will have a perfect musaeum of curiosities; and I shall have to put a Mansarde [sic] roof on to your part of the house to hold them!"[7] What was curious also could be artistic. In assessing the Great Buddha in Kamakura, one globe-trotter noted, "Considering the age and simplicity of the people at that period, it is a remarkable work of art . . . There is no greater curiosity in Japan than this statue."[8] Such taxonomic ambiguities are symptomatic of the nineteenth-century world of trade with and tourism in Japan.

For globe-trotters, a Japanese curio excited visual interest first and foremost because it was anomalous within their own culture. As Aimé Humbert observed: "The most exquisite things among the small figures in ivory to be found in Yedo are incontestably those representing animals, and more particularly the tiger, buffalo, the bear, the monkey, and the mouse. These little art objects, which for us are only *curious,* are an integral part of the outfit of the native smokers of both sexes."[9] Even the most ordinary and banal manifestation of Japanese material culture could arouse the globe-trotter's desire and visual delight.

Whether old or new, utilitarian or not, curios were often distinguished by their reduced scale. "In China and Japan," wrote Charles Coffin, "this word . . . is applied to boxes, trays, bronzes, watch-chains, jewelry, and all small articles."[10] Size was not as much of a practical consideration in the age of sea travel as it is today, but miniatures have always had a special mystique among collectors.

3.1   Utamaro, *Pictorial Sisters (E-kyōdai),* 1799. Wood block print, ōban. Photograph by Mark Sexton; courtesy Peabody-Essex Museum.

Globe-trotters treasured tiny, gemlike curios made of lacquer, ceramic, or ivory for the detail and skill of their craftsmanship. Such miniatures played all the more powerfully for their small scale on the memories and minds of those who acquired them. As Susan Stewart has observed in her study *On Longing: Narratives of the Miniature, the Gigantic, the Souvenir, the Collection*, diminutive size frequently "served as the realm of the cultural other."[11] This ideology was encoded in the appreciation of Japanese curios as well as in their identification with the feminine.

Although both "curio" and "art" were culturally sanctioned and often interchangeable terms for articles that could be purchased in Japan, their adoption could have connotations of class and gender. Curio was a convenient catch-all for globe-trotters lacking the language to describe the visual experiences of their own culture, and by extension, to interpret the more unfamiliar ones of Japan. Whether owing to gendered ideology or to slippage from their status in the European tradition, globe-trotters did occasionally refer to painting and sculpture as art. When a young Bostonian saw the collection of John Walsh, a leading American merchant in Yokohama, he declared his walls to be hung with "chefs d'oeuvre of Japanese art."[12] Men were more likely to characterize their purchases as art, thereby proclaiming to the world that they were discriminating collectors, not merely souvenir shoppers.

The surge in leisure travel combined with enhanced cultural respect for Japan following the 1876 Philadelphia Exposition led to a more broadly based American consensus that *all* products of Japan were artistic. As a result, the word *art* often came to be used to describe many of the same articles earlier tourists had described as curios. The circumstances surrounding this epistemological shift were complex, to be sure, but they were primarily reflective of changes in American, not Japanese, culture. Goods from Japan were esteemed in large part because they were ascribed qualities lacking in those manufactured at home. They were believed to be handmade by craftsmen with an innate aesthetic sense who, unlike their modern Western counterparts, were not motivated primarily by utilitarian or commercial impulses. This idealization of Japan and denial of a commercial aesthetic was part of the constellation of ideas that globe-trotters associated with authenticity.

Curio Street

Unlike their European counterparts, American globe-trotters of the 1860s and 1870s did not go to Japan expressly to form collections of Japanese art, but few returned without souvenirs. The souvenir was indispensable because, as Susan Stewart has written, it "both offers a measurement for the normal and authenticates the experience of the viewer."[13] Personal preferences, the financial means

3.2 Tilt-top table, c. 1799. Brown lacquer with gold lacquer floral patterns. 71.0 x 61 cm. Photograph by Sexton/Dykes; courtesy Peabody-Essex Museum.

at their disposal, and what was available in the limited number of cities and towns they visited guided their selections. What they had seen before their journey and, in some instances, what they saw in the homes of foreign residents while in Japan, could also influence tastes. American expectations of and receptivity to Japanese art and culture, though highly variable, were still further informed by the kinds of goods that had been trickling, then pouring into the country since the beginning of the nineteenth century, often as part of the China trade.

Direct trade with Japan had begun during the Napoleonic Wars, when officials from the Dutch East India Company had chartered American ships to make the annual trip from Batavia to Nagasaki. Notable among these was the *Franklin*, which returned to her home port of Salem, Massachusetts, in 1800 with cargo including knife boxes, cabinets, and tables inlaid with lacquer and mother-of-pearl (fig. 3.2).[14] These domestic furnishings, made in Japan to Western specifications, were functional objects that could be comfortably incorporated into Western domestic environments.

When the *Franklin* arrived in Salem with its precious cargo, the island nation from which it had returned was already well known as the source of lustrous black lacquered goods. Articles protected and decorated with lacquer had been exported from India, China, and especially Japan, for centuries, but those from Japan were especially admired, giving rise to the term *japanning*. European and American craftsmen developed "japanning" techniques and styles in imitation of those used in Japan, but they were forced to find alternatives to lacquer, since the sap from the tree from which it came was not available to them. Consequently, genuine lacquerwares were both sought after and costly.

The attractions and availability of Japanese goods made expressly for the export market grew dramatically after the opening of the treaty ports in 1854. The *Caroline E. Foote,* the first vessel to carry commercial cargo directly to the United States, arrived in San Francisco in 1855. The auction announcement in the *Daily Alta Californian* described the cargo as "rare and curious goods . . . consisting of a large variety of USEFUL AND ORNAMENTAL ARTICLES and of the most beautiful and rare workmanship."[15] The sale was noteworthy enough to merit an editorial in the same paper three days later: "The various articles exposed are perhaps more valuable as curiosities than for intrinsic worth, yet many of them surpass in elegance and workmanship, anything of the same description ever before exhibited in this community." The writer went on to extol the lacquer, cabinetry, and porcelains, giving passing reference as well to "toys for children, fanciful and unique, rich silks and crapes [sic], graceful urns and colored glass, work boxes, [and] painted screens."[16]

Similar auction and sale announcements appeared in East Coast newspapers. Enthusiasm for Japanese arts and crafts was especially high in Boston, Philadelphia, New York, and Newport, cities with a long tradition of trade with the Far East. Many early collectors had ties to naval officials or other Americans who had traveled to Japan or to merchant houses that had been involved in the China trade before the opening of Japan.[17] Most Americans who purchased such exotic wares are unlikely to have been able to distinguish or to have even cared much whether they were of Chinese or Japanese origin.

In 1860, about the time that the first Japanese diplomats were in the United States, an article in the *Boston Evening Transcript* noted, "Anything from Japan awakens interest and excites examination at the present time. We notice in the window of Mssrs. Soule & Jencks' Gallery Sumner Street, a beautiful piece of raised and inlaid work in the shape of a Japanese work table."[18] A decade later the Boston Household Art Company had become an established purveyor of Japanese furnishings.[19] In the 1870s, shops catering to the taste for Japanoiserie were also opening from New Orleans to New York.[20]

Because of this long tradition of exporting to Europe and the United States, merchants and artists in the treaty ports were already well stocked with goods designed to appeal to globe-trotters' tastes. Indeed, the scope of the visitor's purchases was often limited by what local merchants believed they liked. This responsiveness to the perceived desires of foreign customers may have been intensified by the decline of high-end domestic patronage, a change that made artists increasingly dependent on the international market. Those who purveyed their more modestly priced wares along routes well traveled by Japanese, such as the Tōkaidō Road, however, probably had less need to change their ways. Edward Prime was amazed by the succession of shops that lined this thoroughfare between Yokohama and Tokyo: "Little of nature is to be seen, but from the first to the last, it is like a drive through a museum, a grand curiosity shop; the Tōkaidō, the whole twenty-two miles, being a succession of the same beautiful little shops, with neatly-arranged wares, useful and ornamental, which line the streets of all the cities of Japan."[21]

A lacquered table Charley purchased, possibly for use in his Tokyo house, is emblematic of both the continuities and changes in the early Meiji era (pl. X).[22] Like those long favored in New England homes, it is a round tilt-top table with a decorative pattern in gold on black lacquered ground. Its pictorial décor, however, does not consist of a careful arrangement of small clusters of flowering plants, as was typical of the early-nineteenth-century tables exported to Salem. The single branch of flowering wisteria from which a wasp's nest is suspended is in keeping with the kinds of designs favored for lacquerwares made for the domestic market. It is likely that the lacquer artist who created this image drew inspiration from a printed book. The composition resembles an illustration in Utamaro's celebrated *Picture Book of Insects* (*Ehon mushi erabi*, 1788).[23] The signature "Gyokuzansai" appears on the tabletop, but further research is required to determine the artist's identity.

No city was more closely identified with the world of goods available to tourists than Yokohama, whose main thoroughfare, Honchōdori, was popularly known as Curio Street after the numerous shops catering to foreign tastes that lined it. Although globe-trotters often asserted that Yokohama was *not* Japan and complained bitterly about the high prices, they nonetheless made many purchases there. They had little choice. As the French globe-trotter Théodore Duret later wrote:

> The European, who didn't know what to ask merchants or interpreters, since he knew nothing himself, found himself in great difficulty, because there was no way to overcome his ignorance. There were no clues in the shops one entered. Nothing was displayed on shelves. All the objects were instead hidden from view, doubly enclosed, first within bags or covers and then within boxes. The merchant didn't help at all, either by offering objects, or by trying to explain the nature or genre of goods he had.[24]

In the 1860s and early 1870s, Yokohama's curio shops were little more than raised platforms covered with tatami mats, open to the street in front, with the

3.3 Hashimoto Sadahide, *Foreigners Buying Lacquer in Honchō*, from *Record of Things Seen and Heard at the Open Port of Yokohama*, 1862–65. Private collection.

3.4 Felice Beato, curio shop, c. 1870. Albumen print. Miriam and Ira D. Wallach Division of Art, Prints and Photographs, New York Public Library. Astor, Lenox, and Tilden Foundations.

shopkeeper's living quarters in the back. "The outside of these stores," wrote William Perry Fogg, "are by no means imposing. No high marble or granite structure, no plate glass windows, no army of elegantly dressed salesmen are to be seen, but a room perhaps fifteen feet square."[25] This unfamiliar, stagelike setting made shopping an exciting spectacle, akin to participating in a living theater. Since prices were not fixed, bargaining with the storekeeper using hand gestures, facial expressions, and a limited vocabulary of Japanese words was also an important part of the adventure. In the curio shop visitors could simultaneously play the role of cultural insider and outsider, interacting with locals on their terms, while at the same time maintaining their decided economic advantage.

Record of Things Seen and Heard at the Open Port of Yokohama (Yokohama kaikō kenbun shi), a multivolume book written and illustrated by Hashimoto Sadahide between 1862 and 1865, suggests that Japanese were as fascinated by the commercial culture of Yokohama as Western visitors.[26] In one illustration, the artist shows two nattily dressed foreigners examining lacquer samples on the raised platform of a shop in Honchōdori (fig. 3.3). The chair that the enterprising merchant has provided his client is emblematic of the efforts made to adapt Japa-

nese sales practices to Western requirements. By 1874, a European visitor would complain: "Although inhabited by Japanese this avenue has lost all of its character. Instead of Western shop signs, which are long painted tablets inscribed with Chinese characters, there were cloth banners with words like 'Curiosities,' 'English spoken,' or 'Curious shops.'"[27]

The unidentified "Curio Shop" featured in a popular, often-reproduced Beato photograph from the early 1870s discloses none of these changes (fig. 3.4). This frontal view of a tiny shop packed from floor to ceiling with an eclectic array of exotic goods, was designed to appeal to the tourist's commodified fantasies of Japan. The photographer has sought to show how, in the view of Euro-Americans, a curio shop *ought* to appear. This picture fosters the illusion of authenticity by presenting a direct, unmediated encounter between the viewers and the objects they desire. Despite their difference in approach and medium, Sadahide and Beato's pictures consciously capitalized on what was to their respective audiences a culture of strangeness.

What kinds of articles did globe-trotters of the 1860s and 1870s expect to find in Yokohama? Although few collections from this era survive, written and visual sources provide some clues. Most notably, they reveal that, contrary to the popular view today that Japanese wood-block prints and books took precedence, Americans, and many Europeans as well, were eager to collect well-crafted functional or decorative articles that enhanced their personal appearance or the interior of their homes. Decorative metalwork was especially sought after. Coffin, writing in 1869, believed that the high prices demanded for the best bronzes on Curio Street resulted from the admiration they had aroused at the 1867 Paris Exposition. "The finest bronzes are from the province of Couza [?], which lies in the interior. Some are inlaid with silver in arabesque designs, but the prices asked will probably deter most travellers from purchasing. Since the opening of the country to foreign trade everything has advanced in price."[28]

In 1874, Philippe Sichel, a European dealer in Japanese curios *(bibeloteur)*, visited Minoda Chōjirō and Musashiya, the two largest and best-known establishments. Chōjirō had opened an antiques shop in Edo in 1855, but after moving in 1859 to Yokohama, began offering wares crafted by contemporary artists as well.[29] Sichel observed that for the most part the articles on view were not only expensive, but modern. Musashiya, which advertised itself as a purveyor of curios, ivories, and so on, was one of the leading wholesale exporters of arts and crafts. Sichel mentions lacquered cabinets, chairs, boxes for gloves, liqueur chests with characters and crests, and cigar cases. Ultimately he bought only seven "older objects" made of an attractive metal alloy inlaid with gold silver and red copper that portrayed the gods of good fortune.[30]

The less discriminating young Bostonian Benjamin Curtis was captivated by the variety on display in yet another Yokohama shop.

> One of the first places a foreigner should visit is Shobey's silk-store, where the silk articles of all sorts can be obtained at prices which seem incredible. Magnificent bed-spreads, with a monogram exquisitely embroidered on one side; elegant dressing-gowns and smoking jackets of heavy quilted silk; handkerchief-cases, monogram pincushions, scarfs, embroidered handkerchiefs, sofa-pillows, screens,—all these are to be found, of the finest quality and the best workmanship. Near by one can find the largest stock of fans he probably ever saw, the choicest lacquer-work and bronze articles; while the antiquarian will be in paradise looking through collections of old armor, ancient Daimios' swords, and grotesque idols.[31]

The articles tailored to tourist taste that enticed Curtis differed little from those that Americans had been buying in the United States for more than a decade.

Charles Longfellow: The Tourist as Collector

Charley's background prepared him unusually well to appreciate Japanese art and culture. Since the Beacon Hill residences of his uncle Tom Appleton and his own family home in Cambridge were all richly appointed with fine European and American furnishings, paintings, and statuary, he probably had more exposure to the fine arts than many fellow American tourists. The Longfellows' circle of acquaintances, moreover, included many pioneer enthusiasts of Japanese art: the painter William Morris Hunt, with whom Charley would later travel to Mexico; Alexander Agassiz, son of the poet's Harvard colleague Louis Agassiz; various members of the Hooper and Bigelow families; and above all, Charley's maternal uncle, a well-known Boston patron of the arts and early Japanophile, who had lived on the continent for many years, but had no direct experience of Japan.[32]

The contents and scope of Tom Appleton's Japanese collection can only be surmised, but it was apparently quite large even before his nephew left for Japan. A poem titled "Japanese Art. A Cabinet of Ivory" that he wrote about an object, in all likelihood in his own collection, testifies to the high regard in which he held functional yet decorative Japanese imports:

> The world of Magic drops this meteor bright
> To earth, as pattern of her craftsmen there,
> An aerolite from Fancy's upper air!
> Or rather say Titania's cabinet.
> Cobweb I see, and Master Moth alight
> Upon it, with strange birds of plumage rare;
> Pheasants which live; wild swans that dive in air,
> On pearly wings extended, exquisite.
> The ponderous, pygmy doors, whose silver bar
> Is dropped, three little faery drawers unfold,
> Where the Queen's costly robes and jewels are:
> Which open as a spider, snail or leaf we hold,
> All carved in creamy, orient ivory, fair.[33]

This escapist fantasy of Japan as a land of magical enchantment resembling the realm of the fairies Oberon and Titania is a feature of many writings on Japan by collectors who had not traveled to the country themselves. The poem's fervid romanticism has much in common with that of the writings of Appleton's French contemporary Edmond de Goncourt (1822–96). This pioneering French Japanophile recorded his passion for Japanese lacquer, screens, ivories, porcelains, bronzes, and other furnishings in his journal and later, in *La Maison d'un artiste* (1881), his celebration of his residence and its aesthetic décor.[34] Both Appleton and Goncourt disclose the close association between consumerism and the romantic sensibility. As Colin Campbell noted in his study of this phenomenon, romanticism legitimated the pleasures of personal fulfillment, fostering new patterns of consumption that could lead even utilitarian articles to be clothed with layers of emotive meaning.[35]

Although Charley Longfellow was neither a man of letters nor an aesthete, cultural conditioning had made the pictorial arts integral to his apprehension of the world. While many new arrivals described Japan through the lens of photographs, newspaper illustrations, or the pictures on fans they had seen beforehand, Longfellow was unusual in drawing analogies to the work of European painters. To help his family visualize the scenes he encountered on board a ship en route to Hokkaidō, he described a "magnificent sunset—one half of the sea, land, and sky deluged with golden light as in Turner's pictures."[36] And later, in recounting his ascent of Mount Fuji, he compared the "cinders and writhed and contorted rocks" of its crater to Gustave Doré's sketches of Dante's Inferno.[37]

Charley Longfellow's family wealth also predisposed him to collect. What he chose appears to have been in keeping with the tastes of the times, and not unlike the collection formed by the Italo-French globe-trotter Henri Cernuschi. Cernuschi, who arrived in Japan in 1871 with his French travel companion, Théodore Duret (1838–1927), was a banker of Italian birth who had fled to France, where he made a fortune that enabled him to collect on a grand scale. Political turmoil in France prompted his decision to make a world trip. Duret was an influential art critic and friend of many avant-garde painters, including Manet and Whistler, who both painted his portrait. The two globe-trotters traveled extensively in Japan, visiting all the major cities then open to tourists. They returned with thousands of objects, the basis of the Cernuschi Museum, which opened to the public two years after the collector's death.[38] Duret's personal collection of some 1,392 illustrated books and albums entered the Bibliothèque Nationale in Paris in 1899.[39]

Although the full scope and contents of Longfellow's collection can no longer be determined, it is clear that he too bought in quantity. Charley differed from his European counterparts, however, in that he never articulated the aesthetic outlook he brought to his acquisitions. Some of his purchases were made with the aim of furnishing his Tokyo house. Others reveal a penchant for themes, such as views of the sea and boats, beautiful women, or theatrical subjects that resonated with his personal experiences. He also took great delight in humorous and whimsical subjects.[40] Like many fellow Americans, he generally referred to his acquisitions as curios, a word that in his usage often retained the connotations that "curiosity" had in the great age of exploration. Occasionally, he also characterized the paintings and sculptures he saw or purchased as "works of art" or "chefs d'oeuvre," but whether this reflected his own evaluation of them or slippage from the status of these two media as fine arts in the West is uncertain.

Whatever the personal meanings Longfellow attributed to the articles he purchased, there is little doubt that he was a compulsive collector, eager to begin the quest for the trophies of travel. As he declared in a letter to his sister Alice a month after his arrival: "I have not yet bought any things. There are so many, and they are all so lovely, that one gets perfectly dazed strolling through the Japanese town. But before leaving, I must make a foray and capture a few of these pretty things for you and the 'brats.'"[41] Not long afterward, he claimed to have amassed half a shipload. While this was no doubt an exaggeration, a total of thirty cases arrived from Japan and China at the Longfellow house in the fall and winter of 1873–74, prompting Charley's sister to wonder, "Whatever shall we do . . . with the cases of Japanese curios?" The poet was equally concerned about the "screens without end and boxes without number."[42]

Like most globe-trotters, Charley began his hunt on Curio Street in Yokohama. His pocket diary records the names of Musashiya and Minoda Chōjirō, the two shops later visited by Philippe Sichel.[43] Whether or not he bought anything from these merchants is unclear. It is likely that he also explored shops in Tokyo in the hope of finding better range, quality, and value. As Olive Seward observed, this city was "an emporium for the entire empire."[44] Finding the desired goods in Tokyo in the early 1870s was not easy, however, since merchants were as yet ill prepared or unwilling to deal with foreign customers. As quoted above, when Cernuschi and Duret tried to make purchases there, they complained about the limited selection and the indifference of local booksellers. Longfellow does not mention any Tokyo artists by name, but he is likely to have met there members of the Kano school, who, having lost their feudal sinecure, were eager to find new patrons. Artists of the Kano school had once enjoyed the patronage of the ruling elite, and many of its members were still judged the leading artists in the city. Perhaps the "well-known Yedo artist" who painted the birds, plants, and flowers on the sliding doors of Charley's Tokyo house belonged to this lineage.[45] Several works by members of the Kajibashi branch of the Kano school active in the nineteenth century remain in Longfellow House today. They include a hanging scroll showing a man poling a boat under cherry trees by Tanshin Morimichi (1785–1835) and a six-fold screen by Tangen Moritsune (1829–66) offering a panoramic vista of the rolling hills of the Yoshino region covered with profusely blooming cherry trees (fig. 3.5 and pl. VI). Both works are painted in what modern art historians call the "Yamato-e style," a characterization that collectors of Longfellow's generation would not have known.

In his privileged capacity as a member of de Long's entourage, and especially during his journey to Hokkaidō and return to Tokyo, Longfellow purchased many articles not readily available in Yokohama. Acquiring articles outside the limited world of the foreign settlements invested them with added value. Souvenirs from

3.5 Kano Tanshin
Morimichi (1785–1835),
spring landscape, early
nineteenth century.
Hanging scroll, ink and
colors on silk. LNHS.

that remote part of the country were so coveted that Charley and his fellow travelers had to raffle them off to prevent feuds.

Carved wooden spoons, gifts from two young Ainu women in Horobetsu to whom Charley had shown his tattoos, are the first curios mentioned in his journal. Ainu women carved and decorated small spoons for serving soup and larger ladles for stirring the mash when making sake.[46] For the young women who presented them to him, these utensils had practical functions. For Charley, they were personal mementos and emblems of the vanishing world of the Ainu. "They had made [the spoons] themselves, and insisted we should take them as keep-sakes."[47] Ainu spoons, bows, and arrows did not so much assume value in relation to their function within the society that had produced them as in relation to their distance from it.

Many of the goods Charley acquired were utilitarian items of Japanese daily life that caught his eye because they were made of unfamiliar materials, featured exotic subjects, and, above all, were fashioned with uncanny technical and decorative virtuosity. Like his fellow Americans, Charley had a sense of cultural superiority that was tempered by respect for Japanese ingenuity, craftsmanship, and work ethic. Some of these articles were already popular souvenirs among Japanese tourists. In Miyanoshita, the site of hot springs in the vicinity of Hakone, long a resting place for pilgrims preparing to climb Mount Fuji, he purchased inlaid camphorwood boxes that were a local specialty. Although these were functional, tourists—both Japanese and American—valued them as mementos of a particular place and time.

Morioka, a city in modern Iwate Prefecture, which he passed through on the return from Hokkaidō to Tokyo, was famous for articles made of cast iron. Charley and his party were told that the wonderful tea kettles made there "sing but never boil over."[48] The feudal lords of Nanbu domain, of which Morioka was the castle town, were great tea ceremony enthusiasts and had built a foundry on the castle grounds to make the large kettles used for boiling the water. Soon these became a local specialty, much sought after in other parts of the country. In the nineteenth century, local iron casters also began producing the small spouted and handled vessels *(tetsubin)* used for steeped tea. Local lords sometimes presented these as gifts, but they were sold commercially as well. Although Cernuschi did not travel as far north as Morioka, he purchased enough teapots to fill a room in his museum.[49]

After buying a "good singer," the de Long party visited a workshop "in which a dozen nearly naked men were casting the famous tea kettles."[50] Few foreign visitors failed to be impressed by the staggering variety of bronze, lacquer, and ceramic wares produced in Japan, but because of language barriers as well as the limitations on travel still in effect at the time, only the very lucky or well-connected had the opportunity to observe their production. For the tourist collector, watching the process of manufacture not only guaranteed the authenticity of his purchase, but invested it with personal meaning. Such occupational activities (often staged) subsequently became important attractions since they gave tourists the illusion of participating in the culture.[51]

Globe-trotters coveted articles with the patina of antiquity, particularly if they were ascribed noble lineage. There being as yet very little information about individual masters or schools of art, most collectors cared little about the identities of the artists who had created the works they purchased, unless they visited their studios and met them. Age and an aristocratic pedigree, however, were important. Collecting Japanese antiquities gave Americans access to an imagined cultural past that their own nation lacked. Added to this was their satisfaction about saving treasures that they believed might otherwise be lost to posterity.

Western visitors were unanimous in their triumphalist conviction that they were insuring the preservation of Japan's heirlooms. "That is the great trouble of this country," wrote Charley. "One sees so many splendid old things which never will be produced again, as the things from the princes' and nobles' houses are all being sold off—the new fashion being to have everything European. . . . And I only wish I were very rich, if only for the pleasure of buying these splendid things from temples and yashikis [mansions] which in a few years will have disappeared from Japan."[52] He also deplored the destruction of old Buddhist icons, complaining that a "beautiful work of art"—a bronze Buddha on the edge of the lake at Hakone—had "been broken up and sold as old metal."[53] This was a common refrain among Euro-American visitors, although much of what impoverished temples were selling at the time was not of great antiquity. Cernuschi bought an eighteenth-century bronze figure of the Buddha Amida from Hanryūji, a temple in Tokyo's Meguro district, that by present-day standards is a relatively young work. The statue, impressive primarily for its colossal size, was sold to Cernuschi after the temple in which it had served as object of devotion was deconsecrated and became a public school. Longfellow himself acquired a small statue of Kannon Bosatsu dating from the nineteenth century (fig. 3.6).

The de Long party's purchases in Morioka and Sendai, the castle town of the Date family, confirm that travelers could readily buy many articles that had lost their functional value owing to changes in Japanese society. On their arrival in Morioka, the Americans had sent word they wanted to see any curios that might be available, and local merchants brought a sizable collection directly to their rooms. "Some we bought cheap—six fine pieces of old lacquer, an old wedding present from a Daimio to his intended with his and her crests all over them. We agreed to raffle for these in the evening, each getting a prize of more or less value for his ten dollars. I drew a magnificent great tray, but it was so large that

3.6 Seated Kannon Bosatsu, nineteenth century. Gilded and painted wood.
H. 221/4 in. (56.5 cm.). LNHS.

I swapped it with the 'Chief' for a looking glass stand."[54] De Long also got a suit of armor in Sendai.

A handsome lacquer shelf with the crests of two feudal families testifies to Charley's interest in this medium, long a favorite in Japanese exports to the United States, as well as to the desirability of articles from noble households (plate X). The shelf, decorated with an auspicious motif of cherry and pine boughs in lacquer with sprinkled gold designs *(makie),* would have been made as part of the household furnishings for a bride of a feudal daimyo family. The bridal trousseau customarily included three sets of shelves designed to hold clothing, cosmetic articles, writing utensils, and games.

While the members of de Long's group were eager to acquire the trappings of samurai culture, their receptivity to the paintings they were shown was more ambiguous. In Sendai, Charley bought "a picture on silk of a monkey scratching himself, which I think very good, though the others declare it not worth the storage room." He continued,

> My purchase encouraged the merchant to go to his shop and return with two pictures which he proudly hung up for our inspection, but [he] was rather taken aback by the roars of laughter which greeted his chefs d'oeuvre. One was the head of an old fellow with something like a monstrous caricature of Gen. Butler, but the other was the triumph of art. It consisted of a ring about a foot in diameter made by one flourish of the paint brush, in the center of which was a little figure of a big headed man an inch high—and that was all. The merchant said it was painted two hundred years ago by a celebrated artist, and represented an imp (one of seven) enclosed in a thunderbolt that came and led astray the first son of the first Mikado.[55]

So enthusiastic was Charley about this now-lost painting, that he even included a sketch of the "imp" and his thunderbolt in his journal entry.[56] The painting seems to depict Fukurōkuju within a flaming jewel, an auspicious emblem in Buddhist art. One of seven popular deities believed to bring good luck, Fukurōkuju is distinguished by his exaggerated head, a symbol of wisdom, virility, and longevity.

The visitor's eye in Japan was highly selective, and the forms and styles it championed tended to refer back to European and American arts. For some, the strange and unfamiliar motifs and absence of illusionism were insurmountable obstacles to the appreciation of Japanese painting. For others, as discussed below, illusionistic techniques made works inauthentic. Charley's artistic experience may have trained his eye to "see" better than his companions, who probably had had little occasion to view art at home. Was his visual delight in this "chef d'oeuvre" a wholly personal response? Was it perhaps predicated on familiarity with the inventive, comical compositions of artists such as Hokusai (1760–1849), whose work he might have encountered in the United States?

Hokusai was probably the only Japanese artist known by name in the United States in 1871 since John La Farge, an early collector of his prints and illustrated books, had singled him out for special praise in his essay on Japanese art in Pumpelly's *Across America and Asia*.[57] While in Japan, Longfellow in fact acquired several volumes of Hokusai's *Manga,* an encyclopedic compendium of sketches, as well as several of his illustrated tales.[58] For many foreign enthusiasts, such publications became important sources of information, both accurate and inaccurate, concerning Japanese pictorial themes, compositions, styles, and techniques.

Osaka was a city with a long tradition of mercantile activity and presented a wide range of specialties designed for the domestic market. When Mitford visited Osaka in 1867, he noted that he "wished to carry away some of the mei-butsu, special wares, for which the city was famous. Lacquer, quaint pipes of many patterns, fans, and brocade were temptations not to be resisted."[59] During the four days he spent there en route to Kyoto, Charley also made many purchases, listing each item and its price in his pocket notebook.[60] The most expensive were "two gold transparent panelled screens" at 35 ryō. At the time, a ryō was roughly equivalent to one dollar. Next in cost were a group of "storks" at 20 ryō. The remainder, ranging from 13 to 2 ryō, were almost all bronzes: lanterns, vases, candlesticks, lamps, and flower stands. These probably were not made expressly for export, since "stork candlesticks," bronze vases, and other similar utensils had long been manufactured for use in Buddhist temples, in flower arrangements, and in the tea ceremony.[61] The opening in the back of the standing crane still preserved in Longfellow House suggests that it was intended as an incense burner, possibly for perfuming garments (fig. 3.7). Even allowing for the inflated prices often charged foreigners, their cost indicates that they were luxury goods within Japan.

Charley's extravagance reflects the enormous enthusiasm Japanese metalwork excited among Euro-American collectors. Edward Prime, in Japan a year earlier, had declared that the Japanese "excel in working in metals especially in bronzes and in inlay work. I saw in their shops exquisite vases of bronze that were valued at $1200 the pair, the work of which could not be equaled in Paris. The inlaying of metals, as of steel with gold and silver, is carried to the highest perfection, almost making it an art peculiar to Japan. In tempering and fashioning steel blades, the ancient fame of Damascus has been revived among this simple people."[62] Prime may have been particularly sensitive to works in this medium since his brother William Cowper Prime (1825–1905) had traveled and collected in the Near East.[63]

Théodore Duret believed bronze statuary to be one of Japan's greatest artistic achievements. This led his wealthy companion to acquire hundreds of bronze vessels of various subjects, sizes, shapes, and styles. He was especially drawn

3.7 Incense burner in the form of a crane, nineteenth century. Bronze. H. 39 5/8 in. (100.64 cm.). LNHS.

3.8 Kimura Toun, dragon, nineteenth century. Bronze. 41 x 88 cm. PMVP photograph by Degraces; courtesy Cernuschi Museum, Paris.

3.9 Dragon, nineteenth century. Artist unknown. Bronze. 30.4 x 9.5 cm. Photograph by Mark Sexton; courtesy Peabody-Essex Museum.

to small figures of real and imaginary animals—writhing dragons, clusters or tortoises, and perky rabbits.[64] Known in Japanese as *okimono*, such figures originally were made in sizes suitable for display on the shelf within or adjacent to the recessed alcove, *tokonoma*, that was a feature of Japanese residential architecture. Animals of the zodiac and other auspicious symbols predominated. Growing foreign demand, however, fostered the creation of works of larger scale and a wider range of motifs. The fashion for the French sculptor Antoine Barye's (1796–1875) bronze sculptures of animals may have

contributed both to the enthusiastic reception of Japanese okimono and their acceptance as sculpture.

Dragons, which had figured powerfully in the medieval European bestiary, were especially popular among foreign collectors. Cernuschi acquired a large number of such okimono (fig. 3.8). One Charley is likely to have purchased was later donated by his uncle Tom to Boston's Museum of Fine Arts. When it was deaccessioned in 1933, it entered the collection of the Peabody and Essex Museum in Salem (fig. 3.9).

Kyoto, traditionally the source of many luxury crafts for the domestic market, was officially opened to international tourism on the occasion of an exposition held in 1872. Modeled on the international expositions, the event was intended to help the city recover from its economic slump following the emperor's departure and the establishment of Tokyo as the nation's capital. Its goal was to spur tourism, thereby aiding the city's artisans and merchants in developing a new market geared to international clientele. Visitors' responses varied, but many were surprisingly unfavorable. There was general dismay at the high entry fees, absence of labels, and, especially, the paucity of works for immediate purchase. Many objects were samples, on the basis of which prospective buyers could place orders for future delivery. One reviewer noted "all the really valuable articles, or those which have historical or other interest, are not for sale, being lent for exhibition only by Japanese gentlemen."[65]

Charley was among those disappointed by the goods on display. The exhibition, he complained, didn't amount to much, "one being able to see nearly everything that is here exhibited in any dry goods or curio shop."[66] However, he did buy a set of tea and coffee cups with matching saucers from "Minoya Taihe of Gojozaka," a shop situated on the slope beneath Kiyomizu temple, where potters and dealers of the local enamelwares were concentrated. The availability of such goods in Kyoto underscores Japanese potters' responsiveness to foreign tastes. Six years later, Edward Morse wrote, Japanese would refer contemptuously to such wares as "Yokohama-muke," literally, "Yokohama direction."[67]

Although he did not mention them in his journals, Longfellow also made other purchases in Kyoto. Among them, according to a penciled notation in his handwriting reading "Kioto, 1872," is a hanging scroll in ink and colors on silk featuring a pair of birds standing on wave-splashed rocks, a theme that no doubt resonated with his love of the sea. Charley also recorded on the outside of this now badly damaged scroll the identity of its artist, Chikudō. Trained in a Kyoto branch of the Kano school, Kishi Chikudō (1826–97) developed an eclectic pictorial style and range of subjects that later brought him international fame. In the 1880s and 1890s, his renderings of animals, especially tigers, an example of which was displayed at the 1893 Chicago Exposition, were much sought after by Euro-American collectors.[68]

When Longfellow made his purchase, however, Chikudō was probably still unknown to foreign collectors. The information on painters available at the time being rudimentary at best, it is likely that Longfellow purchased this work directly from Chikudō, whose studio was in Kyoto. Unlike globe-trotters of the 1880s, who had access to publications with the names of Japan's leading painters and bilingual art dealers to assist them, Euro-American visitors to the Kyoto exposition had no knowledge of artists' names, seals, or signatures. The first American to publish an essay on Japanese art was the above-mentioned Russell Sturgis. His five-part series, "The Fine Arts of Japan" (1868), was followed a year later by an article in *The Art Journal*, a British publication, by James Jackson Jarves, an American living in Italy who was a pioneer collector of both Italian "primitive" paintings and Japanese art. (This and later essays were the basis of his well-known 1876 publication *A Glimpse of the Art of Japan*.) Other than Hokusai, the only artist mentioned by name in these publications is "BounTiyo," in all likelihood Tani Bunchō (1763–1840), an artist active in Edo.[69] Neither of these articles, however, is likely to have reached a wide audience.

An album of sixty-one scenic views, *meisho*, of Kyoto and its environs by various artists of the city's Kano, Tosa, and Shijō schools of painting is also likely to have been purchased during Charley's visit to this city. It includes sights such as the Thirty-three Bay Hall (Sanjūsangendō), the Bridge over the Uji River, and Mount Takao, long celebrated in literature, painting, and prints. All the places represented were meisho that would have been familiar to the Japanese tourists to whom such albums no doubt had been previously marketed. Since this album has a date corresponding to 1872, it is likely to have been compiled expressly for sale during the brief window when foreigners were allowed to travel to Kyoto. Although Longfellow makes no mention of meisho, his acquisition of this album, along with the very similar one featuring the Eight Scenic views of Omi illustrated in figures 2.16 and 2.17 raises the possibility that he was aware of this Japanese pictorial and poetic tradition.

Japanese porcelains were already well known and much coveted by globe-trotters. Prime asserted that "in some of the arts the Japanese are in advance of other nations. The porcelain of Japan, notwithstanding it takes its name from the Celestial Empire, is rarely rivaled in China."[70] While his nephew was in Japan, Appleton commissioned him to make purchases on his behalf, cautioning him, "If it is true that you can obtain choice objects of art in Japan, something superior and rare, I should like you to invest a thousand dollars for me in such works. Don't get anything common, as I have a good collection and wish only to add things of the best."[71] In Nagasaki, a city known for its porcelains, Charley bought his uncle a pair of vases that are now lost. An assortment of lacquer and tortoise boxes, sake cups, bronzes statuettes, crystal balls, and vases Appleton bequeathed to the Boston Museum of Fine Arts also may have been among the items Charley purchased for him in Japan. Most were later deaccessioned when such "curios" had fallen out of favor.[72]

Contemporary Paintings

The belief that "authentic" Japanese art was in decline and destined to disappear was common among globe-trotters. This attitude spurred them to collect as much as they could "before it was too late," even as they decried the decadence they discerned. Since most had little knowledge or sources of comparison for the objects they saw, they offered only vague explanations for their claims of decadence. In the realm of the pictorial arts, however, the targets of their criticism were specifically representations of "modern" subjects that were incompatible with their romantic image of Japan and the use of illusionistic techniques emblematic of Western influence. As von Hubner wrote:

> I do not think I am mistaken in thinking that the best of the modern drawings (saving some caricatures of locomotives, telegraph posts, strangers in European costumes, with red whiskers, &tc.) are simply feeble reproductions of the past. In these days no one invents anything new. The gift seems exhausted—a characteristic sign of decadence. To prove this inferiority one has only to compare what is done to-day with the works of ancient art, of which the finest are in Europe, where they have been sent by the Dutch from Detsima.[73]

This myth of a vanishing tradition underlay the globe-trotter's eagerness to meet and watch Japanese practice their art: collecting such experiences was as important as collecting rare artifacts. Von Hubner was amazed by the skill and speed of a woman painter called to entertain foreign guests at a banquet.[74] Some years later, Emile Guimet (1836–1918) and his travel companion, Felix Régamey (1844–1907), himself a painter, were astonished by Kawanabe Kyōsai's "performance paintings." Not to be outdone, Régamey challenged Kyōsai (1831–89) to a duel of portraits, an illustration of which was later included in Guimet's *Promenades Japonaises* (1880). Guimet's travelogue prompted other foreigners to visit the talented Kyōsai's studio.[75]

Acquiring a painting directly from the artist certified the work's authenticity, while conferring special authority on and meaning to its owner. As noted above, it is likely that Longfellow bought a painting personally from Chikudō. Cernuschi also purchased an album of paintings directly from Kano Eitoku (Tatsunobu Seisetsusai, 1814–91), whom Duret praised as a practitioner of a purely Japanese style. Eitoku, he claimed, was unlike artists of the new schools who, under the influence of European art, painted sketches *(dessins)* "full of figures in Greek profile."[76]

Duret was not alone in describing Japanese painting as "sketches." In an editorial of 1871, John Black, a longtime resident of Yokohama and editor of *The Far East,* observed: "The Japanese mission who first visited Europe, whilst admiring the pictures in the Louvre, found cause for pitying the barbarians for their realistic productions and for their lack of imagination. They preferred the sketches of their own artists, which with a few masterly touches gave a general idea but left it to the spectator's poetical soul to fill in the picture."[77] Such characterizations are a telling sign that Euro-Americans of the time were not yet prepared to grant Japanese painting, much of which relied heavily on ink outline and light vegetable colors, the status of their own oil paintings. Painting in oil was not an innate activity, but part of a learned pattern of behavior. Sketching, by contrast, was perceived to be spontaneous, unmediated by thought processes. It was an expression of the "natural" aesthetic of the Japanese.

Despite such rhetoric, many globe-trotters, knowingly or not, purchased paintings by living artists whose work was influenced by European subjects, styles, and techniques. Travel, contacts with foreign visitors, and access to a wide range of visual materials from abroad made Japanese painters of the 1860s and 1870s well informed of developments in Europe. In experimenting with European idioms, their aim was not necessarily to cater to foreign tastes, but rather to select and adapt from Western representational practices those strategies that might help them develop new autonomous modes of expression. Several paintings in the Longfellow collection that can be attributed to painters in the Wirgman-Beato circle underscore the conflicting values embodied in ambivalent responses to such works.[78]

Yokohama was a transformative space that produced new cultural relations among Japanese and Western visitors. It exemplifies what Mary Louise Pratt calls "contact zones, social spaces where disparate cultures meet, clash, and grapple with each-other, often in highly asymmetrical relations of domination and subordination."[79] Something of this asymmetry is reflected in responses to the Japanese oil paintings Charley is likely to have purchased from artists in the Wirgman-Beato circle that later hung in his rooms in Cambridge. When the poet Longfellow showed them to a guest in 1881, he observed: "One can see they are Japanese; but it's very hard . . . to tell what else they are intended for. My son is fond of this sort of pictures but to me they look more comical than beautiful." The visitor added: "In truth it was a droll painting to look at but it was in reality too fine a work of art to be so hardly criticized."[80] Despite these diplomatic comments, it is clear that both viewers were discomfited by the Japanese adoption of pictorial techniques that they believed properly belonged to European artists.

The opportunity to learn Western painting and photographic techniques made Yokohama an artistic mecca, much as Nagasaki had been during the Tokugawa period. As the sole port where ships from China, Holland, and Korea were allowed to drop anchor until 1853, Nagasaki had attracted Japanese artists wishing to learn about foreign arts. Most learned the principles of vanishing point perspective, chiaroscuro, and oil painting indirectly, through Chinese painters, or through imported prints and illustrated books. In Yokohama, where there was a larger and more accessible foreign presence, Japanese artists learned through personal contact. Yokohama's Euro-American residents saw the city as a peripheral outpost of Western civilization, but in the eyes of aspiring young Japanese artists, it stood at the epicenter of a new cultural order. Thus, even as they were mediating Japan for Western viewers, Wirgman and Beato also mediated the West for young Japanese eager to learn the techniques of oil painting and pictorial realism. Theirs was one of the flourishing milieux of what the scholar Kinoshita Naoyuki has called the "marriage of painting and photography" (kaiga to shashin no kekkon).[81]

Although he was self-trained, Wirgman became the teacher and role model to young painters including Goseda Hōryū I (1827–92); his son Yoshimatsu (1855–1915), the first Japanese artist to exhibit at a Paris Salon; and Takahashi Yūichi (1828–94), who later became one of Japan's leading oil painters.[82] Wirgman and Beato also influenced Shimooka Renjō, Yokoyama Matsusaburō, and Kusakabe Kinbei, photographers who painted using photographs as visual aids. Kinbei later became known as a purveyor of hand-colored tourist views of Japan, but in the early 1870s, he had a reputation in Yokohama as a painter. John Black wrote that "those who would like to possess good specimens of Japanese art," should acquire works by him. A photograph of two paintings on silk "of the Mikado and his wife," reproduced in this periodical testifies to Kinbei's skill in portraying the figures in the realistic manner in fashion at the time.[83]

Charley Longfellow knew Wirgman well enough to be the target of one of his satirical sketches in *Japan Punch* and to acquire several works directly from him and his pupils.[84] Among these is a small watercolor by the Englishman showing a party where a dancer performs to the musical accompaniment of a group of women and a single man (fig. 3.10). The tray of food and drink, hibachi and pipe tray in the foreground, screen with crane in flight behind the performers, and stone lantern in the misty garden beyond are all synecdoches of Japan that add to the atmospheric mood. Langorous and sensual rather than erotic, the scene invites the viewer of the painting, like the invisible guest, to engage in exotic fantasies. Evocative of the landscape of leisure central to Euro-American perceptions of Japan, this work was a miniature in which its owner could take refuge upon returning home.

The appeal of a pair of paintings of young women that Charley also acquired was similarly rooted in a romanticized vision of Japan (pl. VII). (Originally, these two panels, painted on silk, may have formed part of a set of folding screens discussed in chapter 5.) Their subjects' relatively modest attire and simple coiffures suggest that they are lower-class teahouse attendants rather than high-ranking courtesans, who were distinguished by their front-tied obi. One walks, pulling her surcoat around her while looking back over her shoulder, a typical pose in the genre of paintings of beautiful women, known today as *bijinga*. The other, attired in a striking purple cloak, is also caught in movement, gracefully lifting the hem of her garment from the snow-covered ground with one hand, while clasping a protective umbrella with the other. This pair of paintings, however, is considerably more naturalistic than was customary in the genre of *bijinga* practiced by Hiroshige and other painters of the then-dominant Utagawa school (fig. 3.11). While they adhere to time-honored subject, format, medium, and mate-

3.10　Charles Wirgman, party at a teahouse, c. 1871. Watercolors on paper. LNHS.

rials, the faces appear to have been painted after photographs, and volumetric shading is used for the folds of their garments. The purple aniline dye used to color the robe, in vogue in wood-block prints of the era, adds a further fashionable touch. Although unsigned, these paintings may be attributed on the basis of style to Goseda Hōryū. The slightly foreshortened poses, squat proportions, round faces, and especially the careful description of the kimono pulling over the buttocks and bunching at the sleeves closely resemble a set of six paintings of beauties in the Kōriyama Museum (fig. 3.12).[85]

A small single-panel screen with paintings on silk mounted back-to-back also appears to be a work by Goseda Hōryū or another artist in the Wirgman-Beato circle (pls. VIII and IX). These feature popular scenic places associated with the worship of the goddess Benten. One side presents a moonlit panorama of the beach at Enoshima, a scenic spot near modern-day Kamakura that was popular

3.11   Hiroshige (1796–1858), attr., girl walking in
the snow, Edo period (1615–1868). Hanging scroll,
ink and colors on silk. 311/8 x 12 1/2 in. The
Metropolitan Museum of Art, Howard Mansfield
Collection, Rogers Fund, 1936 (36.100.208).

3.12   Goseda Hōryū, attr., beauty,
c. 1870. One of a set of six hanging
scrolls, ink and colors on silk.
Kōriyama Bijutsukan.

PARADISE OF CURIOS

for outings among both Japanese and Western tourists. In the foreground a group of soberly clad women stroll along the beach, the light from their lanterns casting long shadows before them. A man and dog stroll behind them, and just offshore a boat emerges from the shadowy night. The other commemorates Tokyo's Shinobazu Pond, where an island was the site of a noted Benten Shrine. The foreground is dominated by two colossal lotus flowers, a pictorial device used earlier by the Westernizing painter Odano Naotake (1749–80) in a view of the same spot.[86] Beyond the flowers, two geisha and an attendant peer intently over the veranda of a teahouse at carp in the pond below. In the deep distance clusters of simple wooden houses line the shore. The horizon line is high and the sky enlivened by puffy clouds adapted from western landscape prints.

Small single-panel screens *(tsuitate)* were commonly used in residences and public establishments in Japan, but the red lacquered frame in the shape of a Shinto entry-gate *(torii)* that surrounds these paintings indicates that this one was made for the foreign market. It is likely that it was made as a fireplace screen, the use to which Charley put it upon his return to Cambridge (see fig. 5.14).

Works such as these by Goseda Hōryū and other artists trained or active in Yokohama occupy an ambivalent place within modern Japanese art history. They are often characterized as "Yokohama pictures" (Yokohama-e), implying that as products of the culture of the treaty ports, they are inauthentically Japanese.[87] Their often awkward mélange of styles conflicts with the image of a nation with a well-defined indigenous artistic tradition. Modern scholars know that pictorial illusionism and experiments with oil painting were carried out long before 1853 and that Western techniques were promoted by the Meiji government as part of its effort to "promote industries and increase production" *(shokusan kōgyō)*. Their use in works of the Meiji era is nonetheless taken as evidence of a decline in indigenous artistic values rather than the expression of dynamic cultural interplay. The hostility toward so-called Yokohama pictures also stems from their often erroneous association with a tourist-inspired commercial aesthetic, a view, itself a product of the modernist ideal, that true art must be created outside the marketplace.

Such prejudices are anchored in a persistent Orientalist tendency to see Japanese art as a "tradition to be saved" rather than as part of an ongoing process of "critical and creative recombination."[88] They also underscore the deep-rooted and pervasive unease that works that defy perceived national boundaries may engender both within and without their country of origin. Stylistically, paintings such as those acquired by Charley Longfellow occupy a disquieting cultural borderland because they cannot readily be cordoned off and situated within the modern canon of "Western" or "Japanese style" painting.

The tourist-collector's encounter with Japan was fraught with such ambiguities. While the loss of authenticity in Japanese art since the country had become accessible to tourism was a common refrain among nineteenth-century globe-trotters, authenticity in fact became an issue only following their arrival. As Richard Handler has observed, "Authenticity is a cultural construct of the modern Western world . . . It is an example of the startling degree to which anthropological discourse about others proves to be a working out of our own myths."[89] Japanese artists were accustomed to adapting local products for an international clientele long before the 1860s and 1870s. The advent of tourism, however, unleashed a wave of experimentation that led to the birth of new forms and styles as well as reinterpretations of old ones. Even as tourism spurred Japanese artists to change and reassess their culture in light of visitors' expectations, so too it led tourists to reevaluate theirs. What was "authentic" in the 1870s was no longer so by the turn of the century. In the 1880s and 1890s, critics and professionals in the nascent field of Japanese art history would try to erect a firewall between "tourist" and "high" arts, but the ground beneath them had not yet settled. It is still shifting today.

CHAPTER 4

Embodying Japan

His kimono too short;
The foreigner's hairy legs
Make me laugh.

—Miyao Shigeo,
Senryū, ca. 1911

Clothing figured powerfully in the nineteenth-century Western image of Japan. As a critical component in evaluating Japanese both as individuals and as a people, often in the absence of broader sociocultural information, clothing contributed to the formation of many lasting stereotypes. The construction of personal and national identity through sartorial idioms, however, was not simple or univocal. It was a highly contested cultural terrain that was continually being renegotiated in response to changing requirements.

Since clothing, and its absence, plays a defining role in codifying difference, it is not surprising that both verbal and visual references to it abound in travel accounts from the 1860s and 1870s. Being abroad heightened the response to visual stimuli, and lingering images formed on the basis of physical appearances profoundly shaped travelers' memories of Japan. Most Euro-American visitors were sensitive to generalized sartorial markers of class, profession, age, and sex, although they were unaware of the highly nuanced sumptuary regulations governing the styles, fabrics, and colors of garments of the Tokugawa period. They became keenly attentive to the Meiji government's edicts ordering the adoption of Western dress and hairstyle. An article in *The Japan Weekly Mail* that appeared when male subjects were ordered to cut their topknots *(chonmage)* reveals the importance of physiognomy, body markings, and costume in fixing identity and underscoring otherness. The article asserted, "The philosophy of hair-cutting should rank at least with that of hand-writing, or clothes, noses, thumbs, or any of the other indices of character, and perhaps would be found to have an important bearing on phrenological development."[1]

Tourists and long-term residents alike demanded that Japan be picturesque and were dismayed when it did not meet their expectations. They were especially critical of Meiji bureaucrats who had adopted Western dress as part of an effort to present a modern public face to the world. Globe-trotters wanted to see craftsmen in their striking indigo blue short jackets emblazoned on the back with large stylized characters. They liked the dramatic spectacle of samurai in the ample skirtlike *hakama*, short jacket emblazoned on the shoulders and sleeves with a house crest *(haori)*, topped on formal occasions by a vestlike *kamishimo* (see fig. 1.16). They admired—and coveted—the pair of swords that was once a samurai prerogative. Such clothing and accessories established their wearers' normative roles within Japanese society, but in the eyes of foreign observers, these served instead to establish alterity, becoming synecdoches of the social, political, cultural, and even moral gulf between Japan and the West.

Most visitors to Japan had already formed, through photographs and, especially, illustrations in books and newspapers, impressions of Japanese male and female dress that actual travel to the country did little to alter. The 1860 diplomatic mission to the United States, which made much-publicized visits to cities from coast to coast, had given Americans their first opportunity to see Japanese men for themselves. The shogunal missions to Europe in 1862, 1864, 1865, and 1867 similarly whetted European curiosity. The group that accompanied the 1867 Paris Exposition especially captured the public imagination, since it included the fourteen-year-old Tokugawa Akitake, brother of the ruling shogun, who made appearances in formal court regalia. Three geisha from the Yanagibashi district of Tokyo, the first Japanese women to travel abroad under government auspices, were among his entourage.

Contacts with Western visitors and travel abroad aroused among Japanese complex and often conflicting attitudes toward their indigenous attire. European accessories such as leather shoes, trousers, hats for men, and bows and jewelry for women were already fashionable in port cities in the early 1860s.[2] Local reactions to their adoption were mixed, however. Women who dressed in this way were assumed to be Western concubines or prostitutes and were contemptuously referred to as *rashamen*, Western sheep. In the 1860s, government-sponsored students and diplomats had to pledge that they would wear only Japanese attire, but some found that it set them uncomfortably apart from the Victorian society in which they had to work or study. In 1862, when one member of a shogunal mission "was seen buying Western shoes in Hong Kong, he was considered lucky to receive only a warning and not be sent straight back to Japan."[3] Other

4.1 Charles D. Fredericks, Japanese diplomat in New York, 1860–68.
Salt print. Peabody Museum, Harvard University (photo H 15322).

travelers consciously exploited the rhetorical power of a style of dress that Western observers identified as distinctly Japanese.

Life abroad was emboldening, often encouraging travelers to imagine themselves in new and different ways. Outside the constraints of their own society,
men and women of all nationalities not only flirted with new identities, but
enlisted photography to record their self-fashioning for posterity (fig. 4.1). Just
as some Japanese disavowed their customary dress in favor of clothing that they
thought would help them blend in more successfully in Europe, so too Euro-
American visitors to Japan did the reverse. Some men found the loose-fitting
kimono to be better suited to the hot humid climate of Japan than trousers, shirt,
and jacket, and made it their daily wear. Women, on the other hand, seem to have
donned kimonos only for souvenir photographs.

The introduction and adoption of Western attire overlapped with other processes of sartorial change. Societal changes, especially the abolition of the feudal class system in the Meiji era, contributed to many new trends in Japanese dress. Fashionable young women who studied at newly opened schools, for instance, adopted the baggy trouserlike hakama once worn primarily by men to make visible their seriousness of purpose and special status. Men of all classes were allowed to wear haori and hakama, attire that had once been the exclusive property of a tiny fraction of the population. By the 1880s, in the interest of promoting a sense of national identity, this ensemble would be recognized as the common heritage of all Japanese.

The advent of the word *kimono* was also part of this cultural continuum. Literally, "wearable thing," it came to denote, in a narrow sense, the robe tied with a sash worn by both men or women formerly known as a *kosode*, and in a broader sense, Japanese clothing in general.[4] Precisely when this word came into widespread currency is not known, but like the modern word for art, *bijutsu*, it was probably coined early in the 1870s in response to the introduction of Western taxonomies.

As recent scholarship has shown, clothing is a form of communication, a language whose many meanings may be decoded.[5] These meanings are not fixed, but may be ascribed by the wearer and the context, as well as the viewer. Photographic portraits of Charley Longfellow in various Japanese guises provide a window through which to examine the complex and often ambiguous role that clothing assumed in Western constructs of the Japanese people, their culture, and their art. These reveal how one American, by borrowing elements of the Japanese "social skin," sought to fashion a new self-identity both within and against the constraining environment of New England. Longfellow's cooption of Japanese clothing and tattoos as a form of self-expression, tied up as it was with his personal fantasies, does not necessarily reflect the tastes and experiences of all Western visitors. Yet his self-celebratory photographs were nonetheless shaped by visual conventions and codes of meaning that were widely shared by globetrotters of his generation. They underscore the fact that tourism, even as it fostered differences, also laid the foundations for a new international sartorial pluralism.

Dressing for the Camera

Following his trip to Kyoto in 1872, Charley sent home a stern-faced, studio portrait of himself dressed in haori and hakama, white split-toed socks *(tabi)* and sandals, with a sword at his waist, and a fan in hand (fig. 4.2). In the accompanying letter he playfully noted, "I send you the photo of a gentleman of Kioto, who I met several times in the streets, particularly in the evening."[6]

4.2   Raimund von Stillfried, Charles Longfellow dressed as a samurai, c. 1872. Carte de visite. LNHS.

Although it was only one of several Japanese costumes in which he had himself photographed, and the only one sent home to his family, it was an appropriate choice since it was the form of male dress most Americans were likely to recognize as Japanese.

What kinds of ideas and values did Charley bring to his appropriation of samurai identity? Dressing in Japanese clothing calls into question the conventional connections between self-identity and its trappings. Charley's Occidental facial features reveal one reality, while his costume reveals another. His playfully ironic comments in the accompanying letter show that he knew that his family was in on the joke and recognized the "true" person cloaked in samurai guise. Yet this kind of portrait appealed precisely because it allowed the subject to assume and capitalize on this duality. Homi Bhabha has observed that colonialism, for all its civilizing mission, often exercises its authority through trompe l'oeil, irony, mimicry, and repetition. Mimicry, he observes, "is the sign of a double articulation; a complex strategy of reform, regulation, and discipline, which 'appropriates' the Other as it visualizes power." Since reproduction challenges and destabilizes the authority of the original, it "emerges as one of the most elusive and effective strategies of colonial power and knowledge."[7]

In memorializing himself in this way, Charley was making visible to his family his immersion in Japanese culture and his assumption of the status and privileges of the elite that had dominated Japanese society during the 250 years of Tokugawa rule. His understanding of the samurai class, however, is likely to have been limited—based on personal experiences, as augmented by writings in the Western press and photographs like those purveyed by Beato. Mitford's *Tales of Old Japan* and other fictionalized accounts also contributed to his idealization of the samurai as a chivalrous figure who commanded fear and respect for his military prowess, his loyalty, and his code of honor.[8] While in Japan, Charley read the story of the forty-seven rōnin, Mitford's popular translation and adaptation of the *Kanadehon Chūshingura,* one of the all-time favorite Kabuki plays. Based on a historical event, it recounts the exploits of a group of masterless samurai *(rōnin)* who seek to avenge the death of their lord, who had been forced to commit suicide. Charley was so impressed by Mitford's "record of a curious and fast disappearing civilization" that he also urged his father to get a copy of the book.[9] In a letter to his sister he added, "What I have read was mighty good and shows the Japanese character tip-top."[10] Since the graves of the forty-seven rōnin were within walking distance of the British consulate, it is likely that Charley also visited the site, as did later tourists.[11]

Mitford's perception of the samurai encoded many assumptions about medieval Europe that Charley is likely to have shared. Influential British scholars would continue to interpret the samurai through the prism of their own society well into the twentieth century. Basil Chamberlain, writing in 1904, declared that "'warriors,' 'the military class,' 'the gentry' are perhaps the best English renderings of the word [samurai]; for it was the essence of Old Japan that all gentlemen must be soldiers and all soldiers gentlemen."[12]

Charley's reading of *Chūshingura* and other *Tales of Old Japan* is likely to have been further inflected by his personal experiences in the Civil War. The bullet in his back had done more than leave a lifelong scar. In putting an end to his hopes of a military career, it also dashed his visions of glory. Appropriating for himself the cultural fantasy of the samurai helped to neutralize the psychic pain of having survived the war, when true heroism required sacrificing one's life.

Charley, like Mitford and Chamberlain, wanted to preserve "the essence of Old Japan." In 1872, when his photograph was taken, samurai had been ordered by the government to cut off their topknots. The emperor, to set an example, also began to wear Western military uniform for public appearances. Charley had witnessed the emperor's last appearance in ceremonial court costume and wrote for his family an unusually lengthy and detailed description of his attire. To be sure those at home could visualize the curious court headgear, consisting of "a queer little black silk skull cap with a high knob at the back, from which a strip of figured crepe hangs like a plume," he even supplemented his account with a small sketch.[13]

During the 1870s, high officials increasingly donned Western formal wear, complete with top hats, for governmental functions. Despite these changes, the haori and hakama remained the yardstick by which most Western visitors of the 1860s and 1870s judged the Japanese "aristocracy." This is why they were so scornful when men abandoned or combined it with newly fashionable Western accessories such as bowler hats, umbrellas, or leather shoes. Charley, like most visitors, wanted to see Japan as a static and pristine culture, and was highly critical of efforts to modernize. "They are beginning to imitate Europeans in dress and manners and remind one of monkeys," he complained in one letter.[14] And in another, "They seem to think that European clothes and beer-drinking is going to make men of them, but so far it has had rather the contrary effect, their conceit increasing (if possible)."[15] Many of Charley's peers shared his equation of clothing with moral character.

Having oneself portrayed in native attire was a time-honored tradition among Euro-American tourists. When Americans made their grand tours of Europe, they often affected regional dress or accessories to pose for painted portraits. With the advent of photography, tourists authenticated their experience abroad by going to a studio where they could avail themselves of the selection of costumes kept for the express purpose of dressing for the camera. Photographic portraits had the advantage over paintings of being comparatively inexpensive, ready in a short time, and easily portable. The carte de visite also made it possible for the tourist to have multiple images to send home in letters to friends and family.

In the Middle East, a popular destination throughout the nineteenth century, men often dressed for the camera in Arab garb. The popular travel writer Bayard Taylor included a self-portrait in this guise in one of his publications (fig. 4.3). Many travelers also brought home costumes to wear at masquerade balls and charity bazaars.[16] The same pattern was repeated in Japan. Photos occasionally show men in pilgrim apparel, as William Bigelow had himself commemorated,

4.3 Bayard Taylor in Oriental costume, from Taylor, *A Journey to Central Africa* (New York, 1856).

but the haori and hakama appear to have been the perennial favorites (fig. 4.4). The creation and dissemination of studio images of both Japanese and Westerners in this "traditional" dress continued to inform tourist expectations long after it had disappeared from the streets.

One reason for the popularity of samurai attire among tourists was that it invested its male wearers with a flattering aura of dignity and grandeur lacking in their own clothing. The resulting portrayals are in fact strongly reminiscent of the "swagger portraits" popularized by Van Dyck. As Andrew Wilton has observed, these highly theatrical images "put public display before the more private values of personality and domesticity."[17] This tradition was influential in the development of nineteenth-century portrait photography. Both von Stillfried

4.4 Bigelow as a Buddhist pilgrim, c. 1885. Albumen print. Photographer unknown. Courtesy Museum of Fine Arts, Boston.

and Longfellow were artistic sophisticates who are likely to have self-consciously capitalized on the denotative power of the Van Dyckian portrait, as the Boston painter John Singer Sargent would also. Enacting masculinity in a way that made men objects of display, like women, suggests that in crossing cultures, they were crossing gender as well.

Charley's self-portrait poses a challenge to modern viewers both because of its kitschiness and its promotion of Orientalist stereotypes. Charley's family members, however, are likely to have found it amusing. In their eyes, Japan was primarily a spectacle, making it easy to situate such a picture within a tradition of theatrical portraiture popular in Victorian Europe and America. Henry Wadsworth Longfellow knew Julia Cameron, one of the leading practitioners of this popular photographic genre.

In the late nineteenth century, even as they captured an imagined reality, costume photographs had become indispensable evidence of world travel. By posing as a samurai, Charley has self-consciously created a portrait of himself as someone who has experienced the exotic, idealized world of "Old Japan," and thus as an authority on all things Japanese. His impersonation of a warrior was also tied up with his need for self-dramatization and, especially, his desire to appear before family and friends as a bold adventurer. Japan was no longer a place where one ventured at the risk of life and limb, but it remained dangerous, as Charley pointedly reminded his sister in one letter. In the eyes of many Americans, it was a kind of Wild West, where young men traveled to test their mettle and to discover their true worth. As a samurai, Charley embodied these masculine fantasies of danger and high adventure.

Longfellow assumes a very different, but equally bravura persona in a second carte de visite in which he poses, legs apart, in a stance resembling the stylized *mie* of a Kabuki performer (fig. 4.5). This photograph was taken by Ueno Hikoma, the leading photographer in Nagasaki. The American's cotton kimono, which has been tucked up into his sash to reveal legging-like trousers beneath, and the shortish jacket loosely tied with a brocade ribbon over his chest, suggest a travel costume. Although Charley is already tall by Japanese standards, high wooden geta give him added height. His face is partially masked by a dark hood. His wardrobe is completed by the large paper parasol he holds over his right shoulder.

Charley seems to pay homage here to the chivalrous commoner, *otokodate,* a protagonist in many Kabuki plays and a frequent subject in wood-block prints. The otokodate was a champion of the common people, often taking up their cause in defiance of the haughty samurai. His own dislike of Japanese government officials may have contributed to his identification with this commoner hero and his struggles in the face of an often brutal and unfair bureaucracy. As he wrote

4.5   Ueno Hikoma, Charles Longfellow in the guise of an actor, 1871–73. Carte de visite. LNHS.

4.6   Toshio, 1871–73. Carte de visite. Photographer unknown. LNHS.

his sister, "Nearly entirely the followers of the old Tycoon, or Tokugawa people, were gentlemen by birth and education, while among the present officials, there are more than half almost [who] have been picked up from the gutters and placed in high positions for having done some dirty piece of business with a rascal's cleverness for the present government."[18]

By the 1860s and 1870s the repertory of Kabuki plays featuring such swashbuckling heroes was quite large and varied. Clever, resourceful, yet chivalrous, Banzuin Chōbei of Edo figured prominently in many Kabuki plays. Charley is likely to have been familiar with him, since he is the protagonist of "An Otokodate of Yedo," one of the stories in Mitford's *Tales of Old Japan*.[19] Another exceedingly popular cycle, which had delighted commoner audiences since its inauguration in 1713, featured Sukeroku, a dashing figure who was also something of a dandy. Sukeroku's trademark umbrella, with snake's-eye pattern, made him easy to recognize both on stage and in wood-block prints. Charley shared the fictional Sukeroku's dandified delight in clothes as well as his fondness for relationships with beauties of the pleasure quarters.

Whether or not Charley sought to impersonate a particular stage hero, there is no doubt that he shared his family's love of the theater and amateur theatricals.[20] This may have predisposed him to appreciate Kabuki, whose long performances and complicated plots bored many foreign visitors. He began attending performances in Tokyo soon after his arrival, and was perhaps more taken by the turntable stage than by the melodramatic content of the plays. In his journal, he summarized the first performance he saw as follows: "Girl killing, Ronins, Daimios, Yohama san in a box."[21] His photograph album contains the cartes de visite of Tanoshiki, Shikan, and Narikomaya, three well-known actors of the day. He seems to have especially admired Tanoshiki, whom he characterized as a "Crack actor of Yedo." While none of these cartes de visite feature Sukeroku or other otokodate roles, the actor "Toshio" holds an umbrella strikingly decorated with a Sanskrit inscription (fig. 4.6).

Unlike Kabuki, the parades frequently held and enjoyed as part of seasonal festivals required no knowledge of Japanese tales, and long-term residents and tourists alike were grandly entertained by such spectacles. Festival culture was highly developed throughout Japan, participation being integral to religious life in shrines and temples. Processions often featured men and women in wildly imaginative costumes: fantastic birds, beasts, and insects; heroes from classical literature; battle figures; and even exotic foreigners. Cross-dressing was also common. Such masquerades allowed Japanese participants to express themselves openly and creatively, to poke fun at their social superiors, and more generally, to conduct themselves in ways not permitted in the normal course of life. Although such play-acting appeared to the foreign visitor as little more than boisterous fun, its aim was to attract the attention and please the gods so as to insure their benevolence in the coming year.

Charley himself witnessed several such events. In Nagasaki, he saw a "rum Japanese procession" in which "nearly all singing girls and children [were] dressed in skull caps, red Norfolk shirts and white trousers, to look like Europeans. The more merry had beards stuck on. There was one tall man dressed as a European woman, sun shade, chignon, hat and feathers, hoop skirt and even a veil (the wire grating for a small fire place), and her baggage in a jinrikisha behind her."[22] Later he was equally amused by the festival *(okaicho)* held at Tokyo's great Shiba temple complex to raise money for temple maintenance and repairs. There were "blind priests, with their shaved heads and nothing on but a waist cloth, wrestling together. After which they appeared dressed as soldiers with thin plates on their heads and armed with straw swords, with which they attacked each other furiously."[23]

Charley makes no mention of the procession of eighty Shinbashi and Shiba district geisha dressed as carpenters and other artisans associated with building, who are mentioned in newspaper accounts of the event.[24] This is curious, since his album contains several photographs of them, including one in which, dressed in a workman's indigo blue jacket and trousers, he joins a young geisha in similar attire (fig. 4.7). The young woman seated next to him is one of the geisha from the Yumeirō teahouse.

Carpenters were powerful and highly visible figures in late Edo and early Meiji era Tokyo. Since most of the buildings in the city were made of wood, requiring frequent reconstruction and repairs following fires, earthquakes, and other natural disasters, processions of carpenters following a ridgepole-raising ceremony were a common sight. An article and accompanying photograph in one of the premiere issues of *The Far East* leave no doubt that they were also a favorite attraction among foreigners, not only because of the carpenters' striking indigo jackets emblazoned on the back with red crests, but because "everything they take in hand is done in a manner the reverse of Europeans."[25]

This photograph, in all likelihood taken by a Japanese photographer, highlights the complex relationship that Longfellow had with Japanese culture. Despite the similarity in costume, there is a world of difference between the two "carpenters." While Charley's pictures commemorate a particular time and place, other photographs of women impersonating men of various professions, such as palanquin bearers, suggest that they were part of a popular photographic trend informed by time-honored pictorial conventions.[26] Wood-block prints featuring visual parodies *(mitate-e)* of women engaged in various male artisanal activities were especially common in the nineteenth century. This kind of impersonation also had a long-acknowledged place within the festival and theatrical traditions. Geisha used such cross-dressing as part of a socially sanctioned festival ritual that temporarily destabilized conventional gender distinctions. The visual expectations and delight of Japanese viewers would have been

4.7   Charles Longfellow and geisha in carpenter costume, 1872. Carte de visite.
Photographer unknown. LNHS.

conditioned by their familiarity with this practice. Charley himself, however, is unlikely to have understood these photographs as mitate-e.

Charley has intruded into this Japanese ritual by figuring simultaneously as spectator and uninvited participant. For him, dressing up as a carpenter was little more than a form of recreation. The cloth covering his face, partly hiding his Occidental features, underscores his view of this event as a kind of masquerade party. The facetious inscription "Exiled in Yedo. Hard Luck!" Charley penned beneath this picture is a further reminder that for him, Japan was a place of fun and games.

Going Native

For hundreds of years, Western travelers to the Near and Far East had believed that gaining access to these exotic societies required adopting local attire. This attitude was especially true of those with scholarly aspirations, since to live and look like the members of the culture made one, in modern ethnographic parlance, a "participant-observer." To gain status as a scholar at the Ming court, the sixteenth-century Jesuit Matteo Ricci dressed in the robes of Chinese literati.[27] Bayard Taylor, as we have seen, wore local garb in Arabia. The British scholar Ponsonby-Fane used photographs of himself in hakama and haori as frontispieces in his publications to lend visual authority to his claims that he had experienced authentic Japanese culture and had gained knowledge otherwise inaccessible to outsiders.[28] Such costumes suggested a respect for the host society that was undercut by the wearer's sense of cultural superiority: exercising the option of dressing in the local manner was an implicit part of the rhetoric of imperialism.[29]

Attitudes toward wearing kimonos in public among residents of treaty port Japan were more ambivalent. What they actually did, moreover, was often at odds with the sentiments they expressed publicly. To varying degrees, both visitors and long-term residents brought to bear on this practice prejudices of a political, moral, and cultural nature. Racial and social stereotypes flourished even among those who saw Japan through the lens of romanticism. Class and profession often had a strong bearing on the way people responded as well.

Many Western visitors saw dressing in Japanese clothing through the prism of romantic primitivism. Just as the hakama and haori evoked medieval grandeur, so too the unstructured simplicity and flowing drapery of the kimono evoked a "dialectic of cloth and body" reminiscent of the classical world.[30] Appropriating traditional Japanese dress from this observational standpoint further implied that it was a cultural artifact that needed to be saved, and that the observer had the authority and responsibility to carry out this curatorial task.

Despite its humorous intent, a cartoon in Wirgman's *Japan Punch* of three lounging men, one costumed in Indian, another in Arab, and a third in Japanese garb, suggests that "going native" was not uncommon in the colonial and treaty port environments (fig. 4.8).[31] Such costumes marked their wearers as distinctive vis-à-vis both the West and the East, thus creating a sense of shared community that transcended individual origins. In evoking a cozy room where imperialistic power and privilege is manifested and sustained by male friendships, Wirgman also implies that going native was a sartorial affectation equivalent to the attire worn in private clubs in Europe and the United States.

4.8   Charles Wirgman, "Something like an Asiatic Society," from *Japan Punch*, 1872.

This displacement is not surprising since the men of Yokohama and other treaty ports were indeed members of a kind of "Asiatic Society"—a brotherhood isolated both from the dominant culture and from women of their own background. Like Charley himself, many of the inhabitants of the treaty ports were social misfits who had never put down roots anywhere. The foreign settlement provided them a refuge from the responsibilities of matrimony and fatherhood and fostered the development of strong homosocial bonds. As an all-male substitute for family, it was also an environment in which men could safely negotiate the unresolved complexities and burdens of masculine identity. These unspoken issues were often part of the dynamics played out in the decision to go native.

EMBODYING JAPAN   137

While Japanese men wore haori and hakama for formal occasions, the kimono was, both literally and figuratively, a form of dressing down, since it was customarily worn beneath formal attire. The kimono, like its Edo period precursor, the *kosode,* functioned as casual daily wear for most Japanese men and women. Depending on means, social status, and season, it might be of silk, cotton, linen, or a variety of other fibers. With the exception of the length of the sleeves, the cut of the garment differed little between the sexes. There was, however, considerable disparity in the style and width of the sash—a wide, highly decorative and constricting one for women and narrow, more comfortable one for men. Length was also important.

Most Euro-Americans were insensitive to the norms of kimono length, as Edward Morse discovered to his embarrassment:

> At Enoshima I had a Japanese gown made for me, tied with an *obi,* which looked to me quite grand. It came down to within three inches of the heels; I asked Toyama if it was all right; he smiled and said it was not long enough, it should be two inches longer. Upon pressing him as to how it looked I found it had the same appearance to him that a countryman in our country might have to us with his trousers three inches too short! In other words, it looked "green." Thus their dress, careless as it looks to us with its loose folds and rather girlish appearance, has its precise lines and proportions.[32]

In Western eyes, the loose-fitting cotton kimonos had connotations of personal freedom, leisure, and informality that are made explicit in Charley's recumbent portrait of himself, relaxing in his garden, book in hand (see fig. 2.5). By showing that he was truly at home in Japan, this garment reinforced the image of belonging he sought to achieve by purchasing a house in Tsukiji. It also underscores the Euro-American perception of the Orient as a place of indolent self-indulgence. Indeed, forty years later, the cultural historian Okakura Kakuzō would argue that Sakuma Shōzan (d. 1864), the first Japanese to dress in Western manner, did so because he recognized the kimono's association with such Orientalist perceptions. "It was," he wrote, "the expression of a desire on the part of the progressionist to cast off the shackles of the decadent East and identify himself with the advance of Western civilization. Our kimono meant leisure, while the European dress meant activity, and it became the uniform of the army of progress, like the chapeau rouge in revolutionary France."[33]

The Imperial Rescript ordering Japanese men to wear Western clothing for official ceremonies offers a slightly different, but equally revealing, perspective on the rationale for the Japanese disavowal of indigenous dress. In declaring that men "should no longer appear before the public in these effeminate styles," it acknowledged and sought to overcome the perception, widespread among Western visitors, that there was little difference between male and female dress in Japan.[34] This ambiguity may have contributed to a homoerotic frisson among some Euro-American men.

A photograph of Charley surrounded by five smiling young women and two men clustered around a pole, perhaps part of a gateway, implies that the kimono was also understood to be sexually liberating. By firmly situating the wearer in a different milieu both physically and psychologically, it was a disguise that made it easier to carry out the amorous adventures that were a part of the romance of the Orient (fig. 4.9). By comparison with trousers, shirts, and jackets, the kimono was unquestionably a skimpy body-covering that gave the wearer the appearance of being en déshabillé. Stepping outside one's own culture dressed in this fashion made it easier for men to overcome their personal insecurities and to surrender themselves to sexual pleasures they might have reservations about at home.

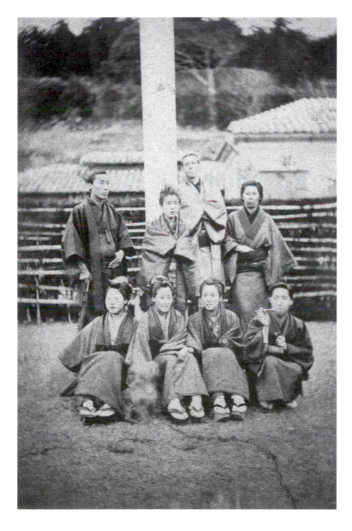

4.9   Uyeno Hikoma, Charles Longfellow in kimono surrounded by women, 1871–73. Albumen print. LNHS.

A genre of "Occidentalist" imagery, in which Westerners in Japanese guise were appropriated as subjects of Japanese observation and entertainment, may be read as visual rejoinders to the threat of such "sartorial kidnapping." These grew out of a tradition of wood-block prints issued in the port cities of Nagasaki and Yokohama since the beginning of the nineteenth century featuring Europeans and Americans in their "customary" attire, engaged in "typical" activities (fig. 4.10). The images popular in the 1870s, however, were doubly exotic since they capitalized on photographic technology. Painted in a highly realistic manner, these often featured foreigners ludicrously decked out in Japanese clothing (fig. 4.11). While some paintings were commissioned by Western clients, many remain in Japan, suggesting that they may have served there as pictorial equivalents of the wax models and other curiosities exhibited at Barnum's New York Museum. Becoming a curiosity was part of the price the tourist paid to see to Japan.

4.10 Utagawa Yoshitomi, *Picture of an American Drawn from Life*, 1861. Wood block print, ōban. The Metropolitan Museum of Art; gift of Lincoln Kirstein, 1959 (JP 3329).

EMBODYING JAPAN

Charley's status as a temporary resident of Japan allowed him to play a double game. In a sense, "going native" was an affirmation of his identification with otherness. On the one hand, he appears to be antiestablishment, criticizing his own culture, while on the other, he is using the trappings of difference to escape it. Yet even as he seems to reject the conventions of his own society and endorse those of an alternative one, he remains both above and outside Japanese culture. Wearing Japanese garments was for him a variation of the narcissistic play-acting he carried out before the camera. It was a form of conspicuous consumption that served simultaneously to differentiate him from more conservative residents of the treaty ports and to draw the attention of Japanese. Despite his local camouflage, Charley knew and took pride in the fact that he was an American.

4.11 Goseda Hōryū (1827–92), attr., foreigner in Japanese costume, 1880s. Hanging scroll, ink and colors on silk. 119.4 x 51.1 cm. Yokohama Museum of Art.

Embodying Japan

Many globe-trotters returned from Japan with kimonos or other exotic clothing as mementos of their travels. Charley himself brought back the carpenter outfit he wore on the occasion of the Shiba festival, customized with his initials in red in the back; a samurai firefighter's wool fire coat *(kajibaori)* and accessories; a short jacket with hand painted design on the inside; and women's kimonos and padded robes *(uchikake)*.[35] He was unusual at the time, however, in that he also lay claim to his experiences in a more intimate and permanent way by having himself tattooed. During his first trip, he had a giant carp ascending a waterfall carved on his back, and during the second, an image of the compassionate deity Kannon carved on his chest (figs. 4.12 and 4.13). In Japan, Charley's tattoos were part of being an outsider playing at being an insider. But unlike the costumes he wore there as a kind of game from which he could choose to withdraw at any time, his tattoos were permanent. Charley returned from Japan with his body irremediably transformed.

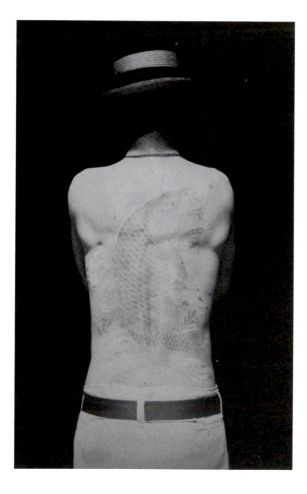

4.12 Charles Longfellow's carp tattoo, 1871–73. Modern print. Photographer unknown. LNHS.

4.13 Charles Longfellow's Kannon tattoo, c. 1885–93. Modern print. Photographer unknown. LNHS.

Descriptions, book illustrations, and photographs of tattooed men leave no doubt that they were nineteenth-century tourist tropes of Japan. Aimé Humbert included a pair of "coolies" with gorgeously tattooed backs in his *Japan and the Japanese Illustrated* (fig. 4.14). Even John La Farge, in the essay he wrote on Japanese art for Pumpelly's travelogue, some fifteen years before he visited the country, celebrated the tattoo, asserting that "in this the most simple means of expression in art" there is a connection "with the designs of Michel Angelo!"[36]

La Farge's comment is noteworthy. In drawing an analogy between Japanese tattoos and Michelangelo's designs, La Farge suggests that Japanese tattooists are artists who celebrate the male body. This observation underscores the role of Japanese tattoos in fostering appreciation of masculine physical beauty. The sight of men so different from themselves baring their decorated bodies no doubt had homoerotic overtones, but it also provoked in Euro-Americans a heightened sensitivity to the potential of aestheticizing their own. Euro-American responses to the Japanese tattoo thus challenge the widely held view that women were the exclusive focus of the male gaze in Japan.

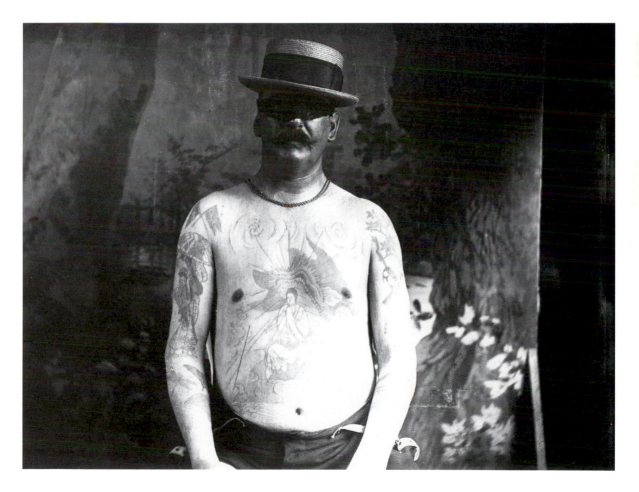

4.14 *Tattooed coolies,* from Humbert, *Japan and the Japanese Illustrated* (New York, 1874).

The running groom, *bettō*, was usually the first tattooed person the traveler encountered (pl. I). Edward Prime wrote:

Everyone who keeps a horse in Japan has a *bettoe* who is inseparable from the horse at home and on the road. In riding or driving he runs with the horse, and is always ready to take him by the head and guide him. . . . The bettoes are as fleet of foot as the North American Indians, and will travel as fast and as far in a day as the horse. They are naked, with the exception of the little strip of cloth around the loins; but, in lieu of clothing, they are often tattooed from the shoulders to the knees in colors, red, and blue, and other dark shades, which gives them a picturesque appearance.[37]

Curiously, despite his keen interest, Longfellow commented on tattooing only when he encountered it among the Ainu, where it was practiced primarily as a rite of passage among women. There he observed, "They have a large pointed moustache tattooed around their lips, the lower as well as the upper, and a tattooed line connects their eyebrows. . . . This tattooing is done when they are about fourteen years old. They also have their arms and the backs of their hands mutilated in the same way. With them it is cut in with a knife, instead of being pricked in with needles as is the usual way"[38] (see fig. 2.15). In the Ainu settlement of Horobetsu, he added, "they were very much amused when I showed them the tattooing on my arm and admired it very much, it being so much better than their own rude work."[39]

Both the circumstances and the subject of this early tattoo are unknown, but it is possible that it was prompted by Charley's enlistment in the Civil War, when many soldiers had themselves marked to show their devotion to their cause and to facilitate identification should they be killed. Martin Hildenbrandt, a German tattooist who had begun to practice his art in New York in 1846, claims to have been in great demand during the Civil War among both Confederates and Union soldiers.[40] Since sailors often had themselves marked during or after long and arduous voyages to distant parts, it is also possible that Longfellow's tattoos commemorate his near victory in a trans-Atlantic race aboard a ship belonging to his friend the newspaper publisher James Gordon Bennett.

Tattooing in metropolitan Japan, however, was of a different aesthetic order than the anchors, dragons, flags, and other emblems typically recorded on the arms and shoulders of soldiers and sailors. In Japan, tattooists, many of them trained in the studios of wood-block print artists, used the torso, arms, and legs as a unified pictorial canvas. During the nineteenth century, even as tattooing functioned as a form of punishment for criminals and outcasts, these elaborate designs became popular among the habitués of the pleasure quarters, theatrical world, and, especially, members of the lower classes in the cities of Kyoto, Osaka, and Edo.[41]

A series of wood-block prints by Utagawa Kuniyoshi (1797–1861) portraying the 108 heroes of the *Suikoden,* issued between 1827 and 1830, is thought to have been a catalyst for the mid-nineteenth-century urban craze for elaborate multicolored pictorial tattoos extending from neck to midthigh and completely covering both back and front (fig. 4. 15). Kuniyoshi's designs were inspired by *The Water Margin,* a fourteenth-century Chinese novel, known in Japan as *Suikoden,* that glorified the lives of a semifictional band of brigands.[42] Like Robin Hood and his followers, these men were countercultural heroes who earned popular admiration because they were loyal to one another and offered assistance to the needy. At a time when Chinese precedent frequently served to legitimate Japanese culture, the *Suikoden* outlaws no doubt lent glamour to the activities of urban hooligans championed by commoners because of their defiance of shogunal authority.

In life as in art, tattoos were distinguishing features of the urban underclass, especially artisans and manual laborers. During the nineteenth century, the fad for ornamenting the body with elaborate multicolored pictorial compositions was particularly popular among men engaged in occupations requiring physical strength, stamina, and the removal of their outer garments during their exertions. Carpenters and firemen were famous for their extensive tattoos. Firemen wore protective clothing made of padded cotton, soaked with water before nearing the fire, that in the heat of action, they shed, often revealing the same tattoos on their bodies that decorated their garments. The motifs they chose were related to their professions: dragons, being associated with water, for instance, were particularly popular among firemen. In addition to their talismanic properties, these tattoos were like badges or uniforms that conferred status and membership while at the same time demonstrating individuality. Because every tattoo is unique, tattooing helped to produce a distinct sense of self within a larger social or occupational framework. Tattoos were also common among palanquin bearers, as represented in a lifelike model now in the Peabody Essex Museum thought to have been acquired by Charley Longfellow (fig. 4.16).

Tattoos conferred prestige among commoners because they gave them status as consumers of culture—a status that was severely curtailed by the shogunal government through sumptuary and other laws that decreed how members of each class could present themselves. Using the body to make a personal aesthetic statement reflected time-honored practice in Japan. During the Tokugawa period, affluent men of the merchant class, forbidden by law to wear silk or have their garments dyed in the colors that distinguished members of the warrior class, expressed their disdain for feudal law and their fashion sense in

4.15   Utagawa Kuniyoshi (1797–1861), *Gen Shōgo, from One Hundred Eight Heroes of the* Suikoden, c. 1827–30. Wood block print, ōban. Anne van Biema Collection.

highly ingenious ways. One popular subterfuge was to wear jackets that concealed costly hand-painted silk linings.

Tattoos were a "social skin" that gave expression to a spirit of aesthetic and political defiance by allowing their bearers to conceal or reveal their self-made persona at will. They gave individuals control over their bodies while fostering a creative self-fashioning that ran counter to the government's aim of keeping people in their prescribed place in society. The shogunal government's recognition of the politically subversive implications of such flamboyant demonstrations of aesthetic consumption underlay their efforts to ban tattoos.

Tattoos continued to have a complex and contradictory relationship to governmental authority after the fall of the Tokugawa feudal regime. The Meiji government, fearing that it conveyed an image of backwardness to the outside world, banned the practice just about the time Charley first had himself decorated. This was part of its "civilization and enlightenment" campaign, which aimed to do away with practices incompatible with Japan's self-presentation as a modern nation-state. This campaign targeted both the residents of metropolitan areas and the indigenous Ainu peoples on Japan's northern periphery, whom the government wished to assimilate. Such attitudes were part of a larger discourse on difference resulting from international travel. The words of the bumbling heroes of Kanagaki Robun's fictional travelogue *Shanks' Mare to the Western Seas* are telling. When they visit Ceylon, they observe, "The women walk around half-naked, with tattoos like swirls around the dirty skin of their faces and lips, like a night-parade of a hundred monsters. There is nothing sexy about them."[43]

The Meiji edict had important consequences for the "masters of carving," *horishi,* who made their living as tattooists, for the designs they carved, and for the many Japanese aficionados of this art. Like any commodity, tattoos were subject to the economy of the marketplace. To survive, artists needed to find new clientele among tourists. Some began advertising in guidebooks, while others attached themselves to curio dealers in Yokohama.[44] As part of these strategies of modernization, traditional tattoo designs also began to change in accordance with Western tastes and the more limited time available for their completion. Globe-trotters had the money to pay for such unique souvenirs of their visits to Japan, but not the year or more generally required to carry out the elaborate tattoos sported by Japanese enthusiasts.

In the Tokugawa period, tattoos had been expressions of up-to-date taste, but in the Meiji they became old-fashioned. They were badges of membership in many traditional professions that would change dramatically or disappear altogether by the end of the nineteenth century. The building profession was being radically altered by the introduction of new Western architectural styles and materials. New firefighting equipment was replacing the time-honored bucket brigades. Trains, telegraphs, and other means of transportation and communication were making running grooms, couriers, and palanquin bearers obsolete. Consequently,

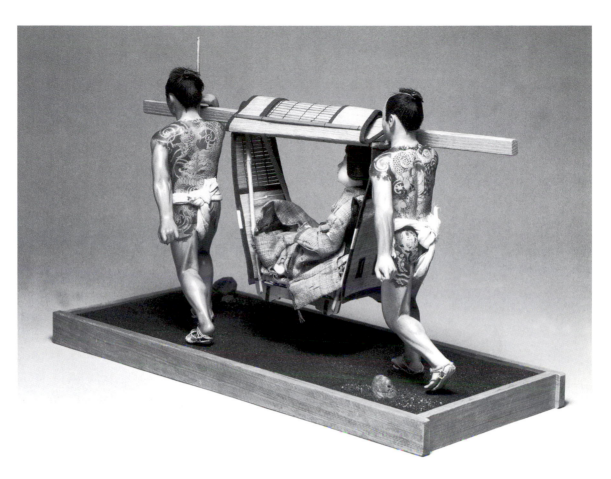

4.16 Model sedan chair and tattooed carriers, 1871–73. Pigments on gesso, textiles, and plant fiber. 47 x 18 x 27 cm. Photograph courtesy Peabody-Essex Museum.

even as they continued to be emblematic of individual resistance to the dominant values of the state, they assumed new meaning in response to the tourist gaze—as tangible evidence of the union of art and life in Japan. They held further mystique because they were understood to be vanishing art forms.

Longfellow never explained his motives for tattooing his back, but the connotations of the motif he chose are revealing. The carp ascending a waterfall was an emblem of virility in both China and Japan, and as such was ubiquitous in the visual arts. Its significance would have been well known to anyone in Japan during the annual celebration of Boy's Day, when giant carp banners were displayed by households with young sons to insure that they become strong and courageous. Nineteenth-century wood-block prints and photographs also indicate that carps, often in combination with heroic youths or other legendary personalities, figured prominently in the repertory of tattoo designs favored by Japanese men.

The choice of this emblem of masculinity, and its placement on Charley's back, where it drew attention to his Civil War scars, may be a manifestation of Longfellow's compensatory tendency to substitute images for genuine achievements. By donning various Japanese social skins he seems to have been appropriating the transformative power ascribed to the art and artists of Japan. To have such a motif carved on one's back also reinforced one of the fundamental messages of the tattoo: masculinity could be achieved only through painful ritual. As Albert Parry has observed, "The very process of tattooing is essentially sexual. There are the long, sharp needles. There is the liquid poured into the pricked skin. There are the two participants of the act, one active, the other passive. There is the curious marriage of pleasure and pain."[45]

Having himself tattooed in Japan in 1872 put Longfellow at the vanguard of a craze that later swept the British aristocracy and fashionable American society. The confluence of forces that contributed to this international vogue included the practice among pilgrims of having themselves tattooed as tokens of their visit to Jerusalem, the widespread publicity following Cook's expedition to the South Seas, British colonial experiences in India, American commercial expansion in the Pacific, and the publicity generated by the celebrated tattooed circus freak Costantenus (also spelled Costentenus) (fig. 4.17).[46] To these one may add one that would seem to apply particularly well to Longfellow. As a perspicacious writer for the *New York Times* explained in 1880: "The practice of tattooing, being a purely savage custom, suggests to the aesthetic Englishman the wild, free life of the isles of the 'sun-down-seas,' and hence to be tattooed is to put one's self in sympathy with Nature, and to protest against the sickly conventionalities of civilization."[47] The common denominator among these disparate developments was a growing fascination with and adventurous travel to exotic parts of the world made possible through Western colonialism.

Articles in British and American newspapers and periodicals of the 1870s and 1880s provide evidence of the steady diffusion of the practice among all segments of society.[48] When Prince Albert and his brother, the future George V, visited Japan in 1881, drawing attention to the special talents of the horishi, they contributed to the Japanese tattoo's transformation into an artistic tourist souvenir. During their five-day shore leave, the two princes visited the studio of Hori-chō, where George had a dragon tattooed on his arm. George Burchett, a British tattooist whose clients included many royals, claimed that King Edward VII had encouraged his teenaged sons to have themselves tattooed in Japan because he himself had acquired one when he visited Jerusalem in 1862.[49] The princes were followed by a host of other European royals, only a few of whom,

4.17 Captain Costentenus, from *The Tattooed Prince Written by Himself* (New York, 1881). Photograph courtesy Ron Becker Collection, Department of Special Collections, Syracuse University Library.

EMBODYING JAPAN

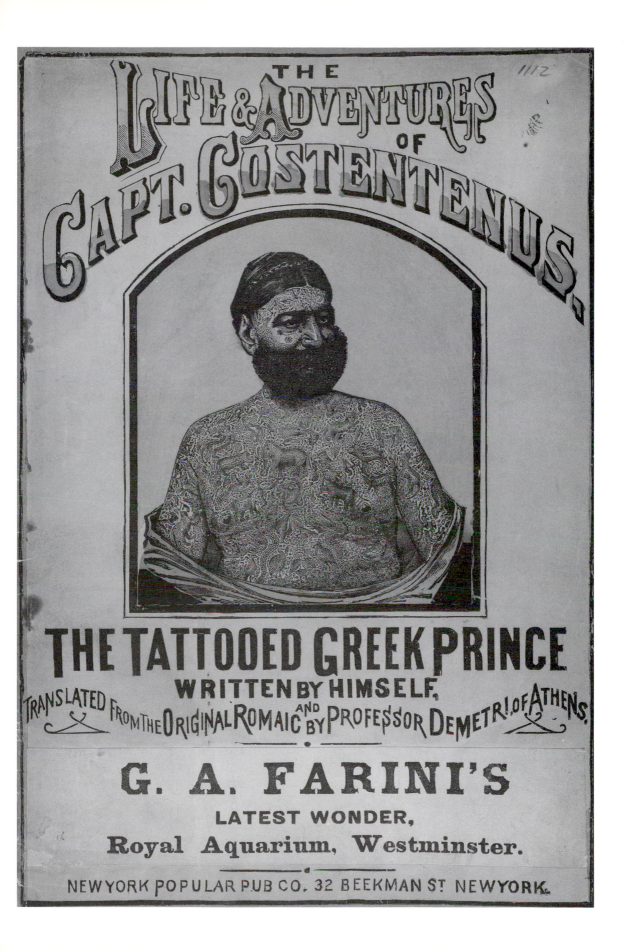

THE LIFE & ADVENTURES OF CAPT. COSTENTENUS.

THE TATTOOED GREEK PRINCE

WRITTEN BY HIMSELF,

TRANSLATED FROM THE ORIGINAL ROMAIC AND BY PROFESSOR DEMETRI OF ATHENS.

G. A. FARINI'S

LATEST WONDER,

Royal Aquarium, Westminster.

NEW YORK POPULAR PUB CO. 32 BEEKMAN ST. NEW YORK.

WITH THE CHINA SQUADRON IN THE EAST—TATTOOING AN OFFICER IN JAPAN

4.18 "With the China Squadron in the East—Tattooing an Officer in Japan," from *The Graphic*, November 13, 1886.

however, were actually tattooed in Japan. The impressive roster included Grand Duke Alexis of Russia, Prince and Princess Waldemar of Denmark, Queen Olga of Greece, King Oscar II of Sweden, the Duke of York, Lady Randolph Churchill, and the Duke of Newcastle.[50] Most chose motifs such as coats of arms, the names of their exclusive clubs, and even scenes of fox hunts as signs of their power and difference vis-à-vis the rest of society.[51]

Before the 1880s, Europeans associated tattooing primarily with the South Seas, India, and Burma, but a fanciful picture that appeared in the *London Illustrated News* on December 2, 1882, confirms that in the popular imagination, following the British princes' visit, the practice became firmly associated with an eroticized stereotype of Japan. It shows a recumbent man, pipe in his mouth, being tattooed while a geisha hovers attentively over him. The procedure is seemingly painless. Four years later, *The Graphic*, another British publication, offered an equally fanciful view of an officer being tattooed before what appears to be a display of Japanese armor (fig. 4.18). This picture, where both observer and observed are male, serves as a reminder that in the military world men could legitimately admire other men's bodies.

Americans emulated their British cousins by embracing the practice with equal enthusiasm. Soon they too were sporting "epidermal dragons and flags . . . to prove they were good sports and brave soldiers of royal blood."[52] Hildenbrandt did a brisk trade among the elite in New York, but he met his match in

Samuel O'Reilly, who pioneered the electric tattoo machine, which made the procedure both faster and less painful.[53] Admiration for the artistry of Japanese tattooists even led an enterprising businessman to attempt to persuade Horichō, unsuccessfully, to move to New York. So famous was Horichō that he was described as the "Shakespeare of tattooing." The author of the same article, writing in 1897, at the height of American Japanism, continued in the same laudatory vein: "Even the prejudice against the barbaric and senseless adornment cannot disguise the fact that [Japanese] design is one of art, and is executed with rare skill."[54]

This is a view that Longfellow held already in 1885, when he revisited Japan and had a second tattoo carved on his chest. The subject appears to be the Buddhist deity Kannon seated in the mouth of a dragon. He may have chosen Kannon because in China and Japan, this deity, who often assumes a distinctly feminine form, was worshipped as the special protector of sailors. Wirgman's explanation of Beato's photograph of a tattooed groom helps explain the significance of the dragon: "The custom of tattooing originated with sendoes or fishermen, who being often employed in the water, imagined that by tattooing their bodies with dragons or other figures, they would frighten away sharks or any sea monsters likely to do them harm."[55] Figures of Kannon seated or standing on the back of a dragon were common in the nineteenth century. Was Charley perhaps inspired by an illustration of this subject in Hokusai's *Shashin gafu* (Pictures drawn from Nature), one of the artist's well-known illustrated books, first published in 1814?[56] If the design on his chest appears rather faint, it may be because there was insufficient time to create the shading, clouds, and other intricately rendered background motifs that customarily make the Japanese tattoo such a rich visual spectacle.

This photograph gives out mixed signals, making it hard to read, both literally and figuratively. On the one hand, Charley has put his body on display for all to see, yet on the other, he has hidden his face behind a mask. This strategy of simultaneously revealing and concealing his identity is perhaps a theatrical gesture, but it is also a pattern of behavior that suggests both pride and shame about his tattoos—and himself.

Japanese tattoos were costly as well as time-consuming. In the early 1870s, a caption to a Beato photo informed viewers that a full-body tattoo cost about $15 (15 ryos or 60 boos), and that red tattooing was the most expensive. Longfellow's journal entries five years later reveal that the tattooist began work soon after his arrival in Yokohama at the end of May, but was interrupted on July 13, when Charley and his friend Charles Weld set off on a cruise to Nagasaki in a borrowed schooner. Work was resumed on October 12 and continued until Longfellow's departure two months later. Even during his absence, Charley had to pay the tattooist Horichō a daily fee of $7.00, a considerable sum at the time.[57] Full body tattoos normally required a year or more to complete, not only because of the artistry involved, but because of the pain and risk of infection. An article in the *Boston Transcript* following Longfellow's return reported that "for that more than three months [he] was in the hands of the tattooer, who did an amount of work on him that is usually spread over a period of three or four years. This caused, of course, a severe nervous shock, which he was only able to withstand by application of hypodermic injections of morphine."[58]

The pain Charley was experiencing at the time dampened neither his enthusiasm nor his pride in what he believed would be a work of art. In a letter to his sister Alice, he announced, "We are now getting ready to come home. Weld has curioes to pack and he and I have finishing touches to be added to some beautiful tatoe [sic] work we have been ornamenting ourselves with. I will give you a private exhibition when I get home. We think ourselves far ahead of Captain Costantenus and we certainly are, as far as art goes, our designs being from celebrated artists."[59]

Costantenus (whose name was spelled in various ways) began his career in the 1860s, but only achieved international celebrity following his appearance at the International Exposition in Vienna in 1873. His body, it was said, was adorned "with 388 animal and floral designs, all carefully executed with elaborate detail and color."[60] His claim that his tattoos were carved in Burma was reportedly confirmed by Max Muller, an eminent scholar of Oriental languages, who detected Burmese writing among the images.[61] When P. T. Barnum brought Costantenus to the United States, he was advertised as "The Living Picture Gallery." Capitalizing on the tattoo's erotic connotations, further publicity claimed that "this wild tattooed man is always much admired by all the ladies."[62]

In comparing himself to Costantenus, Longfellow revealed his pride in his own numerous tattoos. In addition to those on his back and chest, he had on his right arm crossed flags, a kimono-clad woman beneath a parasol, a butterfly, and a dragonfly. His left shoulder was decorated with a branch of maple on which perch a pair of small birds. With the exception of the flags, all these motifs were associated with Japan. Charley apparently sought to differentiate himself from other visitors to that country by the quantity as well as the quality of his tattoos. To him these represented a unique collection of Japanese art.

The analogy to Costantenus also underscores Longfellow's penchant for exhibitionism. Most nineteenth-century travelers to Japan were content to acquire souvenirs in the form of curios or photos they could display in their homes; only a few dared to embody their aesthetic experience of Japan in the form of tattoos. Those who did seem to have been members of the social elite, men who could afford to make spectacles of themselves. Dressing up in tattoos was a form of conspicuous consumption that flaunted status and power. It was a way of making visible a status, or presumed status, outside the class hierarchy. By having themselves artistically tattooed, members of the American aristocracy were, as Marjorie Garber has written in another context, "asserting a

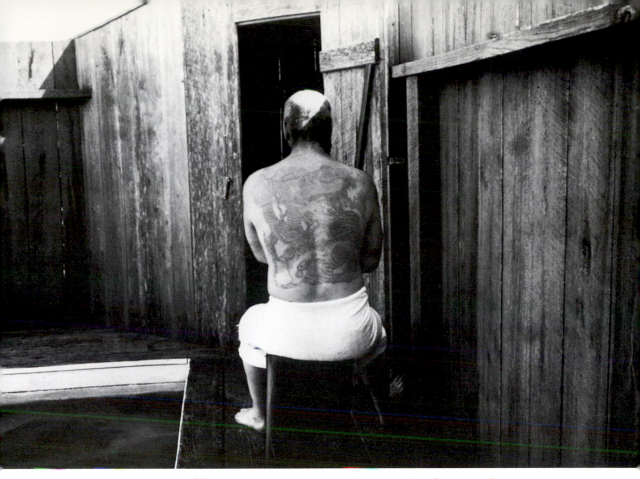

4.19 Charles Goddard Weld's tattoos, after 1885. Modern print. Photographer unknown. Photograph courtesy Peabody-Essex Museum.

class privilege that permitted them to dress up by dressing down—to carnivalize their political or cultural power."[63]

The number of tattooed American "aristocrats" who may be identified by name is small, but they included several members of socially prominent Boston and Philadelphia families. Weld had tiger and dragon in mortal combat carved on his back in Yokohama (fig. 4.19). In 1891, Charley introduced another friend, identified only as Merrill in his journals, to his own tattoo artist, Horichō, and to Horiyasu. The former tattooed a dragon and the latter flowers on Merrill's arm.[64] A few years later, William Henry Furness III, son of the Shakespearean scholar and nephew of the Philadelphia architect, also visited Horichō. Furness announced in the *Harvard Class Report* of 1894 that while in Japan he had been "tattooed artistically down to the waist."[65] He also had himself photographed, front and back, like the subject of an ethnographic study (figs. 4.20 and 4.21). His partial nudity and, especially, his provocative pose astride a chair, clearly invite voyeuristic appreciation of his body.

The subjects and minimalist style of Furness's tattoos underscore the dramatic transformation this art underwent in the late nineteenth century. The tattoo on

4.20 K. Tamamura, William Furness's tattoos (front), 1895. Photograph courtesy University of Pennsylvania Museum, Philadephia (neg. S4–13022).

EMBODYING JAPAN

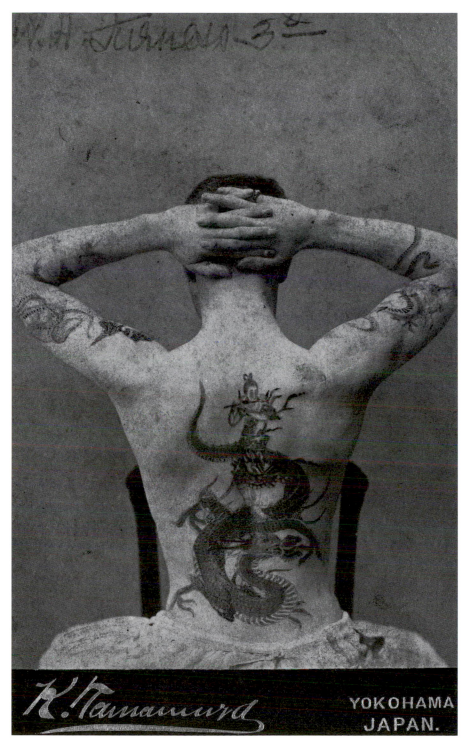

4.21 K. Tamamura, William Furness' tattoos (back), 1895. Photograph courtesy University of Pennsylvania Museum, Philadelphia (neg. S4–139021).

Furness's chest depicts the Thunder God, encircled with drums, which he beats to produce the threatening noises that announce his arrival. This classical motif was popularized abroad through its inclusion in Hokusai's *Manga,* although tourists may have known about it indirectly from an illustration in Aimé Humbert's *Japan and the Japanese Illustrated.*[66] The source of the flute-playing goddess astride a dragon figuring on Furness's back is unknown, but it appears to be a variation of the theme also chosen by Longfellow.

Like other forms of artistic expression, Japanese tattoos are polysemic, assuming whatever meanings the viewer wants to read into them. Even as they were displaced and given new meanings by their display on American bodies, they still had the capacity to express the social, economic, and aesthetic values of Japan. Among the values that remained important in the American context were their connotations of daring, strength, and virility. As we have seen, Charley drew his various creative impersonations of Japan from many different social strata, but these heroic ideals were central to all the alter egos he fashioned for himself.

If the basic symbolism of the tattoo changed little upon crossing sociocultural boundaries, the context in which it was displayed changed significantly. In Japan, the men who wore tattoos were all engaged in productive activities. As emblems of occupational identity, tattoos aestheticized work, but in Europe and America, they aestheticized leisure travel and play. This made them ideal artistic souvenirs for globe-trotters who engaged in sports such as sailing and swimming that offered frequent opportunities for self-display. Sports were a surrogate for work for Charley and many of his friends. In this homosocial context, tattoos became a kind of uniform, a distinctive form of undress by which men of the same class and interests could recognize one another.

Longfellow's self-portraits underscore that Japan was an insulated make-believe, a theatrical space where, as a tourist, he could act out his personal fantasies. Viewing them, one is forcefully struck not only by his infatuation with photography but also with his narcissistic self-dramatization. Although the photographic enactments of paintings and amateur theatricals were popular during Charley's lifetime, his self-portraits suggest that for him, dressing up and down was a kind of performance through which he sought to negotiate his masculine identity. His skillful use of this symbolic pictorial environment also serves as a reminder that travel to Japan in the 1870s was tied up with a new culture of individualism and of the body for men as well as for women.

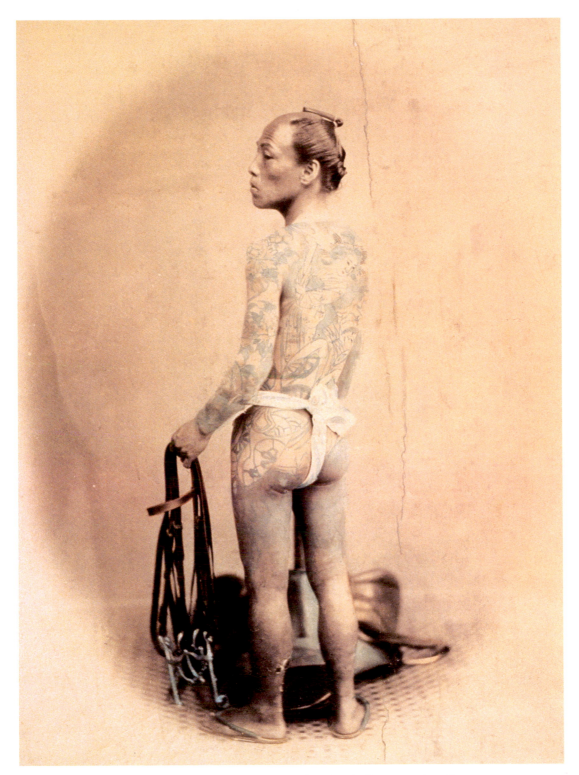

I. Felice Beato, *Groom (Bettō)*, c. 1870. Hand-colored albumen print. Courtesy Longfellow National Historic Site, National Park Service (hereafter LNHS).

II. Felice Beato, teahouse girl, c. 1870. Hand-colored albumen print. LNHS.

III. Raimund von Stillfried, *Ohannasan* with a parasol, 1871–73. Hand-colored albumen print. LNHS.

IV. Raimund von Stillfried, *Ohannasan* playing a samisen, 1871–73. Hand-colored albumen print. LNHS.

V. Raimund von Stillfried, attr., women on veranda of Longfellow House, 1872–73. Hand-colored albumen print. LNHS.

VI. Kano Tangen (Moritsune) (1829–66), spring landscape, late Edo period. Six-fold screen, ink and colors on gold foil. 178.1 x 372.6 cm. LNHS.

VII. Goseda Hōryū, attr. (1827–92), two beauties, c. 1870. Two-fold screen, ink and colors on paper. 166.5 x 124.4 cm. LNHS.

VIII. Fireplace screen, view of Enoshima, c. 1870. Ink and colors on silk. LNHS.

IX. Fireplace screen, view of Shinobazu Pond, c. 1870. Ink and colors on silk. LNHS.

X. Tilt-top table (top), c. 1871. Black lacquer with makie design. H. 37 in. (93.9 cm.), D (top) 22 5/8 in. (57.46 cm.). LNHS.

XI. Shelf. Nineteenth-century black lacquer with gold makie. LNHS.

CHAPTER 5

Domesticating Japan

For the structure that we raise,
Time is with materials filled;
Our to-days and yesterdays
Are blocks with which we build.

—Henry Wadsworth Longfellow,
The Builders, 1849

Globe-trotters brought back from their travels a wide array of arts and crafts large and small, old and new. Divorced from their original contexts, these souvenirs served to write new cultural narratives. These were often long and complex, varied from one setting to another, and could vary further still depending on the reader. Although there were many ambiguities and contradictions in the appropriation of Japan, its material culture was generally interpreted from the collector's rather than the creator's frame of reference. Americans were eager to acquire lacquer, ceramics, bronzes, screens, and other decorative objects that brought exotic flair into their lives and bore witness to their cosmopolitanism. Not all the articles from Japan that become increasingly prominent features in American residences of the 1860s and 1870s were acquired by tourists, of course. Missionaries, doctors, teachers, diplomats, and traders also assembled collections according to their individual means and tastes. American consumers could also buy Japanese goods in Europe and the United States at international expositions and fairs, at curio shops and bazaars, and at auctions and art galleries. Globe-trotters, however, were active participants in a process of "domestication" that helped to consolidate old and trigger new images of Japan.

This process coincided with many changes in American society, among them the emergence of a consumer economy, growing preoccupation with the formation of national identity, and, deeply implicated in both these socioeconomic phenomena, the cult of domesticity. In the decade following the Civil War, as the country evolved from a predominantly agrarian to an increasingly mercantile and industrial society, sensitivity to art and culture expanded dramatically. Even as Americans revered progress, the losses to the nation during the Civil War had made them more sensitive to the value of tradition in their own and other cultures.[1] The colonial revival movement, offering common ground that transcended the divisiveness of the Civil War, was one manifestation of this new attentiveness to the nation's past. Growing anxiety about the impact of science, industrialization, and immigration—developments that caused disruptions and conflicts between city and country, older and newer Americans, and even between one city and another—helped to fuel this nostalgia. At the same time, industrialization contributed to the growth of an urban middle class with the means, education, and aspirations to furnish their homes with, in Katherine Grier's words, "culture and comfort."

Japan was part of the shared experience of both men and women, but its apprehension was distinctly gendered. Victorian ideology promoted the home as a key site for the formation of individual and national identity. Women were assigned a primary role in shaping identity through their virtuous and dedicated care of home and family. The cult of domesticity promoted an ideal of femininity based on a sharp division between public and private life. The home was a haven from the uncertainties of the outside world, an otherworldly place whose values transcended class, ethnic, and regional differences. Yet paradoxically, the home, honored as refuge from the pressures of the marketplace, also became the dominant site for the manifestation of consumerist impulses. As traditional patterns of sociocultural coherence were lost, people turned increasingly to material possessions for personal and family fulfillment. Display of Japanese imports was one way in which the newly affluent middle classes sought "distinction."[2]

Writing of the British framing of "Chinese art," Craig Clunas has observed: "It is impossible to discuss the creation of the broader category of 'Chinese art' in Europe and America over the past hundred years without first accepting the existence of a discourse (and gendered discourse) of China which has its primary locus in the context of domestic consumption, since it is against, or by contrast with, what is done in the home that so much of what happens in the institutional context of museums and of the academy is defined."[3] Much the same could be said of the American framing of "Japanese art."

The aesthetic hodgepodge of exotic articles—Japanese silk, printed book, bronze vase, folding screen of cranes, and a huge conch shell resting on a Turkish rug—in a still life painted in 1879 by Elihu Vedder (1836–1923) is characteristic of the way Japan was understood and appreciated in the United States at that time (fig. 5.1).[4] Japan was not presented in a systematic or didactic way,

5.1   Elihu Vedder, Japanese still life, c. 1879. Oil on canvas. 21 1/2 x 34 1/2 in.
(54.6 x 87.6 cm.). Los Angeles County Museum of Art, Gift of the American Art
Council (M.74.11).

but for its connotations of formal elegance, fine materials, comfort, and sophistication. During the 1870s the curiosity value of articles from Japan was increasingly overshadowed by appreciation of their value in accessorizing the American
home and in connecting their owners to a genteel way of life. In this sense, Japan
participated in the creation of a new cultural idiom closely tied to changing standards of living. Perceptions evolved especially rapidly after the Philadelphia
Exposition, as Japanese goods once restricted to the relatively affluent, became
a part of middle-class culture. Collectors, decorators, critics, dealers, and their
audiences all helped to orchestrate these reformulations of meaning. This incremental process of "domestication" preceded and served as a counterpoint to the
recognition of Japanese art as an aesthetic category within the Western hierarchy of the fine and decorative arts.

   To Americans of the 1860s, Europe was a cultural beacon, beckoning them
to visit and bring home tangible evidence of their exposure to its values. By the
end of the decade, however, as more and more tourists began venturing to destinations in the Middle East and beyond, they sought to acquire emblems of these
distant cultures as well. Because historical and artistic information about these
articles was often lacking, Americans could mold them to their own tastes and
ideals at will. With the approach of the nation's centennial, this trend became

linked to efforts to create a new and distinctive American culture that was not indebted to Europe. With its presentation of goods from around the world, Philadelphia's Centennial Exposition, the first such event in the United States, "unlocked the floodgates of what became a steady flow of goods and fantasies about goods."[5]

A review in the *Atlantic Monthly* leaves no doubt that the Japanese displays whetted American appetites (figs. 5.2 and 5.3).

5.2   Selections from the Japanese section, Centennial Exhibition, from *Harper's Weekly* August 12, 1876.

5.3   Selections from the Japanese section, Centennial Exhibition, from *Harper's Weekly* August 12, 1876.

The Japanese collection is the first stage for those who are moved chiefly by the love of beauty or novelty in their sight-seeing. The gorgeousness of the specimens is equaled only by their exquisite delicacy. . . . Here is the handicraft of those extremest Orientals, five, eight, eleven hundred years old, if we can believe it, with a grace and elegancy of design and fabulous perfection of workmanship which rival or excel the marvels of Italian ornamental art at its zenith; and as one of discernment standing by said, there is no decline nor degeneracy, no period of corruptness and coarseness, such as the Renaissance shows in its decay. . . . The Japanese seem to possess the secret which the modern pre-Raphaelites have striven for without success, the union of detail and effect."[6]

The author of this article extols Japanese art for its design, workmanship, and purported antiquity through the lens of Euro-American concerns about moral and artistic decline that were fostered by the writings of John Ruskin and the Pre-Raphaelites. Other visitors to the 1876 exhibition emphasized the time and cost involved in producing such goods. One vase on view "represented the equivalent of 2,250 days of steady labor for one man, and the $2000 price did not seem excessive."[7] Yet a Japanese viewer dismissed the articles from his country as little more than "playthings."[8]

Despite the enormous enthusiasm Americans of this period professed for Japan, few shared the standards of artistic taste prevailing among Japanese. Nor were they able to recognize the difference between its arts and those of India and China. Even Clarence Cook illustrated a Japanese screen as a work of Indian provenance in *The House Beautiful* (1877), his influential guide to interior décor for middle-class Americans.[9] In any event, most consumers were not particularly concerned with distinguishing between various "Oriental" cultures. The Japan craze was part of an exoticizing trend that encompassed many countries: to help young married women furnish their houses tastefully, yet practically and economically, Cook recommended "picking up" inexpensive and attractive articles whether from India, China, Japan, or Turkey. In the view of European visitors more accustomed to interior décor defined by period styles, this kind of eclecticism was a distinctive feature of American taste.[10]

Rising interest in home décor both shaped and reflected expanded coverage in books and magazines. *Scribner's Monthly* (which later became *Century* magazine) included articles on the subject, bringing a new middle-class audience into the world of art and culture. Like Clarence Cook, the predominantly male authors of these publications often combined the roles of tastemaker, critic, educator, and salesperson. Merchants, eager to capitalize on the trend, stocked the kinds of goods praised in print. By 1891, bazaars and emporia selling goods ranging from bronze cachepots and bamboo étagères to fans and parasols had

5.4 *Much in Little Space,* from Cook, *The House Beautiful* (New York, 1877).

opened across the country, making Japan part of the shared experience of Americans even in rural and frontier towns.[11]

Japan lent itself particularly well to American representational needs, since the wide array of goods it produced could be readily adapted to different environments and economic circumstances. Those of modest means could content themselves with inexpensive yet colorful paper fans, parasols, and lanterns. Middle-class Americans could express their fashionable taste by displaying a porcelain cup or vase in their parlors, while more affluent ones could decorate their residences with large bronzes, lacquers, and folding screens. Regardless of background, there was a pronounced tendency to furnish rooms with an abundance of these fashionable accessories. "Much in Little Space," the caption of one of the illustrations in *The House Beautiful*, leaves no doubt that Cook endorsed this approach (fig. 5.4).

The articles in Cook's illustration—a statue of Minerva, writing table, hanging bookshelf filled with pottery, and Japanese scroll—are emblematic of "that heterogeneous catalogue of things for which the word *bric-a-brac* has been invented." And, he continued,

> these objects, which are coming to play the part in our external life that they have played these many years in Europe and Asia . . . when they are well chosen, and have some beauty of form or color, or workmanship, to recommend them, have a distinct use and value, as educators of certain senses—the sense of color, the sense of touch, the sense of sight. One need not have many of these pretty things within reach of hands and eyes, but money is well spent on really good bits of Japanese workmanship, or upon the workmanship of any people who have brought delicacy of hand and an exquisite perception to the making of what are in reality toys.[12]

Regardless of cost, Japanese furnishings and decorative articles were understood to be beautifully handcrafted rather than machine made. Since they lacked the aristocratic pretensions of their European counterparts, they were especially well suited to the art of everyday life in a democratic nation. They were also, as Cook implied, "feminine," an ascriptive quality linked to Euro-American stereotypes of Japan and its people as small and dainty.

As Victorian ideologies of womanhood promoted a new focus on domestic culture, ownership of Japanese imports became part of rising middle-class feminine identity and aspirations to cosmopolitan gentility. In their assigned role as guardians of culture, women were responsible for bringing beauty and refinement to their homes. Even practical, low-cost furnishings and bric-a-brac from Japan filled these desiderata. Like the domestic interiors that these items enhanced, their symbolic significance was divorced from the real workaday world.

While women acquired articles from Japan as part of a culture of domesticity, men collected them with the aim of forming cabinets of curiosity, collections *d'amateur*, or, in the case of artists, as professional aids. The Boston painter Winckworth Allan Gay used Japanese *objets d'art*, probably sent by his brother, to enhance the artistic ambiance of his studio. Charley's sister Edith, who visited in 1875, described it as a "perfect little bower of lovely Jap things and the amiable man being at home we stayed a long while admiring his curios and lovely pictures of the Nile and Venice."[13]

What Rémy Saisselin has written of France in the 1880s to a large extent holds true of the United States as well:

> By 1880 in France, women were perceived as mere buyers of bibelots, which they bought as they did clothing, in their daily bargain hunting. Men of course, collected too, but their collecting was perceived as

serious and creative. Women were consumers of objects; men were collectors. Women bought to decorate and for the sheer joy of buying, but men had a vision for their collections, viewed their collections as an ensemble with a philosophy behind it.[14]

In the 1860s, American Japanophiles were collecting to satisfy their personal tastes, not with the aim of donating their acquisitions to museums. Museums were still rare in the United States and not yet a primary venue for the encounter with Japanese art. In any event, those museums where the public could see articles from China and Japan were not places for disinterested aesthetic contemplation. Their mission was to entertain and educate the public by the display of objects held up as exotic curiosities. Most were private institutions that served also as marketing tools to advance their founders' material interests. The East India Marine Society, the first American institution to display curiosities from Japan, was formed by donations from merchant traders to provide an institutional setting for the promotion of Salem's trade with India and the Far East. Similar aims underlay the exhibition of some 1341 Chinese artifacts, including three colossal Buddhas, belonging to the prosperous Philadelphia China trader Nathan Dunn (1782–1844), first held at the Philadelphia Museum in 1838. Since the differences between Chinese and Japanese art were as yet little appreciated, there being no regular trade with Japan at the time, it is possible that the collection included some objects from Japan as well. After Dunn's death, P. T. Barnum bought many of his curiosities at auction to add to his New York museum.[15]

Many of the nation's great art museums were founded during the 1870s. Art history also began to be recognized as a professional discipline. Until that time, men of letters often doubled as art critics. Longfellow's friend Charles Eliot Norton, a Dante scholar, also wrote about Gothic churches, an enthusiasm he had developed through the influence of John Ruskin. In 1875 he taught the first fine arts course at Harvard College. By the following decade, decisions about what constituted "art" would be determined by a small corps of experts, many of them men who functioned both as art dealers and advisers to museums and private collectors. They decided what was worthy of a collection and what was not.

In crusading for a museum, Thomas Appleton reminded his fellow Bostonians that their city could not live forever on the glory of literary heroes such as Longfellow and Holmes. "Unless a distinct effort be made now, Boston will lose its place and go behind."[16] Appleton and other civic leaders continued to fill their own residences with elegant furnishings and fine arts from around the world, even as they pushed for the founding of museums to educate and elevate public taste. Although the traditional vision of the cabinet of curiosity was being redefined in this era of global consumerism, men like Cornelius Vanderbilt still relished the sense of dominion that came from displaying their personal collections in a designated room within their homes (fig. 5.5). Their desire to own and display Japanese art implied a degree of respect for the culture that had produced it, but in the context of a private residence, curios were fragments of another world deployed primarily to tell stories about their owners.

Although travelogues suggest that all globe-trotters acquired at least a few curios in Japan, no collections from the 1860s and 1870s survive. Written and visual evidence of the nature of these articles is also limited. Longfellow House thus offers a rare vantage from which to explore how and by whom Japan was culturally represented and in what ways the interpretations of these American representations changed over the last quarter of the nineteenth century. In this domestic context, Charley's souvenirs, now separated from their country of origin, were put to new purposes and assigned new meanings inflected by a host of considerations. Some were specific to his and his family's aspirations, while others reflected broader cultural trends. For Charley, many of these objects continued to function chiefly as personal mementos, markers of his Japanese regression to childhood, but their incorporation into the colonial home of a celebrity poet established a new semipublic framework that aroused in their viewers new ideas about Japanese art and its place in America.

5.5   Vanderbilt's Japan Room, from *Artistic Houses* (New York, 1883).

DOMESTICATING JAPAN

Longfellow House: American Cultural Icon

The house at 105 Brattle Street in Cambridge was already a historic site when Nathan Appleton purchased it as a wedding present for his daughter Frances and her husband, Henry Wadsworth Longfellow (fig. 5.6). Built in 1759 by Major John Vassall, George Washington had made it his headquarters after the wealthy Tory fled to Canada on the eve of the revolution. When the Longfellows moved in, locals called it Craigie House, after the widow who had owned it since 1819. The poet and his wife playfully dubbed it Craigie Castle.

The house's "sacred" association with the nation's founder, one of its chief attractions when Nathan Appleton bought it for the newlyweds in 1843, soon led Frances to set about acquiring Colonial-era furnishings and memorabilia associated with Washington. A copy of Houdon's celebrated marble bust of Washington was one of the first acquisitions of the proud owners of a house where, as Frances wrote her brother Tom Appleton, "Washington dwelt in every room."[17] Furnishing a house in Colonial style, though in keeping with Longfellow's celebration of early American history, was something of a novelty before the Civil War. When his wife began collecting antiques, the art critic John Neal chided her for filling their house with "trumpery antiquities."[18]

5.6 Longfellow House, c. 1870–80. Modern print. Photographer unknown. LNHS.

Frances Longfellow also decorated the interior of the house with European and American paintings and family portraits. A letter of 1857 written to her elder sister living in England, gives an idea of Frances's artistic knowledge and taste:

> I am very glad you were able to get to Manchester in time to enjoy the treasures of Art there heaped up like the jewels in Aladdin's garden. How I envy you seeing these. There is nothing I miss so much in this new world as the best pictures. Music now comes to us, but those cannot, though we are to be favored with specimens of modern English and French art regularly, but I love the "grand old masters," and care not for Ruskin's sneers at them. His school of Pre-Raphaelites miss all the poetry of the art in their foolish mania for detail, and they cannot get the saintly grace of expression when art was a religion and an act of devotion. Charley Norton has written an account of the Exhibition in our new magazine [*The Atlantic Monthly*] which is a little à la Ruskin, not in style but in theory.[19]

After Charley's return, Japanese screens, bronzes, vases, and other articles further enhanced the already eclectic décor. With the approach of the 1876 centenary, the Longfellow home assumed a double pedigree as a national historical and literary shrine, its interior promoted as a cultural model for all Americans.

Not everybody could visit the house, of course. Unlike with museums, entry was not open to the general public. Guests, however, were extremely numerous, both during the poet's lifetime and after his death in 1882. The abolitionist senator Charles Sumner, the writer and Harvard professor James Russell Lowell, the socialite Annie Fields, Charles Eliot Norton, and James Jackson Jarves were all among the Longfellows's circle of friends. International celebrities who paid their respects to the American included Anthony Trollope, Wilkie Collins, and Charles Dickens, who called the year before Charley set off for India.[20] Numerous individuals who at some point traveled to Japan, also visited, among them, Richard Henry Dana II, Bayard Taylor, Isabella Bird, and Sir Edwin Arnold (1832–1904).[21]

The Longfellows' participation in the process of shaping American images of Japan was part of a new exhibitionary culture made possible by the burgeoning of reproductive technologies. Stereoscopic views of the interior, available in the 1860s, along with illustrations in popular books and magazines, were all instrumental in familiarizing the American public with their colonial house. Its appropriation as a model is emblematic of both the cultural prestige of the man of letters and the belief that anyone in America's democratic society could aspire to have a house like the poet's.

American publishers had first turned their attention to the homes of Emerson, Hawthorne, Longfellow, and other notable men of letters in the 1850s. Both Putnam and Appleton, two leading New York publishing houses, featured

Craigie House in their similarly titled *Homes of American Authors* (1853, 1857), primarily with the aim of helping readers appreciate Longfellow's poetry.[22] As an article on Longfellow in *Scribner's Monthly* noted: "We find in all biographies that all writers, even the greatest, are influenced by their surroundings and by the books they read."[23] Publications from the 1870s and 1880s are more voyeuristic, catering to a growing demand for counsel on the do's and don'ts of home décor. The poet's house shows people how they should live by way of example. The growing number of illustrations that accompany many of these books reinforces the message that it is a private, lived-in space that also assumes larger public meanings. The functional values of the furnishings—whether a "grandfather" clock, a chair made from the wood of the "spreading chestnut tree," or a Japanese screen—are subordinated to their value as emblems of good taste for all Americans.

It is easy to dismiss Longfellow as the Victorian poetic equivalent of Norman Rockwell. He is unfashionable today, his critical reputation having been eclipsed by his proto-modernist contemporaries Emily Dickinson and Walt Whitman. Yet during his lifetime he was a celebrity with a literary reputation at home as well as abroad. In *The Song of Hiawatha* (1855), *The Courtship of Miles Standish* (1858), *Tales of Wayside Inn* (1863), and other epic verses, he told moving tales about America that not only appealed to a wide audience but were instrumental in the formation of American cultural identity. William Eliot Griffis offers a telling instance of this. Before the advent of the photographic carte de visite, it had been common practice in Japan to exchange, as personal mementos, fans painted or inscribed by the donor, often with well-known poems. When Griffis was in remote villages he often participated in this ritual by writing in English excerpts from Shakespeare, Milton, or Longfellow.[24] One can only imagine what their recipients made of these poems.

In various ways and to varying degrees, many members of the Appleton and Longfellow families participated in the promotion of Craigie House and the Japanese art within it. Whatever his personal reservations about the direction Charley's life had taken, the poet took every opportunity to express public pride in his son's travels in Japan. He was delighted to learn from a friend that Charley's diplomatic post as Charles de Long's secretary had been mentioned in the *New York Times*. He encouraged the reading of Charley's journals and letters in the presence of family and friends. Charley's reports also may have warmed his reception of Mori Arinori, a member of the Iwakura Mission who visited Cambridge during his tour of the United States. The welcome the poet and his family extended to Yamada Ineyasu (1850–1908), a Japanese student who entered Harvard Law School in 1871, no doubt also reflected the family's personal involvement with Japan. Yamada joined the Longfellows for dinner, played croquet with Charley's sisters, and even taught the poet a few words of Japanese.

Longfellow's growing interest in Japan also bore fruit in his own work. It is possible that his son's travels were a catalyst for his inclusion of translations of several Japanese verses in *Poems of Places,* an anthology on which he began working in 1874.[25] Japan also figures prominently in *Keramos* (1878), one of the most famous compositions of the poet's later years. An elegy to the ceramic arts, it takes the reader on a whirlwind tour of the world. With each turn of the potter's wheel, we travel to another country noted for its ceramics—France, Holland, Spain, Italy, Egypt, India, China, and finally Japan, where both artist and artisan touch the human heart by following in "Nature's footprints."[26]

We must be cautious about attributing the poet's interest in Japanese ceramics solely or even primarily to his son's collection, however. His brother-in-law Thomas Appleton had a large number of Japanese *objets d'art*. Although he was not a collector himself, Longfellow had a general interest in the arts. He was sufficiently aware of Japan as a source of lacquer to joke when urging his son to return home, "We begin to think here, that you are now sufficiently Japanned."[27] His complaint to a visitor that a maid had broken a vase Charley purchased in Japan underscores, if not his sensitivity to its beauty, at least his recognition of its value.[28]

That he became surrounded by an extraordinary panoply of Japanese arts is beyond doubt. The contents of the Japanese cases, which arrived several months before Charley himself, may be surmised from a letter the poet wrote his son on February 19, 1874:

> Your 5 cases of Personal effects by *Benefactor* were passed free. The 15 cases by *Eliza Shaw* came in on Bond and were opened here, or some of them, the Appraiser giving up in despair, and putting on what he thought a fair average duty. We are now opening the other cases, and taking the beautiful things out to keep them from the damp of the Billiard Room where they are stored. Last night the library was gay, with screens. As yet we have come upon no bronzes; but have found a few silks and two splendid bed-quilts. Also two cabinets, not yet unwrapped, and sundry strange little objects which greatly delight Uncle Tom.[29]

Only a small number of these can be matched with articles still in the house. One of the "two cabinets" may be a portable chest *(tansu)* that Charley later installed in his room (fig. 5.7). The latter closely resembles a chest discussed at some length and illustrated in the chapter on the bedroom in Cook's *The House Beautiful* (fig 5.8). Made of soft, light wood in two parts, one standing on the other, its unpainted surface is set off by striking iron hinges and handles. Cook characterizes it as traveling trunk and bureau, ideal for a man to store his shirts, handkerchiefs, collars, and gloves, but Charley's cousin Mary King Longfellow also had one in her house in Portland, Maine (see fig. 5.13).[30]

5.7 Japanese chest
(tansu), c. 1871–73.
Wood. H. 39 3/4, W. 37
1/4, D. 16 1/8 in. LNHS.

5.8 *Grand Combination
Trunk Line*, from Cook,
The House Beautiful
(New York, 1877).

A small sampling of the "sundry little articles" referred to in Longfellow's letter may be discerned in photographs from the 1870s and 1880s. The Longfellows adopted the Japanese practice of displaying flowers in vases suspended from the wall, which was later popularized in the United States by Edward Morse's *Japanese Homes and their Surroundings* (1886).[31] A photograph from circa 1885–92 shows a hanging metal flower container made to simulate woven bamboo suspended from one of the columns in the library.[32] A photograph taken after Charley's death also features a handsome pair of Japanese blue-and-white vases, with a motif of cranes and waves, on the mantelpiece of the "Blue Room," a bedroom on the second floor.[33] Numerous Chinese porcelains, some perhaps dating from before Charley's journey, also figure in photographs and book illustrations from the late 1860s on.[34]

Charles Wyllis Elliott's *The Book of American Interiors* (1876) is the first publication to draw attention to the Japanese screens in the Longfellow home (fig. 5.9). In explaining the purpose of this book, Elliot wrote: "What is attempted here is to give a picture, more or less perfect, of a few interiors which the taste and ingenuity of our people have devised, as the receptacles or treasure-houses for their volumes. No effort has been made to show the most expensive rooms, but such as express a sense of the beautiful in their adaptation to their use."[35] Elliot featured a view of the library with the recommendation that "brilliant Japanese screens and ornaments give life and piquancy to the quiet which sometimes reigns too supreme in the library of the good American."[36] His promotion of the Longfellows' interior décor was hardly disinterested, since he was the manager of Boston's Household Art Company, a shop that purveyed Japanese furnishings. His publication is emblematic of the confluence of taste and marketing that characterized the popularization of much Japanese art in the 1870s.

Stoddard's *Poets' Homes*, published the following year, notes the presence of Japanese screens as well as bronzes in the library, "the most beautiful room in the house; dark and rich in tone, with a look of spacious elegance and home-like comfort." In Longfellow's study, "the most interesting room in the house," he admired an orange tree and near it, what he believed to be an "Egyptian stork," keeping watch.[37] This was no doubt one of "the flock of bronze storks from five to three feet high" Charley had purchased in Japan (see fig. 3.7). The birds in question were in fact cranes, not storks. Emblems of longevity, cranes were among the ubiquitous bird and animal motifs in Japanese painting and decorative arts that prompted Americans to praise Japanese artists for their truth to nature. As may be seen in figure 5.2, they were among the articles featured in the Philadelphia Centennial Exposition. The author of the accompanying article in *Harper's Weekly* asserted that this bronze stork "is one of the most ancient articles in the collection. The figure appears in the ornamentation of many of the vases, and seems to be a favorite model with Japanese artists."[38]

5.9   Library at Longfellow House, from Elliott, *The Book of American Interiors* (Boston, 1876).

Articles Charley brought back also decorated the homes of other Longfellow relatives, furthering knowledge of Japan's art. His Portland cousins Mary King (1852–1945) and her brother Alexander Wadsworth Longfellow (1854–1934) both became Japanophiles. A student of the painter William Morris Hunt, an early proponent of Japanese art, Mary had a modest talent as a watercolorist. Her view of the corner of the poet's library showing the same folding screen recorded in *The Book of American Interiors* testifies to an early interest in Japanese art (fig. 5.10). Alexander, an undergraduate at Harvard College when Charley was in Japan, decorated his dormitory room in Weld Hall with a hanging scroll, fans, prints, and other articles from Japan that Charley had sent him (fig. 5.11). Alexander went on to study architecture at the Massachusetts Institute of Technology, later becoming an associate of H. H. Richardson and a founding member of the Boston Arts and Crafts Society. His early exposure to Japanese art may have been a catalyst for his interest in architectural design and his embrace of the Japanesque.[39]

Charley apparently gave his cousin Mary many paintings and furnishings he had acquired in Japan. Some of these were returned to Longfellow House following her death. Among them is a six-fold screen featuring autumn trees and flowers against a backdrop of bamboo blinds *(sudare)*. While this pictorial motif had been common in screen painting since the eighteenth century, the

DOMESTICATING JAPAN

5.10 Mary King Longfellow, view of the Library at Longfellow House, c. 1876. Watercolor on paper. LNHS.

5.11 Alexander Wadsworth Longfellow's Harvard dormitory room, c. 1875. Modern print. Photographer unknown. LNHS.

5.12 Mary King Longfellow in kimono standing in front of Japanese screen, 1880s. Modern print. Photographer unknown. LNHS.

nineteenth-century version in Longfellow House is unusual in that it features actual set-in blinds rather than painted ones (fig. 5.12).

A photograph thought to date from 1884 shows Mary, dressed in a kimono, standing before this screen. It may have been taken on the occasion of a benefit for needy women and children, billed as a "Japanese tea," that Mary and her mother hosted in Portland. The décor for the event, where tea was served in Japanese cups on Japanese trays, included Japanese fans, lanterns, textiles, parasols, and screens. Visitors paid $1.00 for the thrill of trying on Japanese "dressing gowns"—kimonos Mary had borrowed from Charley to entice women to attend the event.[40] In the 1880s and 1890s Japanese décor was extremely popular for children's parties, dances, ladies' luncheons, church bazaars, and other festive events.[41]

Paintings Charley acquired in Japan also served as models for his sister Edith, his cousin Mary, and their friends. In 1875, Mary was in Cambridge "painting Japanese girls after Wergman [*sic*]."[42] In a letter written to Mary in Portland, Edith offers a vivid description of a screen just completed by their friend Rosie:

5.13   Interior of Mary King Longfellow's Portland house, 1880s. Modern print.
Photographer unknown. LNHS.

I wish you could see Rosie's new screen which she just has finished and
mounted. She has improved wonderfully, working it all out by her own
experience and it is really lovely, and beautifully done. It is four leaves
like the first one, but a good deal taller. It is a lovely shade of light blue
silk, the first leaf to the left has "Fusiyama" below and a stork flying
above, the next to the right pink and white lotus flowers with green leaves
growing in the water, and the next more lotus leaves and flowers and the
bottom and above a full moon just on the horizon casting a broad reflection
across the water and a stork flying across the moon. A vague promontory
of land runs out which is continued in the right-most leaf where there are
three storks in the foreground, standing among reeds on a bank and one
flying above. The blue ground comes in so well for sky and water and the
whale is edged with dark blue.[43]

This Japanesque screen does not survive, but a photograph of a room in Mary's
Portland house in Portland, Maine, gives some idea of the enthusiasm with which
she and other artistically inclined young women embraced Japan (fig. 5.13).
Although such interior décor was a significant component of the popular response
to Japan, with the advent of museums, it would become incompatible with the
promotion of "authentic" Japanese art.[44] In the eyes of male collectors and
museum professionals, the feminine tastes and activities that had contributed
to the domestication of Japan compromised its autonomous aesthetic.

Charley's "Japan Room"

Soon after his return, Charley set out to organize his souvenirs of Japan in a suite of rooms on the second floor of the family residence. Like his photograph albums, these rooms synthesized and compressed spatiotemporal events into a single compact entity. Unlike in the Japan Room in the Vanderbilts' New York mansion (see fig. 5.5), no conscious decorative scheme or aesthetic principles underlay their décor. Decorating his rooms in this manner authenticated Charley's adventures in Japan while also helping to establish an identity independent of his father. Unable to adapt to the vicissitudes of ordinary life, he needed extraordinary places and events around him. The decoration of his rooms helped to recreate in miniature the physical world he remembered in Japan. By the same token, Charley created here a private world where curios functioned as personal accessories that enhanced his masculinity through their association with that exotic "feminine" culture. In this sense, his rooms might be likened to the costumed self-portraits he had taken during his travels.

The personal narrative of Charley's suite does not reflect the kind of artistic or functional hierarchy found in a museum. If there is any organizational principle, it is the fact of ownership and display. Among the heterogeneous articles on view in a photograph from 1874–82, we may make out the "firescreen" painted with a scene of Shinobazu Pond discussed in chapter 3 (see pls. VIII and IX), an ornamental cut-metal lantern resting on the mantelpiece, a photograph album resting in a rack, and lacquer bookshelves covered with an array of bric-a-brac (fig. 5.14). The eclectic, disorderly abundance is reminiscent of the parlor in Charley's Tokyo house, which he had so lovingly described in a letter to his sisters. The long, narrow parlor had a "table in center, porcelain vases in corners and a mantelpiece filled with flowers, mirror over the mantelpiece. Furniture, transoms, and curtains of marron reps [corded fabric], table covered with a glorious confusion of dictionaries, grammars, novels, photo books, newspapers, and, of course, the Japanese pipe and firebox— which is in pretty constant use."[45] Although the arrangement gives the impression of being haphazard, this is misleading. As we have seen, Charley was keenly sensitive to the way he packaged and presented himself. He was equally attentive to his physical surroundings, and the knowledge that his room in the family home would be photographed no doubt spurred him to devote special care in its decoration. This project, moreover, was carried out with the help of his young cousin Alexander, who was himself keenly interested in interior design and décor.

In her study of Japanese taste in America from 1876 to 1916, Jane Converse Brown has observed that rooms decorated in Japanese style during the nineteenth century were generally public spaces that served "as a special form of middle-class display."[46] This was certainly the case at Longfellow House. Charley's quarters had first become showplaces after his return from India. Annie Fields, the

5.14   Charles Longfellow's room, c. 1874. Modern print. Photographer
unknown. LNHS.

wife of the poet's publisher, was taken there in 1871, observing in her diary that
after dinner, "we adjourned to the room of Charles the East-India man, where
we saw many curiosities and had a very pleasant hour before leaving."[47] Fields's
comments suggest that Charley's vision was rooted in the old cabinet of wonders: to enter it was to satisfy one's curiosity about the wider world.

Following the rooms' redecoration in Japanese style, visitors became more
numerous.[48] Stoddard described its now fashionable Japanese décor in his 1877
publication *Poets' Homes:*

> One suite has been fitted up by Mr. Longfellow's son in the Japanese style.
> The wall-paper is of neutral tint, ornamented with Japanese fans in twos
> and threes. The heathen gods frown at you, national arms are collected,
> tables are heaped with Japanese books made on the principle of cat stairs,
> and photographs of Japanese beauties, with buttonhole mouths, and long
> bright eyes abound.[49]

5.15 Charles Longfellow's "Japan Room," c.1890. Modern print. Photographer unknown. LNHS.

Since fans decorated the ceiling rather than the walls, it is possible that Stoddard did not in fact see the second-floor room for himself (fig. 5.15). His reference to them, however, underscores the fan's status as a Japanese cultural trope.

Charley's imaginative use of painted paper fans, each featuring a different pictorial subject, followed Japanese decorative practice. Folding screens decorated with actual fans tumbling down a river or floating on waves had been popular in Japan since at least the sixteenth century. To Japanese viewers, this motif was a visually pleasing, secularized reminder of the Buddhist view that all things in life are ephemeral and subject to change. A nineteenth-century example in Longfellow House testifies that this genre of screen painting also attracted the attention of foreign visitors, although they were unlikely to appreciate its Buddhist connotations (fig. 5.16).

Euro-Americans visitors to Japan would have encountered fans in a wide variety of settings. At the Gankirō brothel in Yokohama, they decorated the sliding doors between rooms, as seen in a wood-block print from the 1860s (see fig. 1.6).

The American merchant-trader Francis Hall observed at about the same time a "not unpleasing though strange mixture" of fans picturing "flowers, landscapes, historical characters, and divinities" on the ceiling of the residence of a Yokohama merchant.[50] The audience hall in the Hamagoten, a palace in Tokyo where official visitors were received, had walls and ceilings decorated "exclusively with huge pictured fans, in many different positions, and so well executed that you might fancy that you feel the air stirred by their motions." The name "Cool-Room" by which this audience hall was known was entirely appropriate, observed Olive Seward.[51] Edward Morse was another American who took note of this distinctive mode of interior décor, although, curiously, he did not mention it in his *Japanese Homes and Their Surroundings* (1886).[52]

5.16 Fans floating on waves, 1860s. Artist unknown. Two-fold screen, ink and colors on paper. 150.9 x 174 cm. LNHS.

The reference in Stoddard's book indicating that the ceiling décor was in place by 1877, makes the Longfellow suite the earliest known example of a "Japan Room" in the United States, but whether or not it exerted any influence on later domestic interiors is unclear. The vogue for decorating with Japanese fans seems to have been well under way in various parts of the United States by the early 1880s. The ceiling in the bedroom of Mr. F. W. Hartt's house in New Jersey was treated in this way. The Japanesque bedroom of a Dr. Hammond in Philadelphia reproduced in an 1883 publication on "artistic houses" featured a row of fans on the walls (fig. 5.17).[53] As William Hosley, the author of *The Japan Idea*, has observed, the random arrangement of fans represents "bric-a-brac interior writ large."[54]

5.17   Dr. Hammond's bedroom, from *Artistic Houses* (New York, 1883).

Further comments appear in *The Home Life of Henry W. Longfellow*, written by Blanche Roosevelt Tucker-Macchetta, a frequent visitor to the household during the last years of the poet's life. Its author, a noted opera singer, was more interested in capitalizing on her friendship with the celebrity poet than in providing an accurate record of his home décor. Nonetheless, her observations suggest that Charley's room was a kind of family museum: "After dinner, the subject of bric-a-brac came up, and the professor invited us to his son Charles' room to see some rare objects, and some Japanese paintings. . . . We entered his son's apartment. It was filled with beautiful cabinets in Japanese work, intricate boxes, fans, chains, carved ivory knick-knacks, and screens innumerable that stood about the place."[55]

In addition to their role as a family showplace, Charley's rooms also served as a kind of play area for his younger sisters and their friends, since some time after returning from Japan, Charley took up residence at the exclusive Somerset Club, situated in the fashionable Beacon Hill district of Boston and visited Cambridge only sporadically. In 1874, after her twenty-first birthday, Edith wrote, she and her friends "adjourned to Charlie's room," and a few days later, inspired perhaps by the Japanese practice of moon-viewing, they donned "Japanese dressing gowns" to stay up and watch an eclipse. There she also "danced the habanera," tried on exotic clothes her brother had brought back from Asia, and played "Japanese" games with her friends.[56]

Circumstances specific to the Longfellow family may have prompted the adoption of Charley's room for fun and games, but Japanese décor was very popular among young American men and women of the 1880s, partly, no doubt, because of its modest cost. A decade after Alexander Longfellow, fellow Harvard student John Coolidge also covered the walls of his dormitory room with prints and paintings from Japan.[57] In a room in an unidentified house in Portsmouth, New Hampshire, photographed in the 1880s, cultural references to Japan are multiplied many times, with rows of fans and parasols covering the walls (fig. 5.18). What is especially striking, however, is the playful tone struck by the two young men who peek out from behind the curtained doorway. One has the sense that they are making fun of the culture embodied in the room, even as they have embraced it wholeheartedly. Such irreverence was much more easily directed toward Japanese than toward European décor. In this "Japanese" environment, young men and women could indulge in play-acting and games that were inappropriate elsewhere.

These rooms are suggestive of the way the idea of Japan as a place for recreation and refuge from the responsibilities of the modern adult world was displaced to America. As noted in chapter 1, long before the arrival of American tourists, Japanese people had been understood to be immature and malleable, like children. Since Japanese infants were never seen to cry, the country, moreover, was admired as a "paradise of children." The delicacy and diminutive

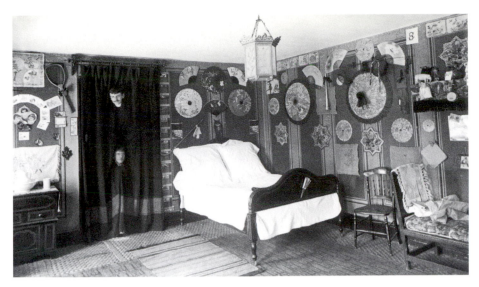

5.18   Room with japanesque décor in Portsmouth, N.H., 1880s. Modern print. Photographer unknown. New Hampshire Historical Society.

scale of Japanese crafts and the prominence of toys among early imports reinforced this image. When she declared that Charley's room was a "Sleepy Hollow kind of place that one loses all track of time and everything else out here," Edith might well have been describing Japan itself.[58]

It is a truism that objects take on different meanings depending on the context in which they are displayed. Charley's rooms presented an armchair traveler's miniature Japan, reinforcing many stereotypical American perceptions of that country. At the same time their décor was a form of self-disclosure by which he organized his experiences, situating them within yet separate from the orbit of family life. By imposing personal order on his chaotic collection of souvenirs, he carved out for himself an important niche in the unfolding myth of the Longfellow family. The display of Japanese screens, bronzes, furnishings, and fans helped to create an aura of cultivation important to Henry Longfellow as a paterfamilias and an American literary icon. Yet Charley was conspicuously absent when his father took guests to his Japan Room. In the poet's eyes, was the room perhaps more presentable to the public than Charley himself? Such a decorative space was a socially and culturally sanctioned achievement, one far easier to deal with than a son who was "japanned." The Japan Room allowed both Charley and his family alike to create and maintain their own personal truths. Yet it was also part of a larger discourse. Connecting Japan to the life of a family with whom other Americans could identify contributed to the democratization of Japanese art and culture. Although such nineteenth-century Japanesque interiors are widely dismissed today as lowbrow and inauthentic, they helped to lay the foundation for Japanese association with a fashionable personal "lifestyle."

Epilogue

> Though Charles Longfellow's remains were cremated in
> Germantown, Pennsylvania, the ashes were returned for
> interment in the family tomb at Mount Auburn Cemetery.
>
> —Undated newspaper clipping,
> Longfellow National Historic Site

In death Charley Longfellow achieved the Japanese-inflected identity he had
sought throughout his life. Although he may have been an unwitting participant in the decision—there being no record of his having requested that his body
be cremated—his cremation was a fitting symbol of his and New England's
embrace of Japanese culture. By the time of Charley's death in 1893, Buddhism
had attracted many adherents. However, he was not among those Americans who
had traveled to Japan in search of nirvana. In the early 1870s, Europeans and
Americans who were prepared to accept Buddhism on its own terms, much less
adopt its precepts, were rare. With the possible exception of Charley's idiosyncratic Kannon tattoo, he did not profess any religious impulses later in life
either. Why then was he cremated?

American interest in Asian religions had first manifested itself in the 1840s
among Transcendentalists and members of the Unitarian church. Emerson,
Thoreau, and Whitman were all drawn to Asian philosophy and religions.
Longfellow was already well enough informed on the subject in 1848 to be sar-
castic about a young missionary "who evidently thinks Calvin is superior to Con-
fucius."[1] The eighteen-line entry in the 1849 edition of *Webster's Dictionary* on
"Boodhism" testifies to both the advent of systematic studies and growing public interest in this religion at the time.[2] Over the course of the next two decades,

publications on Asian religions grew in number, if not always in reliability. By 1872, readers could consult *Oriental Religions and Their Relation to Universal Religion,* a highly regarded three-volume study by Samuel Johnson (1822–82), a Unitarian minister, Transcendentalist, and associate of the poet's brother Samuel Longfellow. Johnson's interpretation stressed Buddhism's compatibility with Victorian values.[3]

Many writings on Buddhism in the 1870s and 1880s, both scholarly and popular, focused chiefly on its Singhalese and Indian rather than Chinese and Japanese manifestations. *The Light of Asia* (1879), Edwin Arnold's poetic account of the historical Gautama Buddha's life, fueled fascination with the Indian founder of this exotic religion. First published in 1879, it became a best-seller both in England and the United States. The sensational reportage concerning Helen Blavatsky (1831–91) and Henry Steel Olcott (1832–1907), cofounders of the Theosophical Society (established in 1875), who converted to Buddhism in Ceylon in 1880, further stimulated public interest. A few years later, Phillips Brooks (1835–93), the liberal-minded Episcopal rector of Boston's Trinity Church, traveled to India, where he visited a Buddhist shrine. In explaining this visit to his family, he declared "in these days when a large part of Boston prefers to consider itself Buddhist rather than Christian, I consider it to be a duty of a minister who preaches to Bostonians."[4]

Writings on Japanese Buddhism in the 1870s fell into two categories. On the one hand, there were censorious accounts of this "heathen" religion by missionaries seeking to plant the seeds of Christianity in the island nation, and on the other, more balanced ones by scholars and diplomats.[5] Commentaries on Japanese religious beliefs, practices, and, especially, divinities also figured in many travelogues, since visits to shrines and temples were part of most visitors' itineraries. Andrew Carnegie stands out among the handful of globe-trotters of the 1860s and 1870s who were sympathetic to Buddhism.[6] The rituals associated with death—funerary rites being a major preoccupation in Victorian society—exerted particular curiosity among Euro-Americans. Aimé Humbert devoted many pages to the subject and even included an illustration of a body about to be cremated under a shroud of rice straw.[7] Such images no doubt fueled fear and horror of a practice that for many Christians brought to mind the fire and brimstone of hell. Such deep-rooted associations made it difficult to make the mental adjustments necessary to accept cremation as a practical solution to the disposal of the body, as it was in Japan, where arable land was scarce and therefore put to use for the living, not the dead.

Although it had deep roots in Greco-Roman and Native American cultures, cremation was reintroduced to the Euro-American public via Ceylon and India. Baron Henry Louis Charles de Palm, a member of the Theosophical Society, was the first to be cremated in a specially constructed crematorium in the United States. It was built in the small town of Washington, Pennsylvania, by Dr.

Francis Julius LeMoyne, a close associate of William Steel Olcott. De Palm's widely reported cremation, which took place in the year of the Philadelphia Centennial, helped to publicize and to set in motion new American responses to the practice. Le Moyne's crematorium, by shielding people from seeing the process, in which heat, not fire, consumed the corpse, would be essential to the American adoption of this form of body disposal.[8]

As Stephen Prothero has written in his *Purified by Fire: A History of Cremation in America*, cremation was part of a paradigm shift in funerary practices and rituals that occurred during the Gilded Age. Like other Asian imports, its emergence as an alternative to embalming and burial in the United States was largely predicated on local conditions and concerns. One of these was the growing preoccupation with eliminating the dangers the corpse posed the living. Dr. Jacob Bigelow (1786–1879), one of cremation's early advocates, saw its adoption as part of a public health crusade that would prevent potential bacterial contamination from diseased or decaying corpses. Such views grew out of the movement to separate the dead from the living that had led in 1831 to the creation of the parklike Mt. Auburn Cemetery in Cambridge, Massachusetts, well outside of the city of Boston. By the 1890s, the "bacteriological revolution was well underway," and cremation became the great purifier, disinfectant, and "only true germicide."[9] This development converged with a more spiritualized understanding of the body and afterlife.

Ironically, the growing emphasis on scientific progress was among the factors that led disaffected members of the New England social and intellectual elite, including Henry Adams, the grandson and great-grandson of American presidents and an influential historian, to seek refuge in Japan and its Buddhist culture. "I myself was a Buddhist when I left America," Adams later declared.[10] His Catholic travel companion, John La Farge, also went to Japan in search of Buddhism, although he would later claim that he did not find nirvana. La Farge envisioned Japan as having a spiritualized geography akin to that located earlier in the Holy Land, and in Nikkō, which by 1886 had become one of the most popular Euro-American tourist destinations, he discovered a numinous landscape to serve as the model for the backdrop for a mural he was to paint for New York's Church of the Ascension.[11]

Economic rather than spiritual needs drove Ernest Fenollosa to Japan in 1878, but both he and William Sturgis Bigelow later became Buddhist converts. They received Buddhist precepts in 1885 at Hōmyōin, a subtemple of Miidera, on the shores of Lake Biwa. Bigelow, who came to be regarded as something of an expert on Buddhism, was later invited to give a series of lectures on the subject at Harvard University. Although these were published as *Buddhism and Immortality* in 1908, his own immortality was achieved primarily as a patron of Buddhist art.[12] His collection of paintings helped to establish the Boston Museum of Fine Arts as the largest repository of Buddhist art outside of Japan. There is considerable irony in this, since in so doing he participated in the process through which Buddhist devotional images were removed from their authentic contexts, secularized, and then resanctified in the museum by their display as aesthetic icons.

From its beginnings in the 1870s, the cremation movement had attracted atheists, freethinkers, Spiritualists, Theosophists, and Unitarians. The latter, among the most sympathetic interpreters of Buddhism, were also the first to embrace cremation, in part because they rejected the elaborate and costly rituals associated with funerals at the time. Supporters also included civic leaders of widely divergent political, social, and cultural backgrounds, primarily in Boston and New York: the businessman William Waldorf Astor; president of Harvard College Charles William Eliot; Phillips Brooks; newspaper editor Charles A. Dana; Andrew Carnegie; and Massachusetts senator Charles Sumner. Leaders in the women's rights movement were also among its advocates.[13]

By the 1890s, cremation was becoming commonplace among many affluent mainline Protestants. Despite its growing popularity, however, when Charley died at the age of forty-nine in 1893, there was not yet a crematorium in Massachusetts. His Unitarian family had to go to considerable trouble to have his corpse transported to Germantown to be cremated by the Philadelphia Cremation Society. Despite advocacy of cremation among Unitarians, nothing in Charley's will or among his family's papers has yet to come to light to explain who made this decision or why.[14] His sister Alice may have played a decisive role, since she cared for him at the family home during the long bout of pneumonia that led to his death. Upon her death in 1928 she too was cremated, as were her brother Ernest and his wife. Their ashes, like Charley's, were all interred in the family plot at Mount Auburn Cemetery.[15]

When a crematorium was finally built on the grounds of Mount Auburn Cemetery in 1900, it was located beneath Bigelow Chapel, a Gothic-style structure built in the 1840s with funds from Jacob Bigelow. It was there that Jacob's grandson William Sturgis Bigelow was cremated following his death in 1926. At his request, half his ashes were buried in the family plot at Mount Auburn Cemetery and half shipped to the temple overlooking Lake Biwa, where he had taken his religious vows. His ashes joined those of Ernest Fenollosa, who had died in London in 1908.[16]

Tourism, collecting, and attitudes toward Japanese culture changed dramatically during the twenty years between Charley's first and last visit. When he arrived in Japan in 1871, most globe-trotters were still confined to the treaty ports and their surroundings. Japanese authorities strictly controlled not only where visitors went but what they saw. Language barriers imposed further limitations on foreign access to the country. By 1885, depending on their means, inclinations, and connections, travelers could go most anywhere. When

Longfellow traveled there with Charles Weld, the two friends cruised the scenic coast from Yokohama, through the Inland Sea, to Nagasaki aboard *The Loiterer,* a fifty-five-foot schooner built in Hong Kong. As a "great favor," Inoue Kaoru, then minister of foreign affairs, granted them permission to call at ports still closed to foreign ships.[17] Their sailing adventure ended tragically on the night of October 16, when a typhoon destroyed *The Loiterer.* Although Longfellow, Weld, and their crew were on shore in Shimoda at the time, their ship and much of its contents, including souvenirs the two men had acquired en route, were lost. Although the nature of Longfellow's acquisitions is unknown, it is likely that they differed from those he purchased during his first trip.

Globe-trotters of the 1860s and 1870s had little guidance in making their purchases, but in succeeding decades, information about Japanese art became readily available in many forms. Guidebooks of the 1880s included lists of representative arts and crafts the tourist might wish to buy as souvenirs, as well as informative synopses of the historical development of Japanese art and its leading schools and artists.[18] By 1894, *Murray's* popular *Handbook of Japan* (already into its fourth edition) even featured a glossary identifying the major deities of the Buddhist pantheon and celebrated personages of Japanese history appearing as subjects in Japanese arts.[19] To better cater to the tourist trade, crafts shops had hired bilingual staff and opened their workshops to visitors. When Longfellow and Weld left their ship for two weeks to travel to Kyoto, Nara, and Osaka, they visited manufacturers of cloisonné, gold and silver inlay work, embroidery, and pottery. In Nara, during his 1891 trip, Longfellow purchased two "sword canes" after watching swords being made by a member of "the famous old house of Sanjo Munechika."[20] Of the many antique shops outside Yokohama described in guidebooks, Yamanaka's in Osaka became a particular favorite among globe-trotters since its name was familiar through its branches in New York, Paris, and Boston. Longfellow and Weld visited this firm as well as that of Ikeda, one of its Kyoto rivals.

Although Longfellow does not mention going there, the permanent museum built in Tokyo's Ueno district in 1882 was also instrumental in altering the tourist's experience and understanding of Japan. When it was inaugurated, it presented a distinctly colonial face, having been designed in Indo-Moorish style by the British architect Josiah Conder (1852–1920), then teaching at the Tokyo Industrial College. As a division of the Department of Agriculture and Commerce, the museum initially had an economic, not artistic, focus. It was a *hakubutsukan,* an institution founded primarily for the study and promotion of the industrial arts and natural sciences, not a *bijutsukan,* a gallery of fine arts. Initially, its collections were limited, consisting of a miscellany of foreign articles designed to instruct the Japanese public about science and technology, archaeological artifacts, a few purchases from Buddhist temples, and a small number of crafts that had been displayed abroad in the context of the international expositions. This changed in 1889, after the museum came under the auspices of the Imperial Household Ministry and was renamed Teikoku Hakubutsukan (Imperial Museum). In keeping with the prevailing ideal of "civilization and enlightenment," displays now aimed to make intelligible nineteenth-century ideas of evolutionary progress. These featured Japanese artifacts, laid out chronologically from ancient to modern. An imperial bullock cart, imperial autographs, and facsimiles of ancient objects used at the court underscored the centrality of the emperor and the aristocracy to ideas of national identity. Like museums in Europe and the United States, the museum in Tokyo also exhibited many reproductions, most notably copies of eighth-century frescoes from Nara's ancient Hōryūji temple. The museum's Fine Arts Department, located on the second floor and featuring paintings in the form of hanging and horizontal scrolls and manuscripts, as well as ancient masks and images, was subsumed within this larger ideological program.[21] Taken in their totality, these displays were intended to convey to museum visitors of all nationalities that Japan was a forward-looking nation with a long and distinguished cultural history.

Developments in the United States, and especially Boston, were also creating a new framework for envisioning Japan. While the Imperial Museum was using the creations of the Japanese people to promote national identity, the Boston Museum of Fine Arts sought to promote civic identity through the acquisition and display of articles of other nations and cultures, including Japan. Its own collection of European oil paintings, statues, and decorative arts being still rather limited, it was heavily dependent on loans, photographs, and plaster casts of famous European works. When the museum began acquiring examples of Japanese arts and crafts soon after its founding, these were primarily ceramics, lacquer, and bronzes purchased from the Philadelphia Centennial Exposition or available through dealers in Europe. The first major exhibition of Japanese art, held in 1880, consisted of 111 examples of Japanese lacquer, 35 textiles and embroideries, 6 examples of wood and ivory carving, 19 bronzes, 18 ceramics, 116 swords, and 177 netsuke on loan from William Sturgis Bigelow.[22] The second exhibition of Bigelow's collection held in 1881, a year before he departed for Japan, also featured articles purchased in Europe and the United States.[23]

At a time when New York was outpacing Boston economically, the museum became the site of a symbolic struggle between old and new money and cultural values. Boston positioned itself as the "city on the hill," an American Athens, where aesthetic taste rather than money assured "distinction." Its citizens' zeal to assemble the nation's foremost collection of Japanese art was part of this larger discourse, since Japan was long idealized as an artistic nation, where artists were not yet caught up in the materialism of modern Western society. Art, moreover, was thought to embody important social and moral values that could improve the character of the increasingly large local immigrant population while at the same time consolidating the authority of the elite who owned or controlled it. As the sociologist Paul DiMaggio has written of the beginnings of this and other cultural institutions in Boston: "The distinction between high and popular culture . . . emerged in the period between 1850 and 1900 out of the efforts of urban elites to build organizational forms that, first, isolated high culture and, second, differentiated it from popular culture. . . . By 1910, high and popular culture were encountered far less frequently in the same settings."[24]

In 1886, following his return from Japan, Weld purchased the bulk of Fenollosa's collection of Japanese paintings, with the understanding that they would eventually go to the Boston Museum. Expectations that Bigelow also would donate his collection led architects involved in the museum's expansion to reserve two large rooms on the second floor for Japanese art.[25] After Bigelow had placed his collection on deposit in the museum, Fenollosa was hired as the first curator of Japanese art. Two years later, Morse, whose encyclopedic collection, already on loan, was purchased by the museum, was named Keeper of Japanese Pottery. He held this position even as he continued to serve as director of the Peabody Museum of Salem, a position he had assumed in 1880. Public attitudes toward the museum's emphasis on Japanese art may have been more complex and contradictory than we now know, but the Weld and Bigelow families' generous donations to the building fund, as well as the families' places in Boston society, no doubt muted any overt opposition to what was still an unusual emphasis on Japanese art.

The 1890 report issued by the Committee on the Museum underscores the pride in these collections:

> No public museum offers so extraordinary a display of Japanese art as is found in the Japanese room and the corridor adjoining, for which we are indebted to Dr. Wm. Sturgis Bigelow and Dr. Chas. G. Weld. The sword guards, the ornaments of gold, and other metal work of exhaustless fertility of design, and remarkable delicacy of workmanship, the carved ivories, netsukes, and bronzes, panels of wood-carving illustrating the legends of Buddha and the fairy tales of old Japan, the textiles, the superb lacquers, will be a perpetual delight to all interested in the creations of that most artistic of all nations.
>
> In the corridor is hung a small portion of the Fenollosa Collection of Japanese paintings, lent to the Museum by Dr. Weld; it combines a complete historical series of original works, illustrating all the schools, and nearly all the leading masters of Japanese pictorial art, from its origin in the VIIth century to the present day. . . .
>
> Here, too, is the Morse Collection of Japanese pottery. In bringing the collection together, Mr. Morse has endeavored to secure specimens of every province in which pottery has been made, including work of every

age; also the work of every maker and every variety of mark; and further, to secure every kind of object made in pottery.[26]

The ideological underpinnings of the extensive display of Japanese art in Boston were complex. As the art historian Michael Baxandall has written: "It seems axiomatic that it is not possible to exhibit objects without putting a construction upon them . . . to select and put forward any item for display, as something worth looking at, as interesting, is a statement not only about the object, but the culture it comes from."[27] In reserving such a large space for Japanese art, Boston was at the vanguard of the movement to promote its study on its own terms. Yet by the same token, the Museum of Fine Arts sought to capitalize on the prestige and authority that followed from possession of authentic treasures from another culture. Japanese art provided Boston with an idiom to compete with other American and European museums. By its artistic choices the museum was also commenting on and implicitly criticizing contemporary developments in Europe. Many of Boston's Japanophile collectors and civic leaders were not progressives: Bigelow and Fenollosa were romantic aesthetes who extolled Japanese art as an alternative to the decadence of its European counterparts. They deplored the very modernist trends that the discovery of Japan had stimulated among some American and European painters.

Fenollosa also used his post at the museum to advance his career as a professional art historian, dealer, and specialist on Japan. Under his direction, the Museum of Fine Arts promoted the Buddhist arts and identification of individual painters, media, and period styles in a way that was still relatively new in the United States. In so doing the museum contributed to the Euro-American reevaluation of Japanese painting within the hierarchy of Japanese arts. The rise of the modern understanding of Japanese art was not the product of any one person, institution, or nation, of course. This process of category formation was incremental and intimately connected with the dynamics of international cultural politics. International acknowledgment that Japanese painters and sculptors deserved the same recognition as their European counterparts coincidentally came about in the year of Charley's death, when Japan was invited for the first time at Chicago's International Exposition to exhibit in the Palace of Fine Arts rather than the Hall of Science and Industry.

Collecting was part of the ideology of imperialism that globe-trotters carried with them in their travels around the world. It combines an attitude or set of beliefs with practices, institutions, and structures that vary from one person to another and from period to period. In the twenty years since Charley first visited Japan this ideology had undergone considerable change and elaboration. By the year of his death, museums, exhibitions, and art professionals increasingly guided the production and consumption of Japanese art both within Japan and abroad. Private collections were being dispersed and reconstituted in museums, where they assumed new public meanings. While individuals could and did still decide what to acquire, what meanings to ascribe, and how to display them, many sought professional or institutional certification. As art history became an autonomous discipline, its practitioners saw themselves as answerable only to their fellow professionals. The views of the professional overrode those of the once admired *amateur d'art*.

Charley Longfellow's attitudes toward Japan represent one specific moment of this evolutionary process. He did not participate in the culturally legitimizing activities of the younger generation of Boston collectors. His "Japan Room" was a self-referential tableau. As arranged and displayed in the Longfellow house, his curios commemorated a family. Collecting remained for him a kind of trophy hunt, focusing on the chase and capture of curios. "We captured a few swords and kakimonos, as souvenirs," he wrote during his 1885 visit.[28] During the same trip, Charley proudly declared to his sister that his tattoos were "artistic." The friends he later guided to "his" tattooist, Horichō, may have shared this view, as did other Americans of the time. This did not mean they accepted tattoos as Art, however. Tattoos shaped personal identity by aestheticizing the body, but they had no exchange value for anyone other than the individual who exhibited them.

Charley Longfellow's activities direct our attention to a key historical juncture in America's relationship with Japan, when the terms of this cultural encounter were being reconfigured in response to a multitude of forces whose impact has been previously ignored or overlooked. Globe-trotters played an instrumental role in this process by appropriating and protecting the material traces of Japanese culture, even as Japanese themselves were beginning to mythologize their own past.

Tourist photographs, curios, and tattoos, however, did not bring full unmediated access to the "authentic" Japan. Authenticity, like memory, is elusive and unreliable. The camera is an instrument that immortalizes the living culture, but it is an imperfect one, since photographs are contingent on the specific historical social and cultural contexts of their creators and viewers. To look at photographs, curios, or tattoos is necessarily a retrospective act. Collecting and display involve choices, displacement, and translation that simultaneously invoke and revoke the past. Collections, moreover, constantly disclose new meanings. Clothing and tattoos tell a cultural story, but it may be a fictional one. By donning samurai attire or having oneself tattooed one may become "japanned," but this does not make one Japanese.

Charley Longfellow reaches out beyond the nineteenth century because he invites us to into an imaginative world that still resonates. By playing out exotic and heroic identities to perform himself, he engages the modern viewer in a dialogue about cultural authenticity that is as contentious today as it was during his lifetime. Longfellow reminds us that, then as now, authenticity is a site of struggle in the name of different agendas and ideologies, one that involves constant mediation between the forces of loss and recovery.

NOTES

Introduction

1. Christine Wallace Laidlaw, ed. *Charles Appleton Longfellow: Twenty Months in Japan, 1871–1873.* (Cambridge, Mass.: Friends of the Longfellow House, 1998), 22. (Hereafter abbreviated as *CAL.*) Unless otherwise indicated, all information about Longfellow's experiences in Japan are based on the journals and letters reproduced herein.

2. Louise L. Stevenson, *The Victorian Homefront: American Thought and Culture 1860–1880* (New York: Twayne, 1991), 64.

3. See Wayne H. Morgan, *New Muses: Art in American Culture, 1865–1920* (Norman: University of Oklahoma Press, 1978).

4. William Hosley, *The Japan Idea* (Hartford, Conn.: Wadsworth Atheneum, 1990).

5. See, for instance, the illustrations accompanying the article titled "Our Japanese Visitors," *Harper's Weekly,* May 19, 1860.

6. Americanist contributions to the field include: John Ashmead, *The Idea of Japan 1853–1895: Japan as described by American and other Travellers from the West* (New York: Garland, 1987) and Christine Wallace Laidlaw, *The American Reaction to Japanese Art, 1853–1876* (Rutgers University, Ph.D. dissertation, 1996). Also useful is Hina Hirayama, *A True Japanese Taste: Construction of Knowledge about Japan in Boston 1880–1900* (Boston University, Ph.D. dissertation, 1999). For an account of the second generation of Japanophiles that included Morse, Fenollosa, and Bigelow, see Christopher Benfey's *The Great Wave: Gilded Age Misfits, Japanese Eccentrics, and the Opening of Old Japan* (New York: Random House, 2003).

7. Horioka Yasuko mentions Longfellow in passing. See her *Okakura Tenshin: Asia bunka senyō no senkusha* (Tokyo: Yoshikawa kobunkan, 1974), 35–39 and 63–65. His travels in Japan are also discussed briefly in the context of Longfellow's writings in Sanehide Kodama, *American Poetry and Japanese Culture* (Hamden, Conn.: Archon Books, 1984), 15–18.

8. In Katherine C. Grier's words, "Victorian" may also be characterized as "the Anglo-American, transatlantic, bourgeois culture of industrializing Western civilization." See her *Culture and Comfort: Parlor Making and Middle-Class Identity, 1850–1930* (Washington, D.C.: Smithsonian Institution Press, 1988), 3.

9. Letter from Charles to Alice Longfellow, 1885 (no date). Longfellow National Historic Site, Cambridge, Mass. (Hereafter LNHS.)

10. Bigelow's address and a reference to the party in 1885 appear in a pocket notebook belonging to Charley that contains addresses and other miscellaneous information (LNHS).

11. Lawrence W. Levine, *Highbrow/Lowbrow: The Emergence of Cultural Hierarchy in America* (Cambridge: Harvard University Press, 1988), 120.

12. Dorothy G. Wayman, *Edward Sylvester Morse: A Biography* (Cambridge: Harvard University Press, 1942), 234.

13. See Musée Cernuschi, comp., *Henri Cernuschi, 1821–1896: Voyageur et collectionneur* (Paris: Paris-musées, 1998) and the articles based on a colloquium at the Maison Franco-japonaise, Tokyo, published in the journal *Ebisu* (numéro hors série, hiver 1998).

14. Richard Handler, "Authenticity," *Anthropology Today* (1986), 4.

1. Globe-Trotting in Japan

1. See annotations in Jules Verne, *Around the World in Eighty Days* (New York: Viking 1996), 97.

2. Aimé Humbert (1819–1900), "Le Japon," in *Le Tour du Monde: Nouveau Journal des Voyages* (Paris: Hachette, 1869), 388–401. *Le Japon Illustré* (1870) appeared in English as *Japan and the Japanese Illustrated*, translated by Mrs. Cashel Hoey and edited by H. W. Bates (New York: Appleton, 1874). This was the edition I consulted. It is also possible that Verne saw the troupe of Japanese jugglers touring the United States and Europe in 1867. See "The Japanese Jugglers," in *Journal of Civilizations*, New York, June 15, 1878.

3. Ludovic de Beauvoir (1846–1929), *Pekin, Yeddo, San Francisco: Voyage autour du monde.* 3 vols. (Paris: H. Plon, 1871–72), and in English *A Voyage around the World.* Translated from the French by Agnes and Helen Stephenson. 3 vols. (London: John Murray, 1870–72).

4. Jacques Siegfried, *Seize mois autour du monde, 1867–1869, et particulièrement aux Indes, en Chine et au Japon* (Paris: J. Hetzel, 1869).

5. Joseph-Alexander von Hubner (1811–92), *Promenade autour du monde, 1871* (Paris: Hachette, 1873); English edition: Joseph Alexander, Baron von Hubner, *A Ramble Round the World, 1871*, translated by Lady Herbert. 2 vols. (London: Macmillan, 1874).

6. Toshio Yokoyama, *Japan in the Victorian Mind: A Study of Stereotyped Images of a Nation, 1850–80* (London: Macmillan, 1987), 116.

7. See John Mertz, "Internalizing Social Difference: Kanagaki Robun's *Shanks' Mare to the Western Seas*," in *New Directions in the Study of Meiji Japan*, edited by Helen Hardacre with Adam L. Kern (Leiden: Brill, 1997), 219–28.

8. J. Scott Miller, *Adaptations of Western Literature in Meiji Japan* (New York: Palgrave, 2001), 18.

9. Cited in Yokoyama, *Japan in the Victorian Mind: A Study of Stereotyped Images of a Nation, 1850–80*, 76.

10. The term *bunmei kaika* was widely used in the 1870s to refer to the Western social, political, economic, and cultural institutions being promoted by the new Meiji government.

11. Edward Dorr Prime, who made a world tour in 1869, noted that while the actual travel time had been reduced to seventy-five days, most people devoted a year to the round-the-world journey. See his *Around the World: Sketches of Travel through Many Lands and over Many Seas.* (New York: Harper Bros., 1872), vii (hereafter referred to as *Around the World*).

12. Charles Carleton Coffin, *Our New Way Round the World* (London: Sampson, Low, Son, and Marston, 1869), 510.

13. Lynne Withey, *Grand Tours and Cook's Tours: A History of Leisure Travel, 1750–1915* (New York: William Morrow, 1997), 271.

14. Benjamin Robbins Curtis, *Dottings round the Circle* (Boston: Osgood, 1876).

15. William E. Griffis, *The Mikado's Empire* (New York: Harper Bros., 1876), 339. Griffis became one of America's leading interpreters of Japan. This book went into ten printings.

16. Basil Hall Chamberlain, *Japanese Things: Being Notes on Various Subjects Connected with Japan* (Rutland, Vt.: Charles E. Tuttle, 1971), 212–15. This book was titled *Things Japanese* when first published in 1890. Chamberlain (1850–1935), a leading British interpreter of Japan, went there in 1873 to teach at the Imperial Naval College.

17. For an example of this antagonism,

see Emile Guimet, *Promenades japonaises* (Paris: G. Charpentier, 1878), 31–33.

18. This is the main point made by Daniel Boorstin in "From Traveler to Tourist: The Lost Art of Travel," in *The Image: A Guide to Pseudo-Events in America* (New York: Harper Colophon, 1967), 77–117.

19. For nuanced discussions of this issue, see James Buzard, *The Beaten Track: European Tourism, Literature, and the Ways of Culture, 1800–1918* (Oxford: Clarendon, 1993), and Jonathan Culler, "The Semiotics of Tourism," in *American Journal of Semiotics* 1 (1981): 127–40.

20. Billie Melman, *Women's Orients: English Women and the Middle East, 1718–1918, Sexuality, Religion, Work* (Ann Arbor: University of Michigan Press, 1982), 102.

21. See James Clifford, "On Ethnographic Allegory," in *Writing Culture: The Poetics and Politics of Ethnography*, edited by James Clifford and George Marcus (Berkeley: University of California Press, 1986), 112–15.

22. See Harold F. Smith, *American Travellers Abroad: A Bibliography of Accounts Published Before 1900* (Carbondale: Southern Illinois University, 1969).

23. Cited in Mary Suzanne Schriber, *Writing Home: American Women Abroad, 1830–1920* (Charlottesville: University Press of Virginia, 1997), 21.

24. William Perry Fogg, *Round the World Letters from Japan, China, India, and Egypt* (Cleveland, Ohio: William Perry Fogg, 1872), introduction.

25. Charles Carleton Coffin, *Our New Way Round the World*, 524.

26. Withey, *Grand Tours and Cook's Tours: A History of Leisure Travel 1750–1915*, 61.

27. Letter dated September 21, 1868, whereabouts of original unknown, photocopy in LNHS.

28. William Simpson, *Meeting of the Sun: A Journey around the World* (Boston: Estes and Lauriat, 1877), 309.

29. Prime, *Around the World*, 114.

30. Cited in Yokoyama, *Japan in the Victorian Mind: A Study of Stereotyped Images of a Nation, 1850–80*, 67.

31. For an example see Melissa Banta and Susan Taylor, eds., *A Timely Encounter: Nineteenth-Century Photographs of Japan* (Cambridge, Mass.: Peabody Museum Press, 1988), 39.

32. See Allen Hockley, "Expectation and Authenticity in Meiji Tourist Photography" (manuscript, 11–14), forthcoming in *Challenging the Past and Present: The Transformation of Japanese Art in the Nineteenth Century*.

33. Raphael Pumpelly, *Across America and Asia: Notes of a Five Years Journey Around the World and of Residence in Arizona, Japan, and China* (New York: Leypoldt and Holt, 1870). For Griffis, see note 15 above.

34. Cited in Masao Miyoshi, *As We Saw Them: The First Japanese Embassy to the United States (1860)* (Berkeley: University of California Press, 1979), 30.

35. *Catalogue or guide book of Barnum's American Museum, New York: containing descriptions and illustrations of the various wonders and curiosities of the world* (1860), 37 and 101–2.

36. Sir Ernest Satow, *A Diplomat in Japan: An Inner History of the Japanese Reformation* (Rutland, Vt.: Charles E. Tuttle, 1983), 25.

37. Margaretha Weppner, *The North Star and the Southern Cross*, 2 vols. (London: Sampson Low, Marston, Low, and Searle, 1876), vol. 1, 234–35.

38. For discussion of gendered travel see William W. Stowe, *Going Abroad: European Travel in Nineteenth-Century American Culture* (Princeton: Princeton University Press, 1994), especially chapter 7. See also Schriber, *Writing Home: American Women Abroad, 1830–1920*.

39. Weppner, *The North Star and the Southern Cross*, vol. 1, 184–95.

40. Ibid., 231–32.

41. Griffis, *The Mikado's Empire*, 371.

42. Hugh Cortazzi, *Victorians in Japan* (London: Althone Press, 1987), 275–89.

43. William E. Griffis, *The Mikado's Empire*, 551–61.

44. *The Journal of Richard Henry Dana, Jr.,* edited by Robert F. Lucid, 3 vols. (Cambridge: Harvard University Press, 1968), vol. 3, 1018.

45. Ibid., vol. 1, xxxviii.

46. Pocket diary, LNHS.

47. See Ishiguro Keishō, *Meijiki no porunogurafi* (Pornography in the Meiji era) (Tokyo: Shinchōsha, 1996).

48. *Harper's Weekly* (December 18, 1858), 816.

49. Andrew Carnegie, *Round the World* (New York: Doubleday, Doran, 1884), 37.

50. Stowe, *Going Abroad: European Travel in Nineteenth-Century American Culture*, 29.

51. William Elliot Griffis, *The Tokio Guide* (Yokohama, 1873), 5.

52. Ibid., 6.

53. See Curtis, *Dottings Round the Circle*, 84–91.

54. *William H. Seward's Travels Around the World,* edited by Olive Risley Seward (New York: Appleton, 1873), 45. See also Andrew Carnegie, *Round the World*, 52–53.

55. Carnegie, *Round the World*, 45.

56. Cited in Neil Harris, "All the World a Melting Pot," in *Mutual Images: Essays in American Japanese Relations,* edited by Akira Iriye (Cambridge: Harvard University Press, 1975), 33.

57. Curtis, *Dottings round the Circle*, 54. Emory Upton (1839–81), who was sent by the U.S. government to study the military, sailed on the same ship as Curtis, and went sightseeing with him in Japan. See Emory Upton, *The armies of Asia and Europe: embracing official reports on the armies of Japan, China, Persia, Italy, Russia, Austria, Germany, France, and England accompanied by letters descriptive of a journey from Japan to the Caucasus* (New York: Appleton, 1878).

58. Prime, *Around the World*, x.

59. Ibid., 121.

60. *The Journal of Richard Henry Dana, Jr.,* edited by Robert F. Lucid, vol. 1, xxxiv.

61. The lecture was on Sept. 29, 1860. See Samuel Longfellow, ed., *Life of Henry Wadsworth Longfellow*, 3 vols. (Boston: Ticknor, 1886), vol. 2, 407.

62. *The Letters of Henry Wadsworth Longfellow,* edited by Andrew Hilen, 6 vols. (Cambridge: Harvard University Press, 1982), vol. 6, 663–64.

63. See Walter Craven, "Winckworth Allan Gay, Boston Painter of the White Mountains, Paris, the Nile and Mount Fujiyama," *Antiques* (November 1981): 1222–32. Gay's brother Arthur was in Kobe during Charley's stay in Japan. See Laidlaw, *CAL*, 118.

64. See note 24, this chapter.

65. The Phillips Library of the Peabody Essex Museum has nine stereocards by Metcalf, whom Morse met on the ship from San Francisco to Yokohama. The two men traveled together while in Japan, most notably to Nikkō. See entries in Morse's diary from June 17, 1877, and following. (My thanks to Luke Gartlan for drawing my attention to this material.)

66. Enoch Marvin, *To the East by Way of the West* (St. Louis: Brand, Brand, 1878), introduction, 15.

67. Adiss Emmet Carr, *All the Way round; or What a boy saw and heard on his way round the world. A book for young people and older ones with young hearts* (New York: Appleton, 1876), 37–38, and 191.

68. Carnegie, *Round the World*, esp. 44–45.

69. *William H. Seward's Travels Around the World*, 63.

70. Jean Edward Smith, *Grant* (New York: Simon and Schuster, 2001), 607.

71. John Russell Young, *Around the World with General Grant: A Narrative of the Visit of General U.S. Grant, Ex-President of the United States to Various Countries in Europe, Asia, and Africa in 1877, 1878, 1879*, 2 vols. (New York: The American News Department, 1879).

72. See Richard T. Chang, "General Grant's 1879 Visit to Japan," *Monumenta Nipponica* 24/4 (1969), 373–92.

73. Young, *Around the World with Gen-*

eral Grant, 569–70, cited in Miller, *Adaptations of Western Literature in Meiji Japan,* 45.

74. Weppner and Bird negotiated foreign travel using contrasting strategies. While the former adopted the style of a well-bred "lady" dependent on gentlemen, the latter became an honorary male, by seeking to prove she could endure the physical rigor of solo travel well off the beaten track. For Weppner's narrative, see note 37, this chapter. See also Isabella Bird, *Unbeaten Tracks in Japan* (Rutland, Vt.: Charles E. Tuttle, 1973). This travelogue was first published in 1880.

75. Ellen Hardin Walworth, *An Old World as Seen Through Young Eyes; or, travels around the world* (New York: Appleton, 1877), ix.

76. Lucy Seaman Bainbridge, *Round the World Letters* (Boston: D. Lothrop, 1882), preface.

77. Ibid., 14.

78. Coffin, *Our New Way Round the World,* 440, 443, 423.

79. Ibid., 509.

80. Walworth, *An Old World as Seen Through Young Eyes; or, travels around the world,* ix.

81. Ibid., 281.

82. Larzer Ziff, *Return Passages: Great American Travel Writing 1780–1910* (New Haven: Yale University Press, 2000), 144–54.

83. See Arrell Morgan Gibson, completed with the assistance of John S. Whitehead, *Yankees in Paradise: The Pacific Basin Frontier* (Albuquerque: University of New Mexico Press, 1993), 351–66.

84. Simpson, *Meeting of the Sun: A Journey around the World,* 344.

85. Carnegie, *Round the World,* x.

86. Bainbridge, the wife of a protestant minister, was among those who disputed its "sweet and wonderful expression," describing it instead as a "stupid silly stare." See her *Round the World Letters,* 54–55.

87. Algeron B. Mitford, *Tales of Old Japan,* 2 vols. (London: Macmillan, 1871).

88. Letter dated January 11, 1860, LNHS.

89. Prime, *Around the World,* 113.

90. Walworth, *An Old World as Seen Through Young Eyes; or, travels around the world,* 288.

91. Marvin, *To the East by Way of the West,* 24.

92. Ibid., 21.

93. Cited in Young, *Around the World with General Grant,* 515. Young was quoting from the poet's *Kéramos* (1878).

94. For a discussion of this aesthetic principle and its impact, see Christopher Hussey, *The Picturesque: Studies in a Point of View* (London: Frank Cass, 1967).

95. Bainbridge, *Round the World Letters,* 53–54.

96. Prime, *Around the World,* 110.

97. Marvin, *To the East by Way of the West,* 69.

98. Walworth, *An Old World as Seen Through Young Eyes; or, travels around the world,* 285.

99. *The Journal of Richard Henry Dana, Jr.,* vol. 3, 1030.

100. For a discussion of these issues see Elisa Evett, *The Critical Reception of Japanese Art in Late Nineteenth Century Europe* (Ann Arbor, Mich.: UMI Research Press, 1982).

101. Carr, *All the Way round; or What a boy saw and heard on his way round the world. A book for young people and older ones with young hearts,* 191.

102. See note 16, this chapter.

103. See letter of June 3, 1866, in *The Letters of Henry Wadsworth Longfellow,* vol. 5, 55; also Richard O'Connor, *The Scandalous Mr. Bennett* (New York: Doubleday, 1962), 54–60.

104. On the trans-Atlantic trip, see Susan Hale, *Life and Letters of Thomas Gold Appleton* (New York: Appleton, 1885), 327; on the trip to Russia and Paris, see Brevet Nathan Appleton, *Russian Life and Society* (Boston: Murray and Emory, 1904).

105. Dickens' wrote this letter at Gad's Hill Place, Monday, July 6, 1868; LNHS.

106. See Comte de Gabriac, *Course*

humoristique autour du monde: Indes, Chine, Japon (Paris: Michel Levy Frères, 1872), 130–31.

107. Longfellow's experiences in India are covered in seven journals dating from October 10, 1869, through January 25, 1870. Christine Laidlaw kindly made available to me the portions of these as well as several letters that she has transcribed. In addition, there is a combination sketchbook/journal from October 1868 to January 1869. The photographs are contained in three albums with engraved titles "Voyage in India and Kashmir 1869." All are in LNHS.

108. See his 1855 sketchbook, LNHS.

109. Alexander Hesler's daguerreotypes of the Northwest, most notably his views of Minnehaha Falls in Minnesota Territory, were catalysts for *Hiawatha*. Robert Taft, *Photography and the American Scene: A Social History 1839–89* (New York: Dover, 1964), 111–12 and 98.

110. Longfellow's account of his transcontinental journey is covered in a journal dating May 8–28, 1871.

111. The 1860 sketchbook is in LNHS.

112. See George Henry Preble, *The Opening of Japan: A Diary of Discovery in the Far East, 1863–1856* (Norman: University of Oklahoma Press, 1962).

113. Longfellow met Taylor in 1846. The two visited and corresponded until the latter's death in 1876. In a letter to Charley dated Dec. 13, 1866, he mentions a visit to Longfellow (*The Letters of Henry Wadsworth Longfellow*, vol. 5, 98).

114. Louise Hall Tharp, *The Appletons of Beacon Hill* (Boston: Little, Brown, 1973), 304.

115. Walter Muir Whitehill, *Museum of Fine Arts Boston: A Centennial History*, 2 vols. (Cambridge: Harvard University Press, 1977) 1, 52–53.

116. Thomas G. Appleton, *Windfalls* (Boston: Roberts Brothers, 1878), 3.

117. Laidlaw, *CAL*, 30.

118. Ibid., 28.

119. *New York Times*, September 21, 1871.

120. See letter of Sept. 10, 1866, in *The*

Letters of Henry Wadsworth Longfellow, vol. 5, 79.

121. See letter of Dec. 8, 1878, *The Letters of Henry Wadsworth Longfellow*, vol. 6, 413. See also O'Connor, *The Scandalous Mr. Bennett*, 125–27.

122. In a letter to his father dated "N.Y. Tuesday, 1871, written from the Bennetts' 425 Fifth Avenue residence," he notes, "I am beginning to doubt whether I shall have money enough to get to Japan with if I can't manage to negotiate a new loan." This letter is in the collection of Houghton Library, Harvard University.

123. Griffis, *The Mikado's Empire*, 371.

124. See letters from Henry to Charley on January 18, 1873, and November 19, 1873, in *Letters of Henry Wadsworth Longfellow*, vol. 5, 646 and 693.

125. This trip, from March to April 1875 is covered in an untitled and much edited handwritten travelogue that Charley may have intended for publication, LNHS.

126. This trip is covered in two journals, dated July 13–August 10, 1885, and August 16–October 10, 1885. My thanks to Christine Laidlaw for making available to me her transcriptions. The last trip is covered in a journal of January 2–May 26, 1891, transcribed in part by Kumiko Yamada. Both are in LNHS.

127. His journal entry of May 12, 1871, notes that he carried one hundred guns during the transcontinental journey, LNHS.

128. Edward Wagenknecht, *Henry Wadsworth Longfellow: Portrait of an American Humanist* (New York: Oxford University Press, 1966), 180.

129. Letter from Edith Longfellow to Mary King Longfellow, November 18, 1870, LNHS.

130. On the nude bathing episode, see Andrew Hilen, "Charley Longfellow Goes to War," *Harvard Library Bulletin* (Spring 1960), 80–81; on the Bennett affair, see O'Connor, *The Scandalous Mr. Bennett*, 129–44.

131. On his Civil War career, see Andrew Hilen, "Charley Longfellow Goes to War,"

Harvard Library Bulletin (Spring 1960): 59–81, and (Winter 1960): 283–303.

132. Nathan Appleton, *Russian Life and Society*, 159.

133. See Jackson Lears, *No Place of Grace: Antimodernism and the Transformation of American Culture 1880–1920* (New York: Pantheon, 1981), chapter 6.

134. Letter from Edith Longfellow to Mary King Longfellow, Nov. 5, 1875, LNHS.

135. Letter from Edith Longfellow to Mary King Longfellow, Oct. 24, 1875, LNHS.

136. Ik Marvel, *Reveries of a Bachelor* (New York: Scribner, 1856), 19–20. I am grateful to Jay Fliegelman for bringing this influential publication to my attention.

2. Picturing Japan

1. See John Urry, *The Tourist Gaze* (London: Sage, 1990).

2. The list is reproduced in John Clark, *Japanese Exchanges in Art, 1850s–1930s, with Britain, Continental Europe, and the USA* (Sidney: Power Publications, 2001), illustration number 8 (hereafter abbreviated as *Japanese Exchanges in Art*).

3. Laidlaw, *CAL,* 199.

4. On early photographers, see Naomi Izakura and Torin Boyd, *Portraits in Sepia from the Japanese Carte-de-visite collection of Torin Boyd and Naomi Izakura* (Tokyo: Asahi Sonorama, 2000).

5. For a chronology of Beato's career, see John Clark, *Japanese Exchanges in Art*, 89–120.

6. For his chronology, see Clark, *Japanese Exchanges in Art*, 121–88. For examples of his work, see Chantal Edel and Linda Cloverdale, trans., *Once upon a Time: Visions of Old Japan. Photographs by Felice Beato and Baron Raimund von Stillfried* (New York: Friendly Press, 1986), and Banta and Taylor, eds., *A Timely Encounter: Nineteenth-Century Photographs of Japan*. It should be noted that many of the photographic attributions in these publications

are open to question.

7. Clark, *Japanese Exchanges in Art*, 136 and 142.

8. See Isobel Crombie, "China, 1860: A Photographic Album by Felice Beato," *History of Photography* 11, no. 1 (Jan.–March 1987): 25–37.

9. On Wirgman, See Clark, *Japanese Exchanges in Art*, 5–58.

10. William W. Stowe, *Going Abroad: European Travel in Nineteenth-Century American Culture*, 29.

11. Prime, *Around the World*, 116.

12. Simpson, *Meeting the Sun*, 315.

13. See *Shashin torai no koro* (The Advent of Photography in Japan) (Tokyo: Tokyo Metropolitan Museum of Photography, Hakodate Museum of Art, and Tokyo Metropolitan Foundation for History and Culture, 1997).

14. This characterization was used by Oliver Wendell Holmes in "The Stereoscope and the Stereograph." See *Classic Essays on Photography*, edited by Alan Trachtenberg (New Haven, Conn.: Leete's Island Books, 1980), 74.

15. Ibid., 88.

16. Von Hubner, *A Ramble Round the World, 1871,* vol. 1, 457–58.

17. Von Hubner, *A Ramble Round the World, 1871,* vol. 2, 68.

18. Coffin, *Our New Way Round the World*, 451.

19. See Heinz K. Henisch and Bridget A. Henisch, *The Painted Photograph 1839–1914: Origins, Techniques, Aspirations* (University Park: Pennsylvania State University Press, 1996).

20. See Arthur H. Crow, *Highways and Byeways in Japan* (London: Sampson, Low, Marston, Searle, and Rivington, 1883), 15, and M. Bickersteth, *Japan as We Saw It* (London: Sampson, Low, Marston, and Company, 1893), 93–94. I thank Allen Hockley for drawing my attention to these sources. The Italian photographer Adolfo Farsari also wrote glowingly of the Japanese colorists in his employ. See Elena dal Pra, "L'Avventura Giapponese di Adolfo Farsari," *Il Giappone* 33 (1993), 52–54.

21. On the complex relationship between photography and painting in Japan, see Kinoshita Naoyuki, *Shashin garon: Shashin to kaiga no kekkon* (On Photographic Pictures: The Marriage of Photography and Painting) (Tokyo: Iwanami shoten, 1996).

22. Curtis, *Dottings Round the Circle,* 95–96.

23. See Donald Keene, "Portraits of the Emperor Meiji," *Impressions* 21 (1999): 17–30.

24. See Ikeda Atsushi, "Meiji no bunkazai kiroku: Yokoyama Matsusaburō; Ogawa Isshin" (Documenting cultural properties during the Meiji era: Yokoyama Matsusaburō and Ogawa Isshin) in Dainichi Art Center, comp., *Nihon shashin zenshū* (Compendium of Japanese photographs) (Tokyo: Shōgakkan, 1983), vol. 9, 149–55.

25. See Ozawa Takeshi, *Nihon no shashinshi: Bakumatsu no denpa kara meijiki made* (History of Japanese photography: From the Bakumatsu to the Meiji Eras) (Tokyo: Nikkon Kurabu, 1986), 158–65.

26. For photographs of an 1872 exhibition of products from Wakayama, see P. F. Kornicki, "Public Display and Changing Values: Early Meiji Exhibitions and their Precursors," *Monumenta Nipponica* (Summer 1994), 187.

27. Elmer Funkhouser, "T. Fukasawa Meiji Era Photographer," *Daruma* 10 (Spring 1996), 12.

28. Laidlaw, *CAL,* 27.

29. Ibid., 51.

30. See Yokohama kaikō shiryōkan, ed., *Bakumatsu Nihon no fūkei to hitobito: Ferikusu Beato Bakumatsu Nihon shashinshū* (Collection of photographs of Bakumatsu Japan by F. Beato) (Yokohama: Yokohama kaikō shiryō fukyū kyōkai, 1987).

31. See Humbert, *Japan and the Japanese Illustrated,* 170 and 177.

32. Laidlaw, *CAL,* 134.

33. Ibid., 135.

34. Dean MacCannell, *The Tourist: A New Theory of the Leisure Class* (Berkeley: University of California Press, 1999), 57.

35. Ibid., 91–107.

36. On the relationship between the photographic gaze, the flâneur, and tourist see Urry, *The Tourist Gaze,* 136–40.

37. The places photographed closely match those described by Captain Henry Craven St. John in his *Notes and Sketches from the Wild Coasts of Nipon, with Chapters on Cruising after Pirates in Chinese Waters* (Edinburgh: D. Douglas, 1880). Some of the illustrations in St. John's publication are based on the same photos in Nogootchi's album. Longfellow owned a copy of this publication.

38. See British Admiralty files ADM 38/7218, subsection SLVO. I am grateful to Sebastian Dobson for supplying this information. His research also brought to light an 1874 reference to a Noguchi Gen'nosuke, who worked as a photographer's assistant in Yokohama in 1874, but whether or not they are one and the same cannot be verified.

39. On photography in Hokkaidō, see Nihon shashinka kyōkai, comp., *Nihon shashinshi 1840–1945* (History of Japanese Photography 1840–1945) (Tokyo: Heibonsha, 1971), 362–63.

40. Ozawa Takeshi, *Nihon no shashinshi: Bakumatsu no denpa kara meijiki made,* 159–61.

41. Hugh Cortazzi, *Victorians in Japan: In and around the Treaty Ports,* 37. Holmes's comments were part of a larger discourse on the racial and ethnic origins of the Japanese.

42. Ibid., 44–45.

43. St. John, *Notes and Sketches from the Wild Coasts of Nipon, with Chapters on Cruising after Pirates in Chinese Waters,* 26.

44. See David L. Howell, "The Meiji State and the Logic of Ainu 'Protection,'" in *New Directions in the Study of Meiji Japan,* 612–34.

45. St. John, *Notes and Sketches from the Wild Coasts of Nipon, with Chapters on Cruising after Pirates in Chinese Waters,* 14–15, and Laidlaw, *CAL,* 51.

46. See Gwyniera Isaac, "Louis Agassiz's Photographs in Brazil: Separate Creations,"

History of Photography 21, no. 1 (Spring 1997): 3–11.

47. Laidlaw, *CAL*, 44.

48. Ibid., 48.

49. Hiroshige designed at least twenty-one series entitled Ōmi hakkei (Eight Views of Lake Biwa) during the 1830s (Charlotte von Rappard-Boon, *Catalogue of the Collection of Japanese Prints, Part IV: Hiroshige and the Utagawa School* [Amsterdam: Rijksmuseum, 1994], 25).

50. I am grateful to Luke Gartlan for alerting me to similarities in background between these photographs and others attributed to von Stillfried. Laidlaw has noted that Longfellow and von Stillfried were on the same ship (see *CAL*, 147).

51. Audrey Linkman, *The Victorians: Photographic Portraits* (London: Tauris Parke Books, 1993), 70–71.

52. Laidlaw, *CAL*, 158.

53. Ibid., 28.

54. Ibid., 178.

55. See Marvel, *Reveries of a Bachelor*, 15.

56. See Kawasaki Seirō, "Rikkyō gakkō no hasshōchi o motomete" (In search of the original location of Rikkyō school), *Toshi mondai* (1999/12): 77–92.

57. Griffis, *The Mikado's Empire*, 550.

58. John R. Black, *Young Japan: Yokohama and Yedo. A Narrative of the Settlement and the City from the Signing of the Treaties in 1868 to the Close of the Year 1879*, 2 vols. (London: Trubner, 1881), vol. 2, 101, 193.

59. Laidlaw, *CAL*, 174.

60. Ibid., 174.

61. Ibid., 158.

62. Ibid., 27.

63. Yanosuke went to the United States in 1872, returning after only seventeen months because of the death of his father. See Fred G. Notehelfer, *Japan through American Eyes: The Journal of Francis Hall, Kanagawa and Yokohama, 1859–66* (Princeton: Princeton University Press, 1992), 4.

64. Laidlaw, *CAL*, 7.

65. Her address is inscribed in the small pocket notebook he carried with him dur-ing his 1871–73 and 1885 journeys. She is identified as Ichikawa Hanna and, after Charley's departure, apparently worked at a teahouse named Momojiya in Mibu, Tochigi Prefecture. He mentions Osarto-san, "now a large girl and quite pretty, [who] came up from Mibu with her husband," in a journal entry dated June 8, 1891.

66. On the parasol as a pictorial trope see Julia Meech-Pekarik, *Rain and Snow: The Umbrella in Japanese Art* (New York: Japan Society, 1993).

67. Linkman, *The Victorians: Photographic Portraits*, 43.

68. Caption attached to photograph in the Spencer Collection, New York Public Library.

69. Ishiguro Keishō, "Warau shashin no rutsu o saguru" (In search of the roots of the photographic smile) in *Bakumatsu Meiji no omoshiro shashin* (Interesting photographs from the Bakumatsu and Meiji eras) (Tokyo: Heibonsha, 1996), 4–22.

70. Urry, *The Tourist Gaze*, 70.

71. See for instance Claudia Gabrielle Philipp, Dietmar Siegert, and Rainer Wick, *Felice Beato in Japan: Photographien zum Ende der Feudalzeit 1863–1873* (Munich: Edition Braus 1991), 180.

72. Ishiguro Keishō, *Zoku Bakumatsu Meiji no omoshiro shashin* (Further interesting photographs of the Bakukatsu and Meiji Eras) (Tokyo: Heibonsha, 1998), 15. The collector Ishiguro Keishichi was Keishō's father. He first published his collection in *Utsusareta bakumatsu* (Photographic records of the Bakumatsu Era) (Tokyo: 1960), vol. 1, 26–27 and 85.

73. This information appears on another photograph of Sokuhe in the collection.

74. Laidlaw, *CAL*, 113.

75. Ibid., 163.

76. See Allen Hockley, "Cameras, Photographs and Photography in Nineteenth-Century Japanese Prints," *Impressions* 23 (2001): 43–63.

77. Susan Stewart, *On Longing: Narratives of the Miniature, the Gigantic, the Souvenir, the Collection* (Durham: Duke University Press, 1993), 43.

3. Paradise of Curios

1. See Thorstein Veblen, *The Theory of the Leisure Class* (Harmondworth: Penguin Books, 1994), esp. chapters on "Conspicuous Leisure" and "Conspicuous Consumption," 35–101.

2. See Joe Earle, "The Taxonomic Obsession: British Collectors and Japanese Objects, 1852–1986," *Burlington Magazine* 1005 (December 1986): 864–73.

3. Russell Sturgis, "The Fine Arts of Japan," *The Nation* (July 2, 1868), 16.

4. Von Hubner, *A Ramble Round the World, 1871,* vol. 2, 96.

5. Marvin Cohodas, "Elizabeth Hickox and Karuk Basketry: A Case Study in Debates on Innovation and Paradigms of Authenticity," in Phillips and Steiner, eds., *Unpacking Culture: Art and Commodity in Colonial and Postcolonial Worlds* (Berkeley: University of California Press, 1999), 143–44.

6. Nicole Coolidge Rousmaniere, "The Accessioning of Japanese Art in Early Nineteenth-Century America: Ukiyo-e Prints in the Peabody Essex Museum, Salem," *Apollo* (March 1997): 23–29.

7. Laidlaw, *CAL*, 165.

8. Prime, *Around the World*, 96.

9. Humbert, *Japan and the Japanese Illustrated*, 304.

10. Coffin, *Our New Way Round the World*, 450.

11. Stewart, *On Longing: Narratives of the Miniature, the Gigantic, the Souvenir, the Collection*, 43.

12. Curtis, *Dottings round the Circle*, 101.

13. Stewart, *On Longing: Narratives of the Miniature, the Gigantic, the Souvenir, the Collection*, 134.

14. For samples of the goods imported to the United States, see *Nichibei koryū no akebono* (Worlds Revealed: The Dawn of Japanese and American Exchange), Edo-Tokyo Museum, comp. (Tokyo: Edo-Tokyo Museum, 1999), 82–92.

15. Cited in Howard F. Van Zandt, *Pioneer American Merchants in Japan* (Tokyo: Lotus Press, 1981), 276.

16. Ibid., 277–78.

17. Laidlaw, *The American Reaction to Japanese Art, 1853–1876*, 84–87.

18. *Boston Evening Transcript*, Sept. 3, 1860, p. 2. Cited in Cynthia A. Brandimarte, "Japanese Novelty Stores," *Winterthur Portfolio* 26, no. 1 (Spring 1991), 2.

19. The shop is mentioned in Clarence Cook, *The House Beautiful* (New York: Charles Scribner's Sons, 1881), 291. For further discussion, see chapter 5 in this volume.

20. Brandimarte, "Japanese Novelty Stores," 6.

21. Prime, *Around the World*, 100.

22. This table or one very similar to it may be made out in the photograph of his veranda reproduced in Laidlaw, *CAL*, 177.

23. For a reproduction of the design in *Ehon mushi erabi* see, Christine Guth, *Japanese Art of the Edo Period: The Artist and the City* (New York: Abrams, 1996), 110.

24. Théodore Duret, *Livres et albums illustrés du Japon réunis et catalogués par Théodore Duret* (Paris: Ernest Leroux, 1900), introduction, ii–iii (author's translation).

25. Fogg, *Round the World Letters from Japan, China, India, and Egypt*, 43.

26. On this publication, see Julia Meech-Pekarik, *The World of the Meiji Print: Impressions of a New Civilization* (New York and Tokyo: Weatherhill, 1986), 40–51.

27. Philippe Sichel, "Notes d'un bibeloteur au Japon," in Max Put, *Plunder and Pleasure: Japanese Art in the West 1860–1930* (Leiden: Hotei Publishing, 2000), 64–65.

28. Coffin, *Our New Way Round the World*, 450–51. Although he does not acknowledge it, Coffin was quoting from W. F. Mayers, N. B. Denny, and C. King, *Treaty Ports of China and Japan: A Complete Guide to the Open Ports of those Countries, together with Peking, Yedo, Hong Kong and Macao, forming a Guide Book and Vade Mecum, for Travellers, Merchants, and Residents in General* (London: Trubner, 1867), 585.

29. Joe Earle, *Splendors of Meiji Japan*

(St. Petersburg, Fla.: Broughton International, 1999), 94.

30. Philippe Sichel, "Notes d'un bibeloteur au Japon," in Max Put, *Plunder and Pleasure: Japanese Art in the West 1860–1930*, 65.

31. Curtis, *Dottings round the Circle*, 74–75.

32. Laidlaw, *The American Reaction to Japanese Art, 1853–1876*, 84–87.

33. Cited in Laidlaw, *CAL*, 198.

34. See the insightful chapter on the Goncourts' legacy in Debora L. Silverman, *Art Nouveau in Fin-de-Siècle France: Politics, Psychology, and Style* (Berkeley: University of California Press, 1989), 17–39.

35. See Colin Campbell, *The Romantic Ethic and the Spirit of Modern Consumerism* (Oxford: Basil Blackwell, 1987).

36. Laidlaw, *CAL*, 43.

37. Ibid., 157.

38. For a discussion of their background, travels, and the collection they formed, see the special issue of *Ebisu* cited in the Introduction, note 13.

39. See note 24 above.

40. Among the items still in Longfellow House are a small number of lacquered and painted shelves, probably made for his Tokyo house; two albums of sketches of actors performing in various Noh plays; printed and hand-painted notebooks with textile patterns and kimono designs; an assortment of illustrated books; a number of unmounted paintings in Otsu-e style; and an unmounted handscroll recounting in an admonitionary tale about a wayward monk. Since many of the books and albums have Japanese dates ranging from the late 1860s and early 1870s, it is likely that Charley bought them during his first trip. Although his journals from 1885 and 1891 as well as the record of his estate suggest further acquisitions, these seem to have been far more limited in scope and are likely to have gone to his rooms in the Somerset Club in Boston rather than to the family home in Cambridge.

41. Laidlaw, *CAL*, 26.

42. Cited in Sarah H. Heald, "'In the Japanese Style,' Charley Longfellow's Sitting Room," *Old-Time New England* (Fall/Winter 2000), 9.

43. The pocket diary is in LNHS.

44. *William H. Seward's Travels around the World*, 74.

45. Laidlaw, *CAL*, 174.

46. William W. Fitzhugh and Chisato O. Dubreuil, *Ainu: Spirit of a Northern People* (Washington, D.C.: Smithsonian Institution and University of Washington Press, 1999), 205.

47. Laidlaw, *CAL*, 69.

48. Ibid., 88.

49. See *Henri Cernuschi, 1821–1896: Voyageur et collectioneur*, 41.

50. Laidlaw, *CAL*, 88.

51. On staged authenticity, see MacCannell, *The Tourist*, 91–105.

52. Laidlaw, *CAL*, 141.

53. Ibid., 150.

54. Ibid., 89–90.

55. Ibid., 97.

56. For a reproduction, see Laidlaw, *CAL*, 39.

57. Pumpelly, *Across America and Asia*, 198.

58. Surviving works at LNHS include, in addition to assorted volumes of his *Manga* (Random Sketches), *Ehon Onna Imagawa* (Women's Precepts) and *Ukiyo-e gafu* (Album of Ukiyo-e pictures).

59. Cortazzi, ed., *Mitford's Japan*, 39.

60. Laidlaw, *CAL*, 118–19.

61. See Joe Earle, *Flower Bronzes of Japan* (London: Michael Goedhuis, 1995), esp. 131–41.

62. Prime, *Around the World*, 120–21.

63. William Prime was also a promoter of the Metropolitan Museum of Art and later became the first professor of art history at Princeton University. See *Art and the Empire City: New York, 1825–1861*, Catherine Hoover, ed. (New York: Metropolitan Museum of Art; New Haven: Yale University Press, 2000), 95–97.

64. See Akiko Mabuchi, "Cernuschi et sa collection d'okimono," *Ebisu* (Hiver 1998): 107–21.

65. "The Kyoto Exhibition," *The Japan*

Weekly Mail, May 4, 1872.

66. Laidlaw, *CAL*, 135.

67. Edward Morse, *Japan Day by Day 1877, 1878–79, 1882–83*, 2 vols. (New York: Houghton Mifflin, 1917), vol. 2, 185–86.

68. For biographical data, see Ellen P. Conant in collaboration with Steven D. Owyoung and J. Thomas Rimer, *Nihonga Transcending the Past: Japanese Style Painting 1868–1968* (St. Louis Art Museum and the Japan Foundation, 1995), 308–9.

69. Laidlaw, *The American Reaction to Japanese Art, 1853–1876*, 165–70.

70. Prime, *Around the World*, 120.

71. Laidlaw, *CAL*, 162.

72. The items were accessioned as numbers 84.251 through 270. Most were sold by order of the trustees. My thanks to Emiko Usui for locating these records.

73. Von Hubner, *A Ramble Round the World, 1871*, vol. 2, 98–99.

74. Ibid., vol. 1, 443–44.

75. Emile Guimet, *Promenades Japonaises Tokio-Nikko* (Paris: G. Charpentier, 1880), 187–92. On Kyōsai's meetings with foreigners, see Timothy Clark, *Demon of Painting: The Art of Kawanabe Kyōsai* (London: The British Museum, 1993), 27–29.

76. Christophe Marquet, "Le Japon de 1871," *Ebisu*, 69–70.

77. John Black, *The Far East*, Nov. 1, 1871. An anonymous reviewer of the 1876 Exposition, writing in the *Atlantic Monthly* (July 1876) voiced similar confusion: "There are other paintings—drawings, sketches, what shall they be called?"

78. On Wirgman and Beato see Clark, *Japanese Exchanges in Art 1850s-1930s*, 5–89. On Wirgman's painting and illustrations, see Kanagawa Kenritsu Hakubutsukan, comp., *Charles Wirgman* (Yokohama: Kanagawa Kenritsu Hakubutsukan, 1990).

79. Mary Louise Pratt, *Imperial Eyes: Travel Writing and Transculturation* (New York: Routledge, 1992), 4.

80. Blanche Roosevelt Tucker-Macchetta, *The Home Life of Henry W. Longfellow: Reminiscences of Many Visits at Cambridge and Nahant, during the years 1880, 1881,* *and 1882* (New York: G.W. Carleton, 1882), 218.

81. See his *Shashin garon: shashin to kaiga no kekkon*.

82. Clark, *Japanese British Exchanges in Art*, 62–66.

83. *The Far East*, January 16, 1872, 193–95. The photograph appears on page 187.

84. In a cartoon entitled "Consular Charges," Wirgman claims "having called 'Boston Charlie' a chargé d'affaires" (erroneously), as one of the "fees" payable to the consulate. See *The Japan Punch* 1873–74.

85. On these artists see Kanagawa Kenritsu Hakubutsukan, comp., *Meiji no kyūtei gaka-Goseda Yoshimatsu* (The Meiji court artist Goseda Yoshimatsu) (Yokohama: Yokohama Kenritsu Hakubutsukan, 1986).

86. For a reproduction of this painting now in the Akita Museum of Modern Art, see Guth, *Japanese Art of the Edo Period: The Artist and the City*, 145.

87. See Nerima Kuritsu Bijutsukan, comp., *Kikuchi Yōsai to Meiji bijutsu* (Kikuchi Yōsai and Meiji art) (Tokyo: Nerima Kuritsu Bijutsukan 1999), 82, and Yokohama Bijutsukan, comp., *Bakumatsu-Meiji no Yokohama-ten* (Yokohama 1859–99: New Visions, New Representations) (Yokohama: Yokohama Bijutsukan, 2000), 6.

88. James Clifford, *The Predicament of Culture* (Cambridge, Mass.: Harvard University, 1988), 12.

89. Richard Handler, "Authenticity," 2.

4. Embodying Japan

1. *The Japan Weekly Mail*, September 23, 1871, 546.

2. George Smith, Bishop of Victoria, was surprised to see women in Nagasaki wearing rings and other jewelry. See his *Ten Weeks in Japan* (London: Longman, Greene, Longman and Roberts, 1861), 167.

3. Andrew Cobbing, *The Japanese Discovery of Victorian Britain: Early Travel Encounters in the Far West* (London: Curzon Press, 1998), 82.

4. On the history of clothing in the

Meiji era, see Endō Takeshi, *Fukushoku kindaishi* (Tokyo: Yūsankaku, 1970). See also Julia Meech-Pekarik, *The World of the Meiji Print,* and Liza Critchfield Dalby, *Kimono: Fashioning Culture* (Seattle: University of Washington Press, 2001), 59–106.

5. Notable studies include Ann Hollander, *Seeing through Clothes* (Berkeley: University of California Press, 1993); Emma Tarlo, *Clothing Matters: Dress and Identity in India* (London: Hurst, 1996); Alison Lurie, *The Language of Clothes* (New York: Random House, 1981); Roland Barthes, *The Fashion System,* trans. Mathew Ward and Richard Howard (Berkeley: University of California Press, 1990); and John Harvey, *Men in Black* (London: Reaktion Books, 1995).

6. Laidlaw, *CAL,* 141.

7. Homi Bhahba, "Of Mimicry and Man: The Ambivalence of Colonial Discourse," in *Tensions of Empire: Colonial Cultures in a Bourgeois World*, ed. Frederick Cooper and Anna Laura Stoler (Berkeley: University of California Press, 1997), 153.

8. His idealization of the samurai continued well after his first trip. The Longfellow House library preserves a copy of Louis Wertheimer, *A Muramasa Blade: A Story of Feudalism in Old Japan* (Boston: Ticknor, 1886), which Charley presented to his cousin Mary King Longfellow in the year of its publication.

9. A. B. Mitford, *Tales of Old Japan,* vol. 1, 2–3. Charley may have read this tale before its appearance in book form in the *Fortnightly Review.*

10. Laidlaw, *CAL,* 122.

11. My thanks to Allen Hockley for drawing this to my attention.

12. Basil Hall Chamberlain, *Japanese Things: Being Notes of Various Subjects Connected with Japan,* 415.

13. Laidlaw, *CAL,* 34; for sketch see p. 39.

14. Ibid., 113.

15. Ibid., 166.

16. Orientalist costumes were popular at masquerade balls. One attendee at the Glasgow Arts Club Ball of 1889 dressed as Hokusai. See Sara Stevenson and Helen Bennett, *Van Dyck in Check Trousers: Fancy Dress in Art and Life 1700–1900* (Edinburgh: Scottish National Portrait Gallery, 1978), figure 103.

17. Cited in Christopher Pinney, *Camera Indica: The Social Life of Indian Photographs* (London: Reaktion Books, 1997), 74.

18. Laidlaw, *CAL,* 167.

19. Mitford, *Tales of Old Japan,* vol. 1, 98–145.

20. See Edward Wagenknecht, *Henry Wadsworth Longfellow: Portrait of an American Humanist,* 68–70.

21. Laidlaw, *CAL,* 32.

22. Ibid., 124.

23. Ibid., 158.

24. See *The Far East*, October 16, 1872.

25. *The Far East*, July 1, 1870, 2–3.

26. According to Sebastian Dobson, a specialist in Japanese vintage photographs, Shimooka Renjō had a particular penchant for photographic *mitate* (personal communication). A photo of the female palanquin bearers was acquired by J. W. Henderson, an Australian banker in Japan from 1864 to 1874. Wirgman provided the *London Illustrated News* of January 13, 1872, with an illustration of a parade captioned "Girls Dressed as Boys."

27. Jonathan D. Spence, *The Memory Palace of Matteo Ricci* (New York: Viking, 1984), 114–15.

28. See, for instance, R. Ponsonby-Fane, *The Vicissitudes of Shinto* (Kyoto: The Ponsonby Memorial Society, 1963).

29. For a more extended discussion of this subject, see my "Charles Longfellow and Okakura Kakuzō: Cultural Cross-Dressing in the Colonial Context," *Positions East Asia Cultural Critique* 8, no. 3 (Winter 2000): 605–36.

30. On neoclassicism and fashion in the nineteenth century, see Hollander, *Seeing through Clothes,* 62–81.

31. The caption "Asiatic Society" suggests that it may have been occasioned by the founding of the British Asiatic Society

of Japan in 1872.

32. Morse, *Japan Day by Day,* vol. 1, 276–77.

33. Okakura Kakuzō, *The Awakening of Japan* (New York: The Century Co., 1904), 150.

34. Cited in Dalby, *The Kimono,* 66–67.

35. With the exception of the fireman's *kajibaori,* which is in the Peabody Essex Museum, Salem, all these clothes are in the collection of LNHS.

36. Pumpelly, *Across America and Asia,* 197.

37. Prime, *Around the World,* 98.

38. Laidlaw, *CAL,* 62.

39. Ibid., 69.

40. Albert Parry, *Tattoo: Secrets of a Strange Art as Practiced among the Natives of the United States* (New York: Simon and Schuster, 1933), 94.

41. On the history of Japanese tattoos see, W. R. van Gulik, *Irezumi: The Pattern of Dermatology in Japan* (Leiden: Brill, 1982).

42. On the tattooed *Suikoden* heroes, see van Gulik, *Irezumi: The Pattern of Dermatology in Japan,* 48–53.

43. Translation by John Mertz , from "Internalizing Social Difference: Kangaki Robun's *Shanks' Mare to the Western Seas,*" paper presented at Meiji Studies Conference, Cambridge, Mass., May 1994.

44. According to an entry dated May 22 in Charles Appleton Longfellow's Journal for January 2–May 1891, Horichō had entered into "a sort of partnership with two young fellows, curio dealers at no 12 Bund." See also Parry, *Tattoo: Secrets of a Strange Art,* 99–100.

45. Ibid., 2.

46. For a discussion of these and other contributing factors, see the essays in Jane Caplan, ed., *Written on the Body: The Tattoo in European and American History* (London: Reaktion Books, 2000). See also Parry, *Tattoo: Secrets of a Strange Art,* 90–110.

47. Parry, *Tattoo: Secrets of a Strange Art,* 97.

48. James Bradley, "Body Commodification? Class and Tattoos in Victorian Britain," in Jane Caplan, ed., *Written on the Body,* 140–47.

49. George Burchett, *Memoirs of a Tattooist* (London: Oldbourne, 1958), 51 and 100. The princes arrived in Japan aboard the H.M.S. *Bacchante* Oct. 24, 1881, not 1882, as Burchett claims.

50. This list appeared in an 1898–99 publication cited in Bradley, "Body Commodification? Class and Tattoos in Victorian Britain," 146.

51. Parry, *Tattoo: Secrets of a Strange Art,* 93.

52. Ibid., 91.

53. Ibid., 94.

54. Citation from *New York World,* Aug. 29, 1897, in ibid., 99.

55. Original caption attached to photograph in the Spencer Collection, New York Public Library.

56. For reproduction, see Jack Hiller, *Hokusai Paintings, Drawings, and Woodcuts* (Oxford: Phaidon, 1978), 58.

57. Charles Appleton Longfellow's journal for July 13–August 10, 1885; unpublished manuscript, LNHS, transcribed by Christine Wallace Laidlaw.

58. *Boston Transcript,* February 23, 1886.

59. Charles Appleton Longfellow's journal for July 13–August 10, 1885.

60. Robert Bogdan, *Freak Show* (Chicago: University of Chicago Press, 1988), 243.

61. Parry, *Tattoo: Secrets of a Strange Art,* 61.

62. Bogdan, *Freak Show,* 249.

63. Marjorie Garber, *Vested Interests: Cross Dressing and Cultural Anxiety* (New York: Routledge, 1992), 66.

64. Journal entries dated May 14 and 22, 1891.

65. Adria Katz, "Borneo to Philadelphia: The Furness-Hiller-Harrison Collections," *Expedition,* 30, no. 1 (1988), 65. Furness's well-to-do friends Hiram Milliken Miller and Alfred Craven Harrison also had themselves tattooed.

66. Humbert, *Japan and the Japanese Illustrated,* 139.

5. Domesticating Japan

1. Michael Kammen, *Mystic Chords of Memory: The Transformation of Tradition in American Culture* (New York: Vintage Books, 1993), 44–48.

2. This term is borrowed from Pierre Bourdieu, *Distinction: A Social Critique of the Judgment of Taste* (Cambridge: Harvard University Press, 1984).

3. Craig Clunas, "China in Britain: The Imperial Collections," in Barringer and Flynn, eds. *Colonialism and the Object: Empire, Material Culture and the Museum* (New York: Routledge, 1998), 43.

4. Vedder is likely to have drawn inspiration for this painting from the many Japanese goods he received from his brother, a physician in Japan from 1863 until his death in 1870 (Laidlaw, *The American Reaction to Japanese Art, 1853–1876*, 22–23).

5. William Leach, *Land of Desire: Merchants, Power and the Rise of a New American Culture* (New York: Vintage Books, 1994), 32.

6. Anonymous, "Characteristics of the International Fair," *Atlantic Monthly* (July 1876), 89–90.

7. Article in *Harper's Weekly*, August 12, 1876.

8. Cited in Yasuo Okada, "The Japanese Image of the American West," *Western Historical Quarterly* (May 1988), 146.

9. See Clarence Cook, *The House Beautiful*, illustration 59.

10. Howard Wayne Morgan, *New Muses: Art in American Culture, 1865–1920*, 59.

11. See Brandimarte, "Japanese Novelty Stores."

12. Cook, *The House Beautiful*, 101–2.

13. Letter of May 6, 1875, from Edith to Mary King Longfellow, LNHS.

14. Rémy G. Saisselin, *Bricabracomania: The Bourgeois and the Bibelot* (London: Thames and Hudson, 1985), 68.

15. Catherine Pagani, "Chinese Material Culture and British Perceptions of China in the Mid-Nineteenth Century," in Tim Barringer and Tom Flynn, eds., *Colonialism and the Object: Empire, Material Culture and the Museum*, 35.

16. M. A. DeWolfe Howe, *Memories of a Hostess, Chronicle of Friendships drawn chiefly from the Diaries of Mrs. James Fields* (Boston: Atlantic, 1922), 115.

17. Letter of August 30, 1843, cited in *Historic Furnishings Report: The Longfellow House* (Harpers Ferry, W.Va.: Division of Historic Furnishings, Harpers Ferry Center, U.S. Department of the Interior/National Park Service, 1999), vol. 1, 40.

18. Cited in Kathleen M. Catalano, "The Longfellows and Their 'Trumpery Antiquities,'" *The American Art Journal* (Spring 1983), 21.

19. Cited in *Mrs. Longfellow: Selected Letters and Journals*, edited by Edward Wagenknecht (New York: Longmans, Green, 1956), 210–11.

20. Ibid., 82–83.

21. This list is based on a transcription of the Longfellow house guest book compiled by Marc Vargas in 1978. Sir Edward Arnold mentions his visit in *Seas and Lands* (London: Longmans, Green, 1892), 101.

22. *Homes of American Authors, comprising anecdotal, personal, and descriptive sketches by various authors* (New York: G. P. Putnam, 1853) and *Homes of American Authors, illustrated with views of their residences* (New York: Appleton, 1857).

23. *Scribner's Monthly* 17, no.1 (November 1878), cover.

24. Griffis, *The Mikado's Empire*, 520.

25. Henry Wadsworth Longfellow, ed., *Poems of Places* (Boston: Houghton Osgood, 1878), Asia vols. 1–3. Volume three, devoted to Japan, includes anonymous poems translated from the Japanese on Mt. Amakagu, Fujiyama, and Yoshino (see pp. 241 and 248). These had earlier appeared in an article on ancient Japanese poetry in *The Westminster Review* n.s. 38 (October 1870): 321–40.

26. *Henry Wadsworth Longfellow, Poems and Other Writings*, 645.

27. Laidlaw, *CAL*, 140.

28. DeWolfe Howe, *Memories of a Hostess, Chronicle of Friendships drawn chiefly*

from the Diaries of Mrs. James Fields, 128.

29. Laidlaw, *CAL,* 185–86.

30. Cook, *The House Beautiful,* 289–91.

31. See Edward S. Morse, *Japanese Homes and Their Surroundings* (New York: Ticknor, 1886), 304–5.

32. Figure 48 in *Longfellow House Report.* The photo dates from 1885–92.

33. See Figure 106 in *Longfellow House Report.*

34. The Chinese porcelains in the view of "Longfellow's Drawing Room" are illustrated in the 1878 *Scribner's Monthly* article cited above.

35. Charles Wyllis Elliot, *The Book of American Interiors* (Boston: James R. Osgood, 1876), 53.

36. Elliot, *The Book of American Interiors,* 71.

37. Richard Henry Stoddard, *Poets' Homes. Pen and pencil sketches of American poets and their homes.* (Boston: D. Lothrop, 1877), 12, 9.

38. *Harper's Weekly,* August 12, 1876.

39. On A. W. Longfellow, see Nancy K. Jones, "The Charles Longfellow Japan Room of 1874 and the Cross-Over from Japanese Decorative Arts into Architecture in late 19th Century American Designs" (unpublished paper). His career is discussed more fully in Margaret Henderson Floyd, *Architecture after Richardson: Regionalism before Modernism: Longfellow, Alden, and Harlow in Boston and Pittsburgh* (Pittsburgh: Pittsburgh History and Landmarks Foundation, 1994).

40. Letter from Mary King Longfellow to Edith Longfellow, March 1884. A painting of a Buddhist deity seated on a tiered lotus pedestal also found its way to Portland. It appears in an early twentieth-century photograph of the poet's sister, who lived in the family home there.

41. Jane Converse Brown, "The Japanese Taste: Its Role in the Mission of the American Home and in the Family's Presentation of itself to the Public as expressed in published sources, 1876–1916," Ph.D. dissertation, University of Wisconsin, 1987, 319–23.

42. Letter from Edith Longfellow to Mary King Longfellow, March 26, 1875, LNHS.

43. Letter from Edith Longfellow to Mary King Longfellow, March 11, 1876, LNHS.

44. On this issue, see Hosley, *The Japan Idea,* 161–82.

45. Laidlaw, *CAL,* 174.

46. Brown, "The Japanese Taste," 284.

47. M. A. DeWolfe Howe, *Memories of a Hostess: A Chronicle of Eminent Friendships drawn chiefly from the diaries of Mrs. James T. Fields,* 216.

48. Letters from Edith Longfellow to Alice Longfellow, October 25, 1874, and Edith Longfellow to Charles Longfellow, March 28, 1875, LNHS.

49. Stoddard, *Poets' Homes,* 12–13.

50. Notehelfer, ed., *Japan through American Eyes,* 345.

51. *William H. Seward's Travels around the World,* 65.

52. Morse, *Japan Day by Day,* vol. 1, 144.

53. The Hartt's house is not illustrated, only mentioned. See *Artistic Houses: Being a Series of Interior Views of a Number of the Most Beautiful and Celebrated Homes in the United States,* with a description of the art therein (New York: D. Appleton, 1883–1884), 59.

54. Hosley, *The Japan Idea,* 173–74.

55. Tucker-Macchetta, *The Home Life of Henry W. Longfellow: Reminiscences of Many Visits at Cambridge and Nahant, during the years 1880, 1881, and 1882,* 215–17.

56. Letter from Edith to Alice Longfellow, October 25, 1874; letter from Edith to Mary King Longfellow, November 3, 1874, LNHS.

57. For a photograph see Hosley, *The Japan Idea,* 112.

58. Letter from Edith to Anne Allegra Longfellow (dated Sunday morning, ca. 1875), LNHS.

Epilogue

1. Cited in Edward Wagenknecht,

Henry Wadsworth Longfellow: Portrait of an American Humanist, 197.

2. The definition is transcribed in Thomas A. Tweed and Stephen Prothero, eds., *Asian Religions in America: A Documentary History* (New York: Oxford University Press, 1999), 111.

3. Thomas A. Tweed, *The American Encounters with Buddhism, 1844–1912: Victorian Culture and the Limits of Dissent* (Bloomington: Indiana University Press, 1992) 19, 21–23.

4. Ibid., 27.

5. For an example of the missionary attitude, see M. L. Gordon, *An American Missionary in Japan* (Boston: Houghton Mifflin, 1892) 209–20. Its author was in Japan in 1872.

6. Tweed, *The American Encounters with Buddhism, 1844–1912*, 44.

7. Humbert, *Japan and the Japanese Illustrated*, 287.

8. Stephen Prothero, *Purified by Fire: A History of Cremation in America* (Berkeley: University of California Press, 2001), 24.

9. Ibid., 55.

10. *The Letters of Henry Adams*, edited by J. C. Levenson, E. Samuels, C. Vandersee, and V. Winner, 6 vols. (Cambridge: Harvard University Press, 1982), vol. 3, 24.

11. John La Farge, *An Artist's Letters from Japan* (New York: The Century Co., 1897), 170.

12. William Sturgis Bigelow, *Buddhism and Immortality*, the Ingersoll Lectures, 1908 (Boston: Houghton Mifflin, 1908).

13. Prothero, *Purified by Fire*, 38 and 20.

14. In "Longfellow's Tattoos: Marks of a Cross-cultural Encounter" (*Orientations*, 1998), I suggested that his tattoos may have prompted the decision to have him cremated, but I no longer believe this to be the case.

15. Personal communication, Janet Heywood, Vice President of Interpretive Programs, Mount Auburn Cemetery, Cambridge, Mass. Although philosophical considerations no doubt played a role, Ms. Heywood has suggested that there may have been practical ones as well. The family's underground vault was sealed following the poet's death, and there was not enough space on the family plot for full casket burials for all his children.

16. Whitehill, *The Museum of Fine Arts Boston: A Centennial History*, vol. 1, 111.

17. Journal entry for July 13, 1885.

18. See Ernest Satow, *A Handbook for Travellers in central and northern Japan*, 2d ed., rev. (London: Murray, 1884).

19. John Murray, *A Handbook for travellers in Japan, by Basil Chamberlain . . . and W. B. Mason*. 4th ed., rev. and augm. (London: J. Murray; Yokohama: Kelly Walsh, 1894), 33–68.

20. Journal entry of May 17, 1891.

21. Murray, *A Handbook for travellers in Japan*, 106–8.

22. Whitehill, *The Museum of Fine Arts Boston: A Centennial History*, vol. 1, 47.

23. Ibid., 108.

24. Paul DiMaggio, "Cultural Entrepreneurship in Nineteenth-Century Boston: The Creation of an Organizational Base for High Culture in America," *Media Culture & Society* 4, no. 1 (January 1982), 33–34.

25. See Whitehill, *The Museum of Fine Arts Boston: A Centennial History*, vol. 1, 68–69, 72–73.

26. Ibid., 82.

27. Michael Baxandall, "Exhibiting Intention," in *Exhibiting Cultures: The Poetics and Politics of Museum Display*, edited by Ivan Karp and Steven D. Lavine (Washington, D.C.: Smithsonian Institution Press, 1991), 34.

28. Journal entry between September 16 and September 30, 1885.

SELECTED BIBLIOGRAPHY

Appleton, Brevet Nathan. *Russian Life and Society*. Boston: Murray and Emory, 1904.

Appleton, Thomas G. *Windfalls*. Boston: Roberts Brothers, 1878.

Artistic Houses: Being a Series of Interior Views of a Number of the Most Beautiful and Celebrated Homes in the United States, with a description of the art therein. New York: D. Appleton, 1883–1884.

Ashmead, John. *The Idea of Japan, 1853–1895: Japan as Described by American and Other Travellers from the West*. New York: Garland Press, 1987.

Bainbridge, Lucy Seaman. *Round the World Letters*. Boston: D. Lothrop, 1882.

Banta, Melissa, and Susan Taylor, eds. *A Timely Encounter: Nineteenth-Century Photographs of Japan*. Cambridge, Mass.: Peabody Museum Press, 1988.

Barringer, Tim, and Tom Flynn, eds. *Colonialism and the Object: Empire, Material Culture, and the Museum*. New York: Routledge, 1998.

Bird, Isabella. *Unbeaten Tracks in Japan*. Rutland, Vt.: Charles E. Tuttle, 1973.

Black, John R. *Young Japan: Yokohama and Yedo. A Narrative of the Settlement and the City from the Signing of the Treaties in 1868 to the Close of the Year 1879*. 2 vols. London: Trubner, 1881.

Bogdan, Robert. *Freak Show*. Chicago: University of Chicago Press, 1988.

Brandimarte, Cynthia A. "Japanese Novelty Stores." *Winterthur Portfolio* 26, no. 1 (Spring 1991): 1–25.

Brown, Jane Converse. *The Japanese Taste: Its Role in the Mission of the American Home and in the Family's Presentation of Itself to the Public as expressed in published sources, 1876–1916*. Ph.D. dissertation, University of Wisconsin, 1987.

Burchett, George. *Memoirs of a Tattooist*. London: Oldbourne, 1958.

Buzard, James. *The Beaten Track: European Tourism, Literature, and the Ways of Culture, 1800–1918*. Oxford: Clarendon, 1993.

Caplan, Jane, ed. *Written on the Body: The Tattoo in European and American History*. London: Reaktion Books, 2000.

Carnegie, Andrew. *Round the World*. New York: Doubleday, Doran, 1884.

Carr, Adiss Emmet. *All the Way round; or What a boy saw and heard on his way round the world. A book for young people and older ones with young hearts*. New York: Appleton, 1876.

Chamberlain, Basil Hall. *Japanese Things: Being Notes on Various Subjects Connected with Japan*. Rutland, Vt.: Charles E. Tuttle, 1971.

Clark, John. *Japanese Exchanges in Art 1850s–1930s with Britain, Continental Europe, and the USA*. Sidney: Power Publications, 2001.

Clifford, James, and George Marcus, eds. *Writing Culture: The Poetics and Politics of*

Ethnography. Berkeley: University of California Press, 1986.

Cobbing, Andrew. *The Japanese Discovery of Victorian Britain: Early Travel Encounters in the Far West*. London: Curzon Press, 1998.

Coffin, Charles Carleton. *Our New Way Round the World*. London: Sampson, Low, Son, and Marston, 1869.

Cook, Clarence. *The House Beautiful*. New York: Charles Scribner's Sons, 1881.

Cooper, Frederick, and Anna Laura Stoler, eds. *Tensions of Empire: Colonial Cultures in a Bourgeois World*. Berkeley: University of California Press, 1997.

Cortazzi, Hugh. *Victorians in Japan: In and Around the Treaty Ports*. London: Althone Press, 1987.

Curtis, Benjamin Robbins. *Dottings Round the Circle*. Boston: Osgood, 1876.

Dalby, Liza Critchfield. *Kimono: Fashioning Culture*. Seattle: University of Washington Press, 2001.

Dana, Richard Henry. *The Journal of Richard Henry Dana, Jr.* Edited by Robert F. Lucid. 3 vols. Cambridge, Mass.: Harvard University Press, 1968.

de Beauvoir, Ludovic. *Pekin, Yeddo, San Francisco. Voyage autour du monde*. 3 vols. Paris: H. Plon, 1871–72.

———. *A Voyage around the World*. Translated from the French by Agnes and Helen Stephenson. 3 vols. London: John Murray, 1870–72.

de Gabriac, Comte. *Course humoristique autour du monde: Indes, Chine, Japon*. Paris: Michel Levy Frères, 1872.

Earle, Joe. *Splendors of Meiji Japan*. St. Petersburg, Fla.: Broughton International, 1999.

———. "The Taxonomic Obsession: British Collectors and Japanese Objects, 1852–1986." *Burlington Magazine* 1005 (December 1986): 864–73.

Edel, Chantal, and Linda Cloverdale, trans. *Once upon a Time: Visions of Old Japan*. Photographs by Felice Beato and Baron Raimund von Stillfried. New York: Friendly Press, 1986.

Elliot, Charles Wyllys. *The Book of American Interiors*. Boston: James R. Osgood, 1876.

Evett, Elisa. *The Critical Reception of Japanese Art in Late Nineteenth Century Europe*. Ann Arbor, Mich.: UMI Research Press, 1982.

Floyd, Margaret Henderson. *Architecture after Richardson: Regionalism before Modernism— Longfellow, Alden, and Harlow in Boston and Pittsburgh*. Pittsburgh: Pittsburgh History and Landmarks Foundation, 1994.

Fogg, William Perry. *Round the World Letters from Japan, China, India, and Egypt*. Cleveland, Ohio: William Perry Fogg, 1872.

Grier, Katherine C. *Culture and Comfort: Parlor Making and Middle-Class Identity, 1850–1930*. Washington: Smithsonian Institution Press, 1988.

Griffis, William E. *The Mikado's Empire*. New York: Harper Bros., 1876.

———. *The Tokio Guide*. Yokohama, 1873.

Guimet, Emile. *Promenades japonaises Tokio-Nikko*. Paris: G. Charpentier, 1880.

———. *Promenades japonaises*. Paris: G. Charpentier, 1878.

Guth, Christine M. E. "Charles Longfellow and Okakura Kakuzō: Cultural Cross-Dressing in the Colonial Context." *Positions East Asia Cultural Critique* 8, no. 3 (Winter 2000): 605–36.

Hale, Susan. *Life and Letters of Thomas Gold Appleton*. New York: Appleton, 1885.

Handler, Richard. "Authenticity." *Anthropology Today* (1986): 3–5.

Heald, Sarah H. "'In the Japanese Style': Charley Longfellow's Sitting Room." *Old-Time*

New England (Fall/Winter 2000): 5–21.

Henisch, Heinz K., and Bridget A. Henisch. *The Painted Photograph, 1839–1914: Origins, Techniques, Aspirations.* University Park: Pennsylvania State University Press, 1996.

Hilen, Andrew. "Charley Longfellow Goes to War." *Harvard Library Bulletin* (Spring 1960): 59–81, and (Winter 1960): 283–303.

Hockley, Allen. "Cameras, Photographs, and Photography in Nineteenth-Century Japanese Prints." *Impressions* 23 (2001): 43–63.

———. "Expectations and Authenticity in Meiji Tourist Photography." In *Challenging the Past and Present: The Transformation of Japanese Art in the Nineteenth Century.* Forthcoming.

Hollander, Ann. *Seeing through Clothes.* Berkeley: University of California Press, 1993.

Hosley, William. *The Japan Idea.* Hartford, Conn.: Wadsworth Atheneum, 1990.

Howe, M. A. DeWolfe. *Memories of a Hostess, Chronicle of Friendships drawn chiefly from the Diaries of Mrs. James Fields.* Boston: Atlantic, 1922.

Humbert, Aimé. *Japan and the Japanese Illustrated.* Translated by Mrs. Cashel Hoey and edited by H. W. Bates. New York: Appleton, 1874.

Iriye Akira, ed. *Mutual Images: Essays in American Japanese Relations.* Cambridge: Harvard University Press, 1975.

Ishiguro, Keishichi. *Utsusareta bakumatsu* (Photographic records of the Bakumatsu Era). Tokyo: Asoka Shobō, 1960.

Ishiguro, Keishō. *Zoku Bakumatsu Meiji no omoshiro shashin* (Further interesting photographs from the Bakumatsu and Meiji Eras). Tokyo: Heibonsha, 1998.

———. *Bakumatsu Meiji no omoshiroi shashin* (Interesting photographs from the Bakumatsu and Meiji eras). Tokyo: Heibonsha, 1996.

Izakura, Naomi, and Torin Boyd. *Portraits in Sepia from the Japanese Carte-de-visite Collection of Torin Boyd and Naomi Izakura.* Tokyo: Asahi Sonorama, 2000.

Kanagawa Kenritsu Hakubutsukan, comp. *Charles Wirgman.* Yokohama: Kanagawa Kenritsu Hakubutsukan, 1990.

———. *Meiji no kyūtei gaka-Goseda Yoshimatsu* (The Meiji court artist Goseda Yoshimatsu). Yokohama: Yokohama Kenritsu Hakubutsukan, 1986.

Katz, Adria. "Borneo to Philadelphia: The Furness-Hiller-Harrison Collections." *Expedition* 30, no. 1 (1988): 65–72.

Kinoshita, Naoyuki. *Shashin garon: Shashin to kaiga no kekkon* (On Photographic Pictures: The Marriage of Photography and Painting). Tokyo: Iwanami shoten, 1996.

Laidlaw, Christine Wallace, ed. *Charles Appleton Longfellow: Twenty Months in Japan, 1871–1873.* Cambridge, Mass.: Friends of the Longfellow House, 1998.

———. *The American Reaction to Japanese Art, 1853–1876.* Ph.D. dissertation, Rutgers University, 1996.

Lears, Jackson. *No Place of Grace: Antimodernism and the Transformation of American Culture, 1880–1920.* New York: Pantheon Books, 1981.

Levine, Lawrence W. *Highbrow/Lowbrow: The Emergence of Cultural Hierarchy in America.* Cambridge: Harvard University Press, 1988.

Linkman, Audrey. *The Victorians: Photographic Portraits.* New York: Tauris Parke Books, 1993.

Longfellow, Henry Wadsworth. *Longfellow Poems and Other Writings.* New York: The Library of America, 2000.

———. *The Letters of Henry Wadsworth Longfellow.* Edited by Andrew Hilen. 6 vols. Cambridge: Harvard University Press, 1982.

Longfellow, Henry Wadsworth, ed. *Poems of Places*. Boston: Houghton Osgood, 1878.

Longfellow, Samuel. *Life of Henry Wadsworth Longfellow*. 3 vols. Boston: Ticknor, 1886.

MacCannell, Dean. *The Tourist: A New Theory of the Leisure Class*. Berkeley: University of California Press, 1999.

Marvin, Enoch. *To the East by Way of the West*. St. Louis: Brand, Brand, and Co., 1878.

Meech-Pekarik, Julia. *The World of the Meiji Print: Impressions of a New Civilization*. Tokyo and New York: Weatherhill, 1986.

Melman, Billie. *Women's Orients: English Women and the Middle East, 1718–1918, Sexuality, Religion, Work*. Ann Arbor: University of Michigan Press, 1982.

Mitford, Algeron B. *Tales of Old Japan*. 2 vols. London: Macmillan, 1871.

Miyoshi, Masao. *As We Saw Them: The First Japanese Embassy to the United States (1860)*. Berkeley: University of California Press, 1979.

Morgan, Wayne H. *New Muses: Art in American Culture, 1865–1920*. Norman: University of Oklahoma Press, 1978.

Morse, Edward S. *Japan Day by Day 1877, 1878–79, 1882–83*. 2 vols. New York: Houghton Mifflin, 1917.

———. *Japanese Homes and Their Surroundings*. New York: Ticknor, 1886.

Musée Cernuschi, comp. *Henri Cernuschi, 1821–1896: voyageur et collectionneur*. Paris: Paris-musées, 1998.

Nichibei koryū no akebono (Worlds Revealed: The Dawn of Japanese and American Exchange). Edo-Tokyo Museum, comp. Tokyo: Edo-Tokyo Museum, 1999.

Nihon shashinshi 1840–1945 (History of Japanese Photography 1840–1945). Nihon shashinka kyōkai, comp. Tokyo: Heibonsha 1971.

Notehelfer, Fred G. *Japan through American Eyes: The Journal of Francis Hall, Kanagawa and Yokohama, 1859–66*. Princeton: Princeton University Press, 1992.

Ozawa, Takeshi. *Nihon no shashinshi: Bakumatsu no denpa kara meijiki made* (History of Japanese Photography: From the Bakumatsu to the Meiji Eras). Tokyo: Nikkor Kurabu, 1986.

Parry, Albert. *Tattoo: Secrets of a Strange Art as Practiced among the Natives of the United States*. New York: Simon and Schuster, 1933.

Philipp, Claudia Gabrielle, Dietmar Siegert, and Rainer Wick. *Felice Beato in Japan: Photographien zum Ende der Feudalzeit 1863–1873*. Munich: Edition Braus, 1991.

Pratt, Mary Louise. *Imperial Eyes: Travel Writing and Transculturation*. New York: Routledge, 1992.

Prime, Edward Dorr. *Around the World: Sketches of Travel through Many Lands and over Many Seas*. New York: Harper Bros., 1872.

Prothero, Stephen. *Purified by Fire: A History of Cremation in America*. Berkeley: University of California Press, 2001.

Pumpelly, Raphael. *Across America and Asia: Notes of a Five Years' Journey Around the World and of Residence in Arizona, Japan, and China*. New York: Leypoldt and Holt, 1870.

Rousmaniere, Nicole Coolidge. "The Accessioning of Japanese Art in Early Nineteenth-Century America: Ukiyo-e Prints in the Peabody Essex Museum, Salem." *Apollo* (March 1997): 23–29.

Saisselin, Rémy G. *Bricabracomania: The Bourgeois and the Bibelot*. London: Thames and Hudson, 1985.

Satow, Sir Ernest. *A Diplomat in Japan: An Inner History of the Japanese Reformation*. Rutland, Vt.: Charles E. Tuttle, 1983.

Schriber, Mary Suzanne. *Writing Home: American Women Abroad 1830–1920*. Charlottesville: University Press of Virginia, 1997.

Seward, William H. *William H. Seward's Travels Around the World*. Edited by Olive Risley Seward. New York: Appleton, 1873.

Shashin torai no koro (The Advent of Photography in Japan). Tokyo: Tokyo Metropolitan Museum of Photography, Hakodate Museum of Art, and Tokyo Metropolitan Foundation for History and Culture, 1997.

Sichel, Philippe. "Notes d'un bibeloteur au Japon." In Max Put, *Plunder and Pleasure: Japanese Art in the West 1860–1930*. Leiden: Hotei, 2000.

Siegfried, Jacques. *Seize mois autour du monde, 1867–1869, et particulièrement aux Indes, en Chine et au Japon*. Paris: J. Hetzel, 1869.

Simpson, William. *Meeting of the Sun: A Journey Around the World*. Boston: Estes and Lauriat, 1877.

Smith, George, Bishop of Victoria. *Ten Weeks in Japan*. London: Longman, Greene, Longman, and Roberts, 1861.

Smith, Harold F. *American Travelers Abroad: A Bibliography of Accounts Published Before 1900*. Carbondale: Southern Illinois University, 1969.

St. John, Captain Henry Craven. *Notes and Sketches from the Wild Coasts of Nipon, with Chapters on Cruising after Pirates in Chinese Waters*. Edinborough: D. Douglas, 1880.

Stevenson, Louise L. *The Victorian Homefront: American Thought and Culture 1860–1880*. New York: Twayne, 1991.

Stewart, Susan. *On Longing: Narratives of the Miniature, the Gigantic, the Souvenir, the Collection*. Durham: Duke University Press, 1993.

Stoddard, Richard Henry. *Poets' Homes: Pen and Pencil Sketches of American Poets and Their Homes*. Boston: D. Lothrop, 1877.

Stowe, William W. *Going Abroad: European Travel in Nineteenth-Century American Culture*. Princeton: Princeton University Press, 1994.

Sturgis, Russell. "The Fine Arts of Japan," Parts 1–5. *The Nation* (July–Sept. 1868): 16–17, 56–57, 76–77, 96–97, 215–16.

Tarlo, Emma. *Clothing Matters: Dress and Identity in India*. London: Hurst, 1996.

Taylor, Bayard. *A Visit to India, China and Japan in the year 1853*. New York: Putnam, 1855.

Tharp, Louise Hall. *The Appletons of Beacon Hill*. Boston: Little, Brown, 1973.

Urry, John. *The Tourist Gaze*. London: Newbury Park, 1990.

van Gulik, W. R. *Irezumi: The Pattern of Dermatology in Japan*. Leiden: Brill, 1982.

Verne, Jules. *Around the World in Eighty Days*. New York: Viking, 1996.

Von Hubner, Joseph-Alexander. *A Ramble Round the World, 1871*. 2 vols. Translated by Lady Herbert. London: Macmillan, 1874.

——. *Promenade autour du monde, 1871*. Paris: Hachette, 1873.

Wagenknecht, Edward. *Henry Wadsworth Longfellow: Portrait of an American Humanist*. New York: Oxford University Press, 1966.

Wagenknecht, Edward, ed. *Mrs. Longfellow: Selected Letters and Journals*. New York: Longmans, Green, 1956.

Walworth, Ellen Hardin. *An Old World as Seen Through Young Eyes; or, travels around the world*. New York: Appleton, 1877.

Wayman, Dorothy G. *Edward Sylvester Morse: A Biography*. Cambridge: Harvard University Press, 1942.

Weppner, Margaretha. *The North Star and the Southern Cross*. 2 vols. London: Sampson Low, Marston, Low, and Searle, 1876.

Whitehill, Walter Muir. *Museum of Fine Arts Boston: A Centennial History*. 2 vols. Cambridge: Harvard University Press, 1977.

Withey, Lynne. *Grand Tours and Cook's Tours: A History of Leisure Travel, 1750–1915*. New York: William Morrow, 1997.

Yokohama kaikō shiryōkan, ed. *Bakumatsu Nihon no fukei to hitobito: Ferikusu Beato Bakumatsu Nihon shashinshū* (Collection of photographs of Bakumatsu Japan by F. Beato). Yokohama: Yokohama kaikō shiryō fukyū kyōkai, 1987.

Yokoyama, Toshio. *Japan in the Victorian Mind: A Study of Stereotyped Images of a Nation 1850–1880*. London: Macmillan, 1987.

Young, John Russell. *Around the World with General Grant: A Narrative of the Visit of General U.S. Grant, Ex-President of the United States to Various Countries in Europe, Asia, and Africa in 1877, 1878, 1879*. 2 vols. New York: The American News Department, 1879.

Ziff, Larzer. *Return Passages: Great American Travel Writing 1780–1910*. New Haven: Yale University Press, 2000.

INDEX

Pages with illustrations are indicated in boldface type.

Staged authenticity, 64–65

Stanley, Henry, 26

Stereocards, **13**

Stewart, Susan, 88, 94

Stillfried and Anderson Company: "geisha on the veranda of a teahouse," 83; prostitute, *1870s*, **19**; samurai, *1870s*, **32**. *See also* Von Stillfried photographs

Stoddard, Richard Henry, 188–89, 191

Storks. *See* Cranes, bronze

Stowe, William, 21

Sturgis, Russell, 91, 112

Suikoden, 147

Sukeroku, 133

Summers, Rev., 24

Sumner, Charles, 178, 197

Sword canes, 198

Sylvia, A.M.S.S., 68, **69**

Tables, **95**, 96–97, **166**

Takahashi Yūichi, 116

Tales of a Wayside Inn (H. W. Longfellow), 179

Tales of Ise, 36

Tales of Old Japan (Mitford), 32, 126

Tamamura, K., **156**, **157**

Tamoto Kenzō, 67

Tangen (Kano Mortisune), 103

Tani Bunchō, 113

Tanoshiki (Kabuki actor), 133

Tanshin (Kano Morimichi), 103, **104**

Tansu (portable chests), 180, **181**

Tatsunobu Seisetsusai, 114

Tattoos: of the Ainu, 68, **71**, **72**, 145, 148; banning of, 148; on coolies, **144**; cost of, 153; as expression of the heroic, 46–47; homoeroticism in, 143; as leisure symbols, 158; of Longfellow, 142, **143**, 145, 149–50, 153–54; in the marketplace, 148; pain of, 150, 153; photographing, 58; on royalty, 150, 152; on running grooms, 145, 153, **159**; as sexual, 150, 154; social status and, 145, 147; sociopolitical significance of, 147–48; as status symbols, 154–55; stereotyping Japanese through, xvii–xviii; tourists and, 148; value of, 202; Western evaluation of, 33

Taylor, Bayard: international travel as imperialism, 29; Longfellow House visits by, 44, 178, 208*n113*; in traditional Arab clothing, 127, **128**, 136

Tea ceremony, 10

Teikoku Hakubutsukan, 198–99

Tetsubin, 105

Theosophical Society, 195, 197

Things Japanese (Chamberlain), 6

Thoreau, Henry David, 194

Tōkaidō, 36, 73, 97

Tokio Guide (Griffis), 21

Tokyo: foreigners in, 16, 77; Imperial Museum, Ueno, 198–99; Longfellow residence in, xii, 47, 74–78, **162**, 187; Shinobazu Pond, 119; tourist sites in, 21

Topknots, 121, 127

Toshio (Kabuki actor), **132**, 133

Le Tour du Monde, 3

Tourists: Americans in Japan; xi, 9–13, 15–22; architecture in Japan, 22; and art collecting; xvii, xx–xxi; British, 34; conspicuous consumption and, 10, 39; curios and, 89–91; domestic Japanese, 34, 36; in *1880*s Japan, 198; in Europe, 10; expatriates views of, 5; guidebooks for, 21; influence on public attitudes of; xvi, 8; Japanese abroad, xv, 4, 12; journals by, 23–24; as missionaries, 24; as photographers, 51; sex and, 16; and smiling women, 83; tattooing of, 148; in traditional Japanese clothing, 124–36; transportation and facilities for, 20–21; travel articles by, 10, 26, 28; travelers vs., 7; as visitors to known places, 29, 52; woman as, 15–16

Transcendentalism, 194

Travelers, 7. *See also* Tourists

Travelogues, 28–29

Treaty ports, 137

Trollope, Anthony, 178

Trousseaus, 108

Tsuitate, 119

Tucker-Macchetta, Blanche Roosevelt, 192

Turkey, 172

Uchida Kyūichi, 54, 58, 74, **79**

Ueno Hikoma, 54, 130, **139**

Ukiyo-e, 46

Unitarianism, 40, 194, 197

Upton, Emery, 206*n57*

Urry, John, 51, 83

Utagawa Kunisada II, **27**

Utagawa Kuniyoshi, **146**, 147

Utamaro, **92**, 97

Vanderbilt, Cornelius, 175, **176**

Van Dyck, Anthony, 128, 130

Van Rensselaer, Kilian, 23

Vases, 182

Vassall, John, 177

Veblen, Thorstein, 89

Vedder, Elihu, 168, **169**, 217*n4*

Verne, Jules, 3–4, 50

Victorian era: Buddhism's compatibility with values of, 195; cult of domesticity, 74,